NOT ON ANY MAP

Not On Any Map

ONE VIRGIN ISLAND, TWO CATASTROPHIC HURRICANES, AND THE TRUE MEANING OF PARADISE

MARGIE SMITH HOLT

RE:WRITE BOOKS, NEW YORK, NY

This is a memoir.

Everybody has a story. This one is mine, and it's just one story. In writing about a culture that is not my own, I have worked hard to do so with sensitivity, accuracy, and respect. Some names and identifying details have been changed to protect the privacy of individuals, but all the events are true and retold to the best of my reporting abilities and recollections. Some people have asked me to use their real names, which I take as a sign that I got things right. Mostly. As my old boss at Skinny Legs once told me, "Stories are not always accurate, especially in St. John and Coral Bay in particular. But such is life."

Library of Congress Control Number: 2022919275

ISBN: 979-8-218-06807-3

ISBN: 979-8-218-06808-0 (Ebook edition)

re:Write Books, an imprint of Get Me Rewrite LLC, NY, NY 10024

GETMEREWRITE.BIZ

MARGIESMITHHOLT.COM

Front Cover Art: "Weather Coming" by Billie Denise Wright

Back Cover Art: "Johnson Bay II" by Billie Denise Wright

Cover Design: William Stelzer

Map: Bryan McKinney

Interior Design: Created with Vellum

Printed in the United States of America

For Coral Bay

It is not down on any map; true places never are.
—Herman Melville, *Moby Dick*

The mind is its own place, and in itself
Can make a Heav'n of Hell, a Hell of Heav'n.
—John Milton, *Paradise Lost*

ST. JOHN

WELCOME TO CORAL BAY

Maho Bay

Trunk Bay

TO TOWN

Bordeaux Mountain

Cruz Bay

Reef Bay

Hurricane Hole

East End

Leduck Island

Salt Pond Bay

Ram Head

18.3 North 64.7 West

LEGEND

1. The Triangle
2. The Moravian Church
3. Skinny Legs
4. The Dinghy Dock
5. Silver Cloud
6. Shipwreck Landing
7. Cliffhanger House
8. Love City Mini-Mart

CONTENTS

PROLOGUE

One night in November of 2006 I was on a tiny sailboat in the middle of the Atlantic Ocean, no land in sight, and looking up at a sky so full of stars they dripped to the horizon and reflected in the sea, which, if I leaned over far enough, I could touch.

The vessel was 30 feet long. That's about two car lengths. The distance you're supposed to park from a stop sign. Five average-sized men, lying head to toe, stretch about 30 feet. Track and field Olympians can jump 29 feet. If Jesse Owens were alive today, he could probably jump the length of the boat I was on. Thirty feet is a long way to jump, but it's not a lot of boat.

The only other person on board, the captain, was sound asleep below. He was a romantic, this sailor, a young guy with a very old soul who built the boat himself "according to tradition," which meant the hull was wood, the sails were hand-stitched, and we were navigating with pencils, rulers, and paper charts. Looking at the sky of the ancients above me, it was easy to imagine I was one of them. I hadn't seen land in days. I was alone at the tiller and with my thoughts. I was pondering the Universe. Contemplating the Great Questions. Until I had to pee, and then my brain had to concentrate on not falling overboard while pulling down my pants and using the bucket that doubled as a bathroom. Grabbing the lifelines, I silently cursed the person who tricked me into this 2,800-mile transatlantic trip on a boat with no engine, no refrigeration, and no toilet by christening the journey an Odyssey.

Do it, goddamn it, do it! he had urged. *You could drown and disappear forever. But at least you would have died during the exhilarating act of living! This is my dream!*

Good to know it was somebody's. Because it wasn't mine.

One of the sailors at the dock from where we set sail called me an *aventurera.* An adventuress. A word no one, ever, had used to describe me.

I was from Philadelphia, a place known for lawyers, not adventuresses. My dream had been more like Having It All, Traditional Version: Successful career. Husband. Children. And I had gotten so close.

I had the great apartment and an exciting, sometimes even glamorous, job as a TV news reporter. I covered murders and mob trials, elections and politics and corruption, championship games, and weather. Lots of weather. Blizzards, floods, heatwaves, Nor'easters, and the occasional tornado. I covered all the big stories in a big, gritty city—and had shelves of awards to prove I was good at it. When the TV news business changed and I was forced out to make way for younger, cheaper talent, I got lucky and landed a high-profile PR job. That was fine because it came with predictable hours, and I was ready to start a family. I had met, just in time, the man I thought I was going to marry. Until, on our last New Year's Eve together, I learned he had been out shopping not for a ring but a new gig. In Baghdad. I wanted to have kids and spend summers at the Jersey Shore. He wanted to be a war correspondent in the desert. And that was the end of that story. Turned out Philadelphia had adventurers after all.

Heartbroken, I threw myself into work, a strategy my friend and co-worker Jasmine, Jazz for short, thought was deranged. She was the colleague whose invitation to go out "for just one" after work usually meant an evening that didn't end until the bars closed. Jazz believed what I needed was a vacation, an opinion she expressed in the doorway of my office every few days for what seemed like months. One morning, probably after one of those "just one" nights, and definitely to shut her up, I handed her my VISA and told her to book a trip anywhere in the Caribbean. She chose St. John in the U.S. Virgin Islands, a place I knew nothing about.

The first day of vacation, we learned there had been layoffs that morning at work. Our friend Ellen had been let go. Jazz suggested we take something back to cheer her up. But what? A sarong? A bracelet? What Ellen needed was a job. So we spent the next seven days swimming and scuba diving, immersed in some of the bluest water on the planet. And at night, we tried to find Ellen a job.

It started as a joke. *Hey! Let's find Ellen a job in St. John! She can work here, and we'll come visit her. That'll be cool.*

Everywhere we went—every bar, every restaurant, every shop—we asked people if they had any openings because our friend needed a job. And everywhere we went, everyone told us yes! They're always looking for good help! Locals extolled the virtues of their island. Newcomers explained how they ended up there, and why. We heard stories about what they had escaped—cold weather, bad relationships, boredom—and what they had found, or were hoping to find: Love. Sunshine. The meaning of life. Then they gave us their bosses' cell phone numbers.

It all sounded so enticing. So easy. People looked happy, and stress-free. St. John seemed to be some kind of magnet, attracting like-minded beings who had figured something out. Jazz and I spent the return flight babbling about our own nascent desires to try out island life—a bottle of rum and a bag of tacky souvenirs for Ellen safely stowed in the overhead compartment.

Then it was back to the real world. Planned and practical. Profound enough. A place where any sporadic urge to chuck it all and run off to some island was always balanced out by the belief that following your bliss is a whole lot easier with a nice salary.

But something had taken root. Not wanderlust, exactly, but a longing for something—more. My life was full—friends, family, good job—but was it enough? I felt like I'd left a piece of myself behind in that blue water. Could I really do it? Go back, to live? Was that gutsy or just nuts?

One day, while swapping vacation stories at the office, another co-worker, recently returned from hiking in the Rockies, said she thought she'd like to have her ashes scattered there when she died. This prompted some banter about where others would like to make their final resting places. No one talked about where they might like to spend their remaining living days. Wasn't that nuts?

I took inventory of the signs. My last single college friend had just announced she was pregnant. I couldn't stop thinking about two colleagues in the local press corps, not that much older, who had recently died, both suddenly and within weeks of each other. Life can change in an instant. Everybody in my family was healthy. It was an appropriate time to leave my job. I didn't have children. I did have a little cash. There was nothing stopping me. I was essentially free of responsibility. I might never have this much freedom again. What if I didn't take a chance and regretted it later? Carpe diem, and all that.

What's the worst that can happen? I kept asking myself. *If it doesn't work out, you'll come home, get another job, rent another apartment. Big deal. The worst that can happen is you spend the winter in the Caribbean.*

A few weeks after the vacation, after a lousy day at work, we got serious. Jazz and I sat at the bar at the Good Dog in Philadelphia on a sweltering July night and outlined all the reasons to ditch a Good Job and go work on a dive boat. (*Reason #1: Life is short. This is not a dress rehearsal!*) We really did scribble the notes on a napkin.

Jazz was already thinking about what type of business we could open if we liked island life and decided to stay. Not me. I thought soaking up some sun and avoiding deadlines for a while was enough of an objective. I would surround myself with people who disagreed, but I didn't know that yet. St. John would be more sea change than sabbatical, but I didn't know that yet, either.

I did know from trying to find Ellen a job that many new islanders went down on vacation and never went home, but that wasn't our style. We needed a plan. Options. St. John was small. Maybe too small. The U.S. Virgin Islands made sense because we'd be citizens with fewer obstacles to working, so we set our sights on St. Croix, the largest of the U.S. Virgins. We booked a second trip. Not a vacation, a fact-finding mission. A search for housing and employment. We even took our resumes.

Sitting on the beach at the Buccaneer Hotel in Christiansted, we combed through the classifieds in every newspaper we could find. There were just two ads for employment:

Wanted: Lifeguard

Qualifications: Must be over 18. Must be strong swimmer.

Glad we brought those resumes.

Wanted: General manager for 60-unit condominium/resort complex

General manager of a 60-unit condo complex? I'm not qualified for that, I thought to myself.

"General manager of a 60-unit condo complex?" Jazz read out loud. "How fucking hard can that be?"

That right there. That was the difference between Jazz and me.

St. Croix was a bust. Something was missing. The vibe was all wrong. Maybe this wasn't such a good idea after all. But we had two days left so we decided to go back to St. John. Wasn't that where we felt the pull to do this?

We took the sea plane to St. Thomas and ferried back to St. John, instantly familiar. You could almost hear the click. We got a room at Gallows Point, the condo complex in the want ads. Jazz didn't get the job, but she did get the locals rate for another trip down, and it was during that trip that she would find us a place to live: a house called the Cliffhanger. Beginning with a cliffhanger should have been my first clue that some plot twists were in store.

We didn't find work, but we did manage to track down one of the boat captains we had met on vacation. He told us not to worry so much and offered to stow our scuba gear until we returned. And that was that. We were committed. It was August and on our last night we lay on the beach and watched the Perseid meteor shower, and everything felt right.

The next three months were spent addressing the details—quit job, sell car, sublet apartment—and answering questions. Lots of questions.

What are you going to do? sneered the ex. *Swab the decks?*

I didn't know. Maybe.

Is this some kind of a mid-life crisis or something? one of the millennials at work wanted to know.

I'd be turning 40 on my next birthday so, mathematically, yes. But was it still a crisis if I was having fun?

And the one that got asked the most: *Aren't you worried about hurricanes?*

On the list of all the things I worried could go wrong—and it was a list I made and studied ad nauseam—hurricanes didn't even make the top 10.

I worried about not having a paycheck. I worried that something bad would happen to my mother and I'd be too far away to help. I worried about health insurance. I worried about blowing up my resume and never having a "real" job again. I worried I'd drain my savings and be too broke to ever have a kid. I worried I was making a terrible, humiliating, irreparable mistake. Hurricanes? I had covered hurricanes as a reporter and knew they came with warnings, and time to prepare, maybe even evacuate. Plus, where I was going, there hadn't been a big one in ages. So no, I wasn't worried about hurricanes.

But I should have been.

PARADISE
(PART ONE)

I

A PRETTY OK PLACE

The first thing you notice is the color of the water.

"The Elixir," my landlord called it, a nod to the perceived healing properties of the liquid embracing the droplet of land I had decided to call home. But you don't have to believe in healing, or the supernatural, or magic, or anything, really, to look at that blue and know there is something special about it. There's no argument, it's not up for discussion. Empirically, it is astounding. And if you look at it long enough, you will start searching for other adjectives, because blue—simply blue—doesn't quite cut it. How about azure? Turquoise? Maybe aquamarine or teal. Cobalt or sapphire. "Forty-two shades of blue" one of my island neighbors used to say, before 50 shades of anything was even a thing. She was a Bostonian, that neighbor, so she pronounced it "fotty-two" and to this day, that's how I think of the color of that water. Fotty-two shades of blue.

The 42 shades—part Caribbean Sea, part Atlantic Ocean—surround the minuscule, 20-square-mile island of St. John. There is a tiny but fierce percentage of the world's population that is truly, madly, deeply in love with St. John. This includes most of the few thousand people who live there full- or part-time, and vacationers who visit and fall under her spell. Pretty much everybody else has never heard of the place.

No wonder, since it's so small. It's so small, most maps don't even name it, which might explain why people are prone to mispronounce the name, calling it St. John's, with an "s," which is the capital of Newfoundland (an island, yes, but Canadian, not Caribbean), and also the capital of Antigua (closer, but still a different country). St. John is so small, you can walk from one end to the other in less than a day, which hundreds of people do every year in a race called 8 Tuff Miles. St. John is so small that if, for example, you were watching The Weather Channel and the meteorologist pointed to one of those satellite images and said it showed a massive hurricane barreling toward, say, Florida, you probably wouldn't even notice that said storm was already smack over the island because the entire place would be completely obscured from view.

But on a good day, when the weather is fine, St. John strongly resembles paradise. I say resembles because how you define paradise is subjective—that's sort of the point of all this—but St. John ticks all the standard boxes: rugged, volcanic terrain swaddled in dense green vegetation. Colorful flowers blooming. Stately palms standing sentry over white sand beaches. And, everywhere you turn, marvelous views of all those blues. It's like hallucinating paradise. When you fantasize about quitting the daily grind and running away, St. John is the kind of place you run to. In a different time, you might have said it looked just like a postcard, but these days it could be your screensaver, the one labeled "Caribbean Vacation" or "Tropical Escape," an image so idyllic, you think it must be fake—doctored, at least—but it's a no-filter situation. That's really what it looks like in "America's Caribbean." St. John is a U.S. territory and, just to clarify, when that meteorologist on The Weather Channel pointed to Florida on that map and said that massive hurricane was about to hit the United States, he was wrong. It already had.

I used to be one of the people who had never heard of the

place, but I know now that this is how you find it: Head southeast from the Florida Keys and you'll hit Cuba, Hispaniola (Haiti and the Dominican Republic), and Puerto Rico, the land masses getting progressively smaller as you go. Just east of Puerto Rico are the Virgin Islands—some American, some British—all situated at the top of an arcing chain of tiny specks on the map known as the Lesser Antilles. The first speck, just to the right of Puerto Rico, is St. Thomas, and just to the right of that is another speck. That's St. John. St. John is also one of the Leeward Islands, which are part of the West Indies, which is a name that reminds us that for centuries, people have been confused about where exactly this part of the world actually is.

St. John was "discovered" first by the indigenous Taíno and Caribs, who give the sea its name; then by Columbus, who sailed by on his second voyage in 1493 and dubbed the islands "The Virgins" in honor of the Christian martyr St. Ursula and her 11,000 virgin followers; then by the Danes who colonized and enslaved Africans to work their sugar plantations; then by American billionaire Laurance Rockefeller who bought up land in the 1950s and gave it to the U.S. government for a national park; and eventually, in 2004, by me, on vacation with Jazz.

I went from never-heard-of-the-place to spellbound in a week's time and, not long after what was supposed to have been just a little getaway, found myself transitioning from tourist to transplant. I bought a one-way ticket; crammed two suitcases full of clothes, hats, and sunscreen; and left Philadelphia on precisely the type of damp, drizzly November day that sent Ishmael off to see the watery part of the world. And then, though I had been planning the move for months, I spent the entire flight down wondering what the hell I was thinking.

Everybody fantasizes about this! Or so people kept saying, in the weeks leading up to my departure. Yes, everybody *else*. Racking my brains, I tried to remember the signs I was so sure pointed me toward that plane. I think I was supposed to be in search of something ... more. More exciting! More fun! More meaningful. I had a vague recollection of intense, heady talks about shedding social convention, pushing limits, and seeking life-altering experience, happiness—rapture, even! But all that had gotten a bit lost, buried in the pre-move rush.

Maybe it was in my notes. I take good notes.

I opened my journal and read, for the umpteenth time, the quotes taped on the inside cover:

The moment one definitely commits oneself,
then Providence moves too. All sorts of things occur to help
one that would never otherwise have occurred ...
Boldness has genius, power, and magic in it. Begin it now.
—(Attributed to) Goethe

Leap and the net will appear.
—Zen saying

I was no Zen master, but since committing to this move the previous June, all sorts of things had been falling into place. And I could only pray that Providence would keep moving because I was no longer staring out the airplane window at all the blue below. We had landed.

We landed in Charlotte Amalie, St. Thomas, because St. John is so small, there's no airport. The cabin doors opened, and a blast of warm, humid air filled the plane. I was in the cheap seats and deplaned right out the back, down the rickety stairs, and onto the steaming tarmac. I love the heat. On vacation it sweats that top layer of stress right out of my body. But this wasn't a vacation.

I could have used a drink but declined the free rum punch offered by the costumed airport greeters. I wanted to look like I belonged. Virgin Islanders don't act like they're on spring break or at a Jimmy Buffet concert. West Indian culture is conservative. Bathing suits and bare skin are for the beach. Conversations begin with civilities, starting with a hearty "Good afternoon!" for the taxi driver who would take me and my essential belongings to the ferry dock.

St. John is accessible only by boat, and only by ferry or small boat. Like the planes, the cruise ships all go to St. Thomas. It's a 45-minute drive to the ferry dock in Red Hook where the boats leave on the hour. Tourists sit up top for the sun and the view; locals sit down below for the air conditioning. I sat up top. The ride was a quick 20 minutes across Pillsbury Sound, and we had an escort from a brown booby, a tropical seabird, coasting on the boat's updraft.

We docked in Cruz Bay, St. John's port of entry, all brightly colored shops and restaurants and open-air bars. After disembarking, I was greeted again, not by rum punch but by something I had not noticed before: a statue of a man brandishing a machete and sounding a cry of freedom via conch shell. The first successful slave revolt in the New World was on St. John, in 1733, though emancipation wouldn't come for another 100 years. Sugar mill ruins pock the island, reminders of a bloody and shameful past.

I knew that from the dock I could turn left and follow the coast to a string of pristine beaches: Honeymoon, Hawksnest, Cinnamon, Maho. St. John is two-thirds national park. The open-air safari taxis would be lined up at Trunk Bay, famous for its underwater snorkel trail and regularly making lists of the world's best beaches, waiting to take day-trippers to the dock so they could ferry back to St. Thomas and their cruise ships. If I drove inland, past the palms and the sea grapes, I'd find miles of hiking trails meandering through verdant forest. To see the rest of Virgin Islands National Park you need snorkel gear. The stingrays and turtles, vibrant coral reefs, and psychedelic fish are all under the sea.

But I wasn't a tourist, and I wasn't going where the tourists went. I was going all the way across the island to the east side of St. John—the "other" side—headed for a locale so sleepy it didn't even rise to the level of village. I was going to live in a place called Coral Bay.

I had hoped to live in Cruz Bay and get a job in one of the dive shops, but we couldn't find housing "in town," as the main port was referred to, so Coral Bay it was. St. John is about the size of Manhattan with a fraction of the population. The whole island —or "The Rock" as the St. Johnians call it, as in, "If he hasn't been off The Rock in 15 years, stay away from him ..."—is basically one small town. But a lot of folks in Cruz Bay, some of whom seemed to think they actually lived in Manhattan, looked down on "backwater" Coral Bay, referring to it as "the country," as in, "Good luck living way out there in the country. All you'll meet is stoned hippies and toothless old sailors with long gray hair. Why'd you move out there, anyway?"

The citizens of Coral Bay shrugged off the disdain. The who-would-want-to-live-there feeling was mutual. They took great pride in their down-to-earth enclave, welcoming strangers even as they sized them (us) up. And they never asked why. People back home said Jazz and I were brave and called us their heroes, but down there we were nothing special, just two more of many who had done the exact same thing. Two more who probably wouldn't make it.

There are no traffic lights on St. John and just two ways to get to Coral Bay, three if you count by boat: North Shore Road, the scenic drive, full of switchbacks, past the beaches; and Centerline, which bisects the island and is the most direct route. When you leave Cruz Bay and drive out Centerline Road, the air gets cooler as you head up toward Bordeaux Mountain, the highest part of St. John. Just before you come down the other side, about half-way, there used to be an overlook, next to a little restaurant called Chateau Bordeaux, where the tourist taxis would stop for photo ops. A bougainvillea-lined fence separated the shoulder from a precipitous drop down the mountain, but it was worth risking vertigo for the backdrop, a luscious sweep of Caribbean Sea, the British Virgin Islands (BVI) in the distance, and, closer in, the East End of St. John and Coral Bay.

I got my first glimpse of "the country" just down the road

from that overlook. From the bird's-eye view I could see all the sailboats in Coral Harbor; a smattering of houses nestled in the green; the distinctive red roof of Emmaus Moravian Church; and Hurricane Hole, the peaceful, protected cove where boats aren't allowed to anchor overnight except in bad weather. Because I moved down in November—a rainy month, still technically hurricane season—early views of my new home often included a rainbow, sometimes two, as if the lily needed gilding. "Ridiculous excess," to quote Shakespeare, but God, it was stunning.

Continue down Centerline and when you hit the T intersection at the bottom of the hill, you're in Coral Bay. Locals call that spot the Triangle. There was a big *Welcome to Coral Bay* chamber-of-commerce-type sign there, boasting the names of so many businesses you'd swear you were rolling into a thriving metropolis, but look around and you wouldn't see much. If you kept going straight, past the church and the fire station, eventually you'd dead-end at East End. Make a right at the Triangle, toward Salt Pond, and in a few miles you'd hit Lameshur Bay, where, if the roads connected, which they don't, you'd be almost back to Cruz Bay. It's a classic "you can't get there from here," adding to the isolation. Again, just fine with the locals.

Once you knew where to look, though—and, more importantly, what days or times to show up—you'd find a solid half-dozen places to eat and drink in Coral Bay. Names hinted at menu and location: Sticky Fingers, Shipwreck Landing. If it was Wednesday night, you might find Puerto Rican Pete rolling sushi at Voyages. Island Blues was packed when Debbie Did Karaoke on Mondays. The M & M Donkey Diner ("Kick-Ass Food!") was the place to get breakfast, but not before 10 a.m. If you were lucky, you could get fried chicken and Johnnycake at Vie's Snack Shack or roti at Sputnik's bar, delicious West Indian dishes worth the hunt, but getting harder to find. A new place called Aqua Bistro was just getting ready to open.

St. John's nickname is Love City and when all else failed, you could pick up beer and a few groceries at the Love City Mini

Mart. You could also rent kayaks and snorkel gear at Crabby's, book a trail ride at Carolina Corral, make phone calls or check your email at Connections, shop for hats and T-shirts at Jolly Dog or Mumbo Jumbo, buy a leather bag at Awl Made Here or a dress painted by Sloop Jones, and fuel up at the one gas station, if they had gas.

At the center of it all was Skinny Legs. Modestly billing itself as "A Pretty OK Place," Skinny's was the best spot on the island for a cheeseburger and the unofficial town hall of Coral Bay. It was also the so-called "living room" for dozens of sailors who lived on their boats in Coral Harbor. Just like St. John didn't have cruise ships, Coral Bay didn't have superyachts or luxury motor-boats. What it had, mostly, were modest sailboats. Some of the boats in the harbor were—let's be charitable and go with "scrappy"—but there were also beautiful vintage wooden boats. There was a deep appreciation for traditional boatbuilding, some-thing I learned quickly because it's all the boys at the bar talked about: *Boats boats boats!* That and the weather.

There was no marina, although there'd been talk of one forever, and an ongoing battle to prevent one. Coral Bay is a natural harbor. Boats were tied to mooring balls, or anchored, and boaters came ashore by dinghy—inflatable rafts with low-horse-power outboard engines, or rowboats. Instead of a marina, Coral Bay had the Dinghy Dock. Located essentially in Skinny's back-yard, the Dinghy Dock was a simple wharf—part stone dating back to Danish times, part cracked concrete. Tied up at the Dinghy Dock you'd find an assortment of small vessels of varying condition and buoyancy, some of which, at first glance, appeared to be the remnants of a shipwreck but were, in fact, somebody's ride home.

It's worth noting that even back then, many of the locals told me I had already missed the heyday of the place, some earlier, groovier time when there was, presumably, even less going on and things were "better"—whatever that meant. It was a familiar lament. Colleagues in every newsroom I ever worked in told me I "just missed" the glory days of that business. If it was true that I had also missed the boat in Coral Bay, at least I could consider myself fortunate to have some of the old guard around to tell me all about it. Besides, it wasn't all gone. Iconic West Indian elders like Miss Lucy and Guy Benjamin were still alive. Miss Lucy oversaw the pig roasts at her famous full moon parties, where she named the pigs after her staff. Mr. Benjamin sang in the choir at the Moravian Church, and the elementary school that was named for him was still open, full of Coral Bay kids. Doug and Moe, the affable founders of Skinny Legs, were still running the joint. The classic sailboats *Liberty*, later featured in a Johnny Depp movie, and *Breath*, built on St. John's East End, floated in a harbor cradled by unblemished hillsides. Visitors could stay in treehouse-like tents at the Maho Bay Campground, eco-tourism before it was trendy. There was development, but not the "over" kind. Everybody knew everybody. There hadn't been a major hurricane in a decade and, though nobody knew it, there wouldn't be another for 13 more years.

Jazz and I moved into a house with a name. The Cliffhanger was built into a bluff overlooking Coral Harbor. It was a 60-foot drop to the bay, which, at that time of year—the start of the season—was freckled with sailboats. If you were on one of those sailboats looking back at the land, you would see that Cliffhanger was not a misnomer. The house clung to the rock face like a grav-ity-defying mountain climber with a precarious toehold in a crevice or two. What feat of engineering kept it suspended, I do not know.

Had I seen the house from the water, I doubt that I would have moved in. But our view wasn't from the water, it was of the water, and, in this case, ignorance was truly bliss because the Cliffhanger's view was to die for. Rising behind the boats and turquoise water were the rolling hills of the East End and, peeking over the top, the unspoiled tip of Tortola in the BVI, a swath of emerald velvet embellishing blue sky. Just beyond, though you couldn't see it, was Norman Island, purported to be the inspiration for Robert Louis Stevenson's *Treasure Island*. Even in the 21st century, there was a whiff of pirate in the air, a sense that something exhilarating, maybe even dangerous or lawless, was also just out of sight.

The Cliffhanger was divided into two apartments and ours, upstairs, had two bedrooms and two baths separated by a living/kitchen area. The home was sparsely furnished, but every room opened onto an expansive deck that wrapped around three-quarters of the house. A lone pelican skimmed past, buzzing the deck, so often it was like having a pet. We started calling him (or them) Sid. The indoor critters—geckos and lizards, flying cockroaches, the occasional scorpion—would take a little more getting used to, and would not be named.

Despite the relatively primitive nature of our new habitat, I didn't immediately miss the swanky trappings of city life because Jazz, it turned out, had brought them with her. She arrived ahead of me with new linens, gourmet kitchen supplies, and Stanley—another co-worker who came for a few days to help move it all in. Philadelphia Stanley was an urbane, natty gentleman predisposed to cashmere and bespoke suits. Coral Bay Stanley performed his duties dressed in shorts, sandals, and—gasp!—a baseball cap. Coral Bay couture, I would soon learn, was an oxymoron, at least in the crowd I'd be hanging out with. I'd have no use for any of the "resort wear" I'd bought for vacation—unless I wanted to be mocked as a tourist. Stanley's shirt was seersucker, so he hadn't entirely let himself go, but in less than 24 hours, he was halfway to what would become my new uniform.

There was, apparently, interior decorating to be done. While I was unpacking, I heard Stanley in the next room exclaim, "Look! Here's that exquisite amber ball I brought you from Harrods last year!" and "Oh my God, where shall we put these fabulous Guatemalan pillow covers?"—two phrases surely not uttered in any other recently arrived islander's home that month, or, at least not in the homes of any islanders planning to be employed soon in the service industry. My luggage had been stuffed with rain pants, slickers, and all-weather boots. I owned quite a collection of outerwear, thanks to my career as one of those television news reporters who stands outside in bad weather, telling you not to go outside because the weather's bad. I shipped foul-weather gear; Jazz packed artwork. My carry-on was a laptop; hers was a candelabra. We made a good team.

Stanley hauled trash to the dumpster, killed scary bugs, and generally helped ease the adjustment period by running interference between two headstrong and strung-out women. My only contribution to interior design had been the hula lamp—a going-away present from a journalist friend. When the light bulb heated up, the hula girls on the neon purple shade spun in frenetic circles. It was an apt metaphor.

When we needed a break from settling in, we drove two miles down the road to Salt Pond, the closest National Park beach, for a swim. A short hike from the parking lot took us down to a crescent of white sand hugging a pool of calm, clear blue water. The Elixir. Only there did the stress of moving start to melt away. We'd swim with schools of blue tang, maybe spot an angelfish or a gang of squid. After snorkeling we'd go home, blast Van Morrison singing about the water from the speakers, and "dangle," which meant sitting on the Cliffhanger's deck benches, legs and feet hanging over the edge, high above the water, and watching the boats sail into the harbor. The natural beauty was ethereal, and that was just the daytime view. The stars deserve a chapter of their own.

My first night I fell into bed, drained but anxious, not quite able to absorb my peculiar surroundings. The minute the sun went down, bugs and frogs got together to jam. I listened to a chorus of invisible insects backing up shrill tree frog soloists, whose only lyric was their name: *Co-QUI! Co-QUI!* When I couldn't sleep, I tiptoed out onto the deck and looked up. There were billions of stars, most unrecognizable to an urban stargazer, but that hazy glow paint-brushed up the middle had to be the Milky Way. Several hours later, so deep in the night the bugs and frogs were quiet, I woke to hear the subtle rumble of the surf, waves licking at the stones on the beach far below. I looked out again. That time I saw the Big Dipper—upside down, but a lodestar. A cool, tropical breeze brushed across my bare skin, blew through my hair. I took a deep breath. *Drink the wild air's salubrity*—another quote copied in my journal. Emerson. Was this what he was talking about?

The first order of business was figuring out how things worked. WAPA, the Virgin Islands Water and Power Authority, was notoriously unreliable. Power outages were frequent. We would get the coffee maker brewing as soon as someone was up in case we lost the juice, eventually switching to a French press and water boiled on the propane stove. There's a definite learning curve for city dwellers who rarely encounter, let alone master, things like water pumps, propane tanks, and generators. All of that would need to be demystified through a little trial and error and a lot of assistance from our preternaturally self-sufficient neighbors. I don't know if they were straight-up helpful or charged with setting the odds on whether the new girls had the right stuff to cut it, but someone was always willing to lend a hand.

Even brushing your teeth was different: Turn the water on to wet the toothbrush. Turn the water off. Brush. Spit. Turn the water back on just long enough to rinse. Turn it off again. We were surrounded by water, but there wasn't enough of it. Thus, the ubiquitous signs in bathrooms throughout the Caribbean: *In the land of sea and sun, we never flush for number one!*

Rain was an obsession, and a topic of daily conversation: How much fell last night, and how would that affect the day's business, the unpaved roads, or your cistern. The Cliffhanger, like most homes on the island, was not connected to a public water system. Rainwater was collected in gutters on the roof and stored beneath the house in a cavernous tank with, in our case, a slow leak. Conservation was paramount. That meant lathering up in the shower and turning the water off until I was ready to rinse;

waiting until after a good rain to do the laundry; and yes, no flushing for number one. I was told if we learned the sounds the plumbing made, we'd get a warning when the cistern was running low, but the only noise I ever noticed was a deep, foghorn-like groan every time we opened a tap. I lived in fear of being branded the idiots who were constantly running out of water.

Virgin Islanders drive on the left. No one's really sure why— perhaps a tradition left over from some European occupation, although the island's been American territory since 1917—but the *St. John Guide Book* suggested adhering to this "quaint custom" since "everybody else does." Driving had a bit of a death wish element to it and catapulting off a cliff while gaping at a jaw-dropping panorama seemed a distinct possibility. All the roads are narrow, with steep inclines and hairpin turns. Factor in the big Paradise Gas trucks and OASIS water tankers and VITRAN (Virgin Islands Transit) busses that regularly came barreling around the corner—in the middle of the two lanes—sometimes with horns blaring, more often without warning; and tourists driving on the wrong side of the road; and the locals, proficient little speed demons, whipping by in their Jeep Wranglers and Suzuki Sidekicks; and the feral donkeys, goats, mongooses (Mongeese? A local told me the plural is "mongoose dem"), dogs, cats, pigs, chickens, and roosters that populated the road—not the roadside, the road—and it qualified as blood sport. The posted speed limit—20 mph, except where it was 10 mph—was taken as mere suggestion. It wasn't uncommon, we heard, to see drivers take the turns so fast they'd flip over in their jeeps. Then they'd get out, flip the car back over, get back in, and keep going.

Ask for directions and you'd find navigation to be unorthodox. Dumpsters were landmarks. As in, "Turn right at the blue dumpster and you'll see the container (yes, like the kind that goes on a ship) where Tropical Tim lives." Road signs alerting drivers to the presence of speed bumps might be placed after the bump. Other road signs tended toward the creative. (Crab) Dip. (Skinny) Dip. (Big) Dip(per). Another prominent landmark was a towering fork—the kind you eat with—made of concrete, placed tines up, and painted blue. A literal fork in the road. It was also legal to drink and drive but get caught without a seatbelt and you'd be fined $250. One day we stopped by to see Coconut Charlie, the Cliffhanger's property manager, and pick up some boxes; Charlie sent us home with two open cans of Heineken and a warning to buckle up.

The drive from Cruz Bay to Coral Bay took a neophyte, if I was feeling intrepid, about 35 minutes, just enough time to start feeling adequate in the driver's seat. Then I'd arrive at the Cliffhanger and have to park. The driveway sloped downward on a 45-degree angle and was barely wide enough for one car squeezed in between a concrete retaining wall on one side and a drop to the house on the other. The margin of error was zero. Oh, and you had to back in. May the Force be with you. I experienced many more what-the-hell-was-I-thinking moments while trying to park in front of my new home.

Walking wasn't for cowards, either. I once asked a woman on the ferry if we could walk to the Westin from the dock. It looked close on the map. "Well, I THINK you could walk," she replied. The "h" in *think* floated away, her West Indian lilt as buoyant as the blue water beneath us. "But. There is—a HILL." A hill, indeed. What's that expression about San Francisco? When you get tired of walking, you can lean against it. That also applies to St. John. That "hill" on the way to the hotel is referred to locally as Jacob's Ladder.

One night, after I'd been on island a while (long enough to know that you drop the article: you're not "on the island," you're "on island"), I walked into the parking lot at Skinny Legs to find a neighbor sitting in the driver's seat of my beat-up, red Suzuki Sidekick.

"My car won't start!" she wailed.

"Uh, Caroline?" I said. "That's my car."

This is what happens when there are only three makes and models on the island. In retrospect, I should have given her the keys. I'd never seen Caroline's car, but it's a good bet I'd have won in that trade. I had owned a nice car back in Philly, but shipping was cost-prohibitive, and it seemed more practical to buy a car with four-wheel drive. Easier said than done.

It took a while to find a car, mostly because it took a while for it to sink in that those index cards posted on the bulletin board at Connections advertising a *Great Island Car!* for sale didn't mean what we thought. *Great Island Car!* is a euphemism. The hood might be held on with a bungee cord. Or you might have to reach out the window and open the door from the outside. Or the road might be visible through rusted-out holes in the floor. A *Great Island Car!* would, however, have a cup holder. You might be missing a standard feature—brake lights, for example, or a muffler —but every car had cup holders (to take full advantage of the fact you could drink and drive). (On the left.)

We almost bought a Jeep from a fisherman named Lunker. It was a real Thelma-and-Louise job, an old-model, army-green Wrangler that had a leaky transmission and no inspection sticker but came with an almost-full bottle of Southern Comfort stowed in the console. ("Dudes. That's your free gift with purchase," our salesman drawled.) We met Lunker at JJ's Texas Coast Café across from the ferry dock one morning, after he came in from fishing, and waited while he took a phone call. ("Whoa, dude, so nine-toed Walter is now eight-toed Walter?") Every third word out of his mouth was vulgar. He was entertaining until we told him we needed some time to think about the car. Then he called us the mother-fucking cocksuckers who jerked him around for half a day. Hey, it wasn't our fault he required multiple self-service road-side stops just to get the thing going. On the plus side, while discussing the deal over beers at the Quiet Mon Pub, the bartender told a great story about growing up in New York and roller-skating down the planks of the Guggenheim when the museum was under construction.

Hitchhiking was safe, but no guarantee of getting to work on time, much like VITRAN, which adhered to a strictly nebulous schedule. After a neighbor asked if we were on the "rent-to-own" plan with the expensive rental we'd been driving for several weeks, we applied ourselves and found the Suzuki. The "Pirates for Hire" bumper sticker was a selling point—distracting from the spare tire, ripped to shreds—and the windows all rolled up, explaining the enthusiastic *Dry Car!* descriptions on some of the index cards. Windows that rolled up meant we wouldn't come back from the beach to find roosters sitting in the driver's seat. The car was quirky but dependable, chugging up those optimistically named "hills" that felt near-vertical. Even the radio worked. Although it only got one station, and it played a lot of Supertramp.

Still, if you owned a *Great Island Car!* something was always broken. (Hoods secured with bungees, doors that don't open from the inside, and rusted-out floorboards were not considered broken.) Our car had no rearview mirror and, after our first accident, didn't turn left. When you absolutely needed to get something fixed, you stopped at Skinny's to find Slug, the only mechanic on our side of the island, who evidently had a two-year waiting list for an appointment. He promised to look at our car, but we could never figure out if he said he'd do it "Sunday" or "someday." I drove a lot of circuitous routes to avoid turning left.

One morning, pulling out of our driveway, Jazz and I almost got run over by Willie, one of the aforementioned speed demons. We learned later that he had already had two accidents near the Cliffhanger, one of which sent him hurtling all 60 feet down to the water. The wipeout left him with a nasty scar on his left leg, which he told everyone was a shark bite. After that, before we pulled into the road we would look left, look right, and look out for Willie. And here's a misconception about the alleged "laid-back island attitude" that needs clearing up: While it's true that sometimes you had to wait patiently while two cars traveling in opposite directions stopped—blocking all traffic on both sides of the road—so their drivers could have a confab, at other times—while you were driving a safe speed to avoid donkeys and mongoose dem, etc.—someone would be tailgating you. There might only be a handful of cars on the roads but, rest assured, one of them would be on your ass the entire way from Cruz to Coral Bay.

Occasional journeys to "town" were necessary for things we couldn't get or do in Coral Bay. Nobody delivered anything to your doorstep. If you wanted something, you had to go and get it. We might need something from St. John Hardware or Caravan Auto Parts. A trip to the bank or the post office could be an all-day affair. Ditto for grocery shopping. Coral Bay didn't have a supermarket and food prices on the island were ludicrous, so most people made regular excursions to Kmart or Cost-U-Less on St. Thomas. (Or St. Trauma, as some St. Johnians liked to call it; the neighbors returned the favor by calling us St. Yawn.) Shopping was the great equalizer. It didn't matter if you were working-class or the owner of a multi-million-dollar villa. Everyone shopped at Kmart.

Getting onto the car barge was a free-for-all. Aggressive driving habits were an asset. If you didn't pay attention, the barge might start to take off while you were still driving on. We could ward off road rage, we'd been advised, by stopping first at Cap's Place, across from the car barge dock, and grabbing a couple of ice-cold Presidentes for the ride. Add up shopping time, drive time on St. Thomas, the 40-minute (each way) barge trip, and the round-trip drive from Coral Bay to Cruz Bay and grocery shopping took about six hours, but if your timing was good, you got to ride home on the boat with the live palm trees and the bar that sold Coronas after 4 p.m.

Cell service ranged from clear-as-the-water to non-existent. The contract for our new phones stated that we had unlimited minutes with other Cingular customers, but that was a little phone company inside joke since most calls got cut off after two minutes. After a while it felt not only normal but also reasonable that you couldn't make a phone call whenever you wanted. (Well, reasonable to me. Jazz never stopped trying. Here is a "phone conversation" I overheard many nights on the Cliffhanger deck:

"Hello?" Pause. "Hi, Chica! I miss you! How's life in ... Hello? Hello?" Pause. "Hello?") No phone was no big deal when some days you had no power. Or water. My cell phone never rang but it had voicemail, so theoretically I could get messages, provided all circuits weren't busy when someone called, and the caller wasn't deterred by the operator recording, which was in Spanish. It took an hour and a half to get the phone ordered and set up, which wasn't bad by island standards, and as a bonus, the saleswoman invited me to the Veterans Day breakfast at her church. Holidays were big. A holiday shut down all public services and many commercial businesses about once every two weeks.

We spent one afternoon at Innovative, the Virgin Islands cable/telephone company, signing up—and paying—for cable and a landline for dial-up internet service. (Broadband had just arrived in Coral Bay around that time, thanks to a U.S. Department of Agriculture Rural Development Grant, the same program that would get parts of Appalachia connected. Score one for the folks who insisted we were living in the sticks.) Two weeks later, we still had neither. Our service order for the cable had us listed for a house call ... someday.

The Cliffhanger had a rusty mailbox emblazoned with what looked like an official street address but that didn't mean we got mail. We were told the U.S. Postal Service had some sort of off-the-books arrangement with a dedicated St. Johnian who had faithfully delivered the mail in Coral Bay for years. He, however, had apparently been out of commission since throwing his back out a few weeks earlier and, since the entire route was in his head, no one could fill in. The locals kept dropping by Connections, a cramped and lively office that served as the information/communications/scuttlebutt center, hoping anything important would turn up there.

Communication with the outside world more or less a farce, Jazz and I focused on getting to know our neighbors, inserting ourselves into their conversations and crashing their parties. We had seen the ad for the Rotary Club's "Flavors of St. John" while perusing the "Deals on Wheels" classifieds in the *St. John Tradewinds*. The Saturday night event at the Westin—one of only two resorts, both on the Cruz Bay side—featured every major restaurant on island. It was a charity event and a $100 ticket, not exactly in the budget for the new lifestyle, but maybe we'd get jobs out of it. Cocktails: 6:30. Flavors: 7:30. Dress: Island Fancy.

What constituted "Island Fancy?" I had left the little black dresses and tasteful news anchor attire behind but packed one "just-in-case" outfit—diaphanous flower-print sheath, pastel pink stilettos—I thought might fit the bill.

Before heading out, we stopped to see Dirt Digger Darlene, who lived in the Cliffhanger's downstairs apartment with a beast of a dog named Wyatt. Darlene worked construction, cut hair, and referred to herself as a "tough island bitch."

My first introduction to Darlene didn't go well. Jazz and I were walking down her stairs with armfuls of laundry, on our way to the washing machine on her floor that the landlord—who lived off island—said we should use. This was information he had neglected to relay to Darlene. Inconvenienced and annoyed, Darlene confronted us on the landing and began running through her mental list of everything that was wrong with the Cliffhanger, Coral Bay, and Caribbean life in general. She couldn't comprehend why we wanted to live there. "I came on vacation and never left," she explained, as we stood there, shifting our weight from leg to leg, smiling stupidly, and trying not to drop our mildewy towels. "You *chose* to move here. Do you understand the difference?" We didn't but nodded anyway. It sure sounded like an insult, but to confuse the issue further, Darlene followed up by saying she thought what we were doing was "cool as fuck."

Dirt Digger Darlene had spent most of her life in Tulsa where she acquired four husbands, half a dozen kids, an outrageous laugh, and a tattoo on her lower back of an angel who, in turn, had a "Kiss This!" tramp stamp. She loved the Dixie Chicks and said "Praise the Lord and pass the ammunition" was her motto.

She was wildly impressed that we seemed to know more people after two weeks than she'd met in two years, and while she didn't know quite what to make of us, her mothering skills kicked in and she sort of took us under her wing. (Though she never did let us use her washer.)

Wyatt barked maniacally, announcing our arrival.

"Shut up, Wyatt!" Darlene hollered as she slammed the sliding glass door behind her and turned to greet us on the deck, juggling a bottle of tequila and three shot glasses. She looked at me and her eyes bugged out. "Whoa! You could get laid in that dress."

Maybe mothering isn't exactly the right description. But Darlene snapped photos like it was prom night and toasted our big night out. "Here's to two new pirates of the Caribbean!" she cackled, before downing her Cuervo Gold, collecting our empty glasses, and shooing us up the driveway.

I swapped my pink heels for flip-flops for the drive into town, but that strategy fell short. Party dresses and *Great Island Cars!* do not mix. There was no AC in our Suzuki, and the windows didn't roll up unless you physically lifted the glass into place, an impossible maneuver with both hands clutching the steering wheel to curve around unfamiliar, treacherous mountain roads. And I believe I mentioned it was the rainy season? Five minutes into the ride, the brilliant sunshine disappeared and water gushed from the sky, streaming in the open driver's side window and drenching my wispy chiffon. Struggling to see past the sheets of rain blanketing the windshield, I dared to take one hand off the wheel only for the second needed to thrust my sunglasses back on my head and swipe a dripping strand of hair out of my eyes. Jazz was riding shotgun and laughing hysterically, trying to help navigate by sticking her head out the window, the better to see any obstacles ahead. We arrived at the hotel a full hour later, wrung out our dresses in the parking lot, and headed to the tent on the beach with a new understanding of "Dress: Island Fancy." Another inside joke. But it was worth it, as we chatted up the owners/chefs/potential future employers of almost every restaurant represented. It wasn't hard. When you're newcomers in a small place, everybody wants to know who the hell you are.

"You two are brave to come out to this," one prominent businesswoman whispered as she walked by. "Welcome to The Island."

The brave part, it seemed, wasn't uprooting your life and moving to a tropical outpost. It was facing up to the people who already lived there. St. John had about 4,000 year-round residents at the time, first and foremost West Indian families who had been there for generations. But there were also settlers from elsewhere: recent college graduates and comfortable retirees, Vietnam vets, single adults who left good jobs in offices to work on boats, young couples with children who were tired of the commercialism back wherever they came from. Coral Bay had its share of all of them, and plenty of gray-haired stoned hippies, too. Although there were very few true expatriates (they can't vote for president, but Virgin Islanders are all United States citizens), certain places in Coral Bay had an expat feel, with eccentrics from all economic backgrounds who were staunchly anti-authority and made sharp distinctions between themselves and those other Americans who lived "stateside." These Caribbean islands, which have seduced sailors for centuries, retain their pull. Modern-day adventurers, nature-lovers bewitched by the sheer beauty, and free spirits seeking some sort of paradise or another all live in fragile harmony with ancestral islanders—mothers and fathers, grandparents, great aunts and uncles, sons and daughters—descended from the enslaved.

Many of the "born here" St. Johnians shared prominent family names: Marsh. Smith. Samuel. Everyone else was anonymous. Almost no one I met in those early days had a last name and asking was taboo. There were 10 Toms in Coral Bay (just two short of a calendar, the locals sighed): St. Croix Tom and Cruzan Tom (who lived in St. Croix longer than St. Croix Tom, but St. Croix Tom had the moniker first) and Dozer Tom (the only guy who could forge a driveway into those insane rocky inclines) and

Jersey Tom and Tom-Who-Keeps-Getting-Kicked-Off-The-Boat-Because-Ginny-Is-Going-Through-Menopause. Everyone had a nickname: Stinger. Pirate Bill. Long-Haired Ken. Bank Robber Ritchie. Mean Jean. Little Will. Bob Who Drinks Coke. Rumor had it St. John was fertile ground for the Federal Witness Protection Program, so that might have explained the no-surname thing. Actually, if it was true, it explained a lot.

Coral Bay residents swapped partners with alacrity and disarming ease. You needed a flow chart to keep up. Many a new neighbor's current significant other used to be married to, had romantic entanglements with, or was recently jilted by somebody else in the neighborhood. Surprisingly, this was not problematic. Erstwhile couples co-existed amicably on the same small hunk of rock, often scouting out their next liaison in plain view of their former lovers.

"There goes your future ex-husband," Jazz would wisecrack every time a guy would flirt with me at the bar at Skinny Legs.

"New girls can date anyone they want," Mollie at Connections informed us. It seemed a good idea to wait, though, and explore local platitudes such as *The odds are good, but the goods are odd!* This did nothing to deter the gossip mill, which churned out regular speculation about who the new girls might be sleeping with. There was no fighting this. Eventually I started responding by saying that, why, yes, I *was* having sex with every man I was seen with. Strangely, this seemed to satisfy people and the questions stopped, bringing us to another oft-heard tenet: *Nobody cares what you do on St. John. They just want to know about it.*

That, I suppose, is why I started writing it all down. People just wanted to know about it. I never thought about how soon it might all be gone.

2

SKINNY LEGS
18.4°N, 64.7°W

I f you wanted to know what was going on in Coral Bay, you had to go to Skinny Legs. Everybody went to Skinny's.

The first time I saw Skinny Legs was on the dive vacation when I first visited St. John. Jazz had a friend on St. Croix who came over for the day and rented a car to show us around the "rustic" part of the island. We must have arrived in Coral Bay in mid-morning, before the lunch crowd livened things up.

We pulled into Skinny's parking lot—where donkeys grazed amidst crappy, trash-bag-bandaged jeeps—walked in, and digested the scene: A bar and a dozen or so tables with plastic chairs, random sports memorabilia tacked up here and there, and a dirt backyard with a horseshoe pit and a small makeshift stage. The roof was an old sail. Lots of outstanding island bars are little more than glorified shacks, but this one was missing a few key elements. No beach. No view of the water. No delightful breeze. It did have a vague smell of swamp. There were more chickens than humans. A few conspicuous regulars were hunched over the bar. Behind them, hanging from the rafters, was a homespun mobile of unpaired flip-flops, dangling from a sign that read "Lost Soles." And I had just one thought: Who would live here?

Skinny Legs did not look like the center of anyone's universe, but it was about to become the center of mine. Because, almost immediately, I landed a coveted waitressing job. And then I had to start explaining to people who wanted to come down to visit that my new life in the Caribbean wasn't spent sitting under a palm tree, sipping frozen cocktails. For starters, Skinny's didn't even have a blender. Or any palm trees.

"You're working at *Skinny's*?" incredulous employees of lesser establishments would demand. "How'd you get a job there?"

My original plan was to try to work at St. John's big water sports company so I could dive every day, but that was impractical since the boats left from Cruz Bay, the day started at the crack of dawn, and getting to the other side of the island was always a crap-shoot. Moreover, new friends assured me that if I got a job bartending or waiting tables, I'd make more money and work fewer hours, leaving plenty of time to go diving for fun. I'd never waited tables or tended bar, but everyone said I didn't need experience, just personality.

Believe it or not, we sort of thought the Cliffhanger came with jobs. Our new landlord had introduced Jazz to his friend Pat who, along with her husband, Dennis, owned the Shipwreck Landing restaurant, conveniently located a leisurely, five-minute walk down the hill from the Cliffhanger. Pat, it was implied, would be able to use both of us for a couple of bartending and waitressing shifts a week. This was a key factor in our decision to sign the lease. There weren't many employment options in Coral Bay, and we knew we'd be vying for jobs in a pool of energetic 20-somethings with service industry skills out the wazoo.

"She doesn't care that we don't have experience?" I asked Jazz when she relayed the news of her alleged house/jobs score.

"Well, I didn't tell her that. Besides, it's all about personality anyway."

After moving in, we went to see Pat about our jobs. We ambled down the hill to Shipwreck where Pat, an ex-banker from New Jersey, was hard at work varnishing, somehow managing not to mess up her perfectly manicured nails. She looked up from her task and, blatantly uninterested in our personalities, asked what kind of experience we had. I don't remember what we said, but Pat said she didn't need any additional help and made an unconvincing offer to call if anything changed. The exchange lasted two minutes. We turned around and trudged up what suddenly felt like a much steeper hill, back to the Cliffhanger.

Rejected but resilient, we next set our sights on Skinny Legs. Best friends Moe and Doug were the founders and co-owners but Doug, we were told, had been seriously ill so Moe was calling the shots, with a little help from the no-nonsense Mean Jean behind the bar. Jean was from Texas and one of the nicest people you could ever hope to meet. One theory on how she got baptized "Mean" was that, back when she was drinking, she loved to dance, even if it meant she was the only one out on the dance floor. *Mean Jean the Dancing Machine.* "I kinda miss that," she would say with a wistful sigh, referring to the dancing, and the whiskey.

After getting divorced, Mean Jean moved to paradise with two suitcases, her six-year-old son, and $400. She had read about Virgin Islands National Park in the library back home. When she arrived in 1979, St. John was a place with just four telephones—three at the dock, that didn't always work, and one at the police station. Back then you could sit at the end of the ferry dock and fish or look at the stars.

Mean Jean met Doug and Moe when they all worked together at the Back Yard in Cruz Bay—a bar so epic even the Coral Bay folks raved about it—and liked to say she knew them when they both had hair. Around the time the men decided to open their own place, Mean Jean had just read Tom Robbins's *Skinny Legs and All*, and the title resonated. Moe, the runner, always wore sneakers. Doug favored white knee socks with his shoes. The restaurant's logo was a sketch of the two men from the waist down, lanky limbs poking out of their distinctive footwear. Down at the Triangle, there used to be a bench, by the bus stop, supported by replicas of those same two pairs of skinny legs—sneakers, socks, and all.

Moe was a New Englander who rooted for the Patriots and religiously ran the Boston Marathon. He was tall, lean, and, at the time, bald, having recently shaved his head for a fundraiser for an employee with cancer. Jazz and I accosted him at work and, this time primed to prevaricate, asked for jobs.

Moe looked at the two of us skeptically. "What kind of work are you looking for?"

"Waitressing," I said.

"Bartending," Jazz said.

"You have waitressing experience?" he asked me, point-blank.

"Yup."

"How about you? You've bartended before?"

"Uh-huh," Jazz stammered. "I've tended bar."

"Let me rephrase that," he said. "Have you ever poured drinks for money?"

"I learn fast and I don't talk back," I offered, stealing a line from a reporter friend who told me that got him a job on a boat in Hawaii once.

"Sometimes you should talk back," Moe said.

I didn't know what to say next. Couldn't he see we had personality?

"I really need experienced people," Moe explained. "We get so busy in season."

We stood there until Moe said he might have something for one of us and gave us the old "come back tomorrow." Later, Jazz decided Skinny Legs was a little too low-class for her, and magnanimously offered to let me have whatever job might surface. When I stopped back the next day, Moe said he might be able to use some help on Sunday because Skinny's had football on Sundays and football drew a crowd. He promised to call if he needed someone extra to work.

The next day, no call.

The day after, no call.

I went back down to Skinny's to find Moe in person.

"Hey!" I said, cheerfully. "Did you try to call me? Because my phone never works here."

Moe looked puzzled. "Was I supposed to call you?"

"You said you might need me to work on Sunday because it's football Sunday, everybody here is from New England, I'm from Philly, you were hoping to branch out a little ... remember?"

Moe said come in tomorrow to train.

I rushed home to tell Jazz I got the job.

"That's awesome!" she exclaimed. "What will you be doing?"

"I don't know."

"How much do they pay?"

"I don't know."

"How late do you think you'll work?"

I didn't know. I didn't know anything except that I was supposed to be there at 10 a.m. the next day. I didn't ask any questions because I was afraid he'd change his mind. And once I got home, I was really afraid because the next day I had to be a waitress and I'd never waited tables in my life.

I immediately got on the phone and called my best friend from college, Trish, who was also the best—OK, only—waitress I knew, and who probably would have been part of this Caribbean caper except that she was seven months pregnant.

"Help!" I pleaded. "I just lied and said I had waitressing experience and now I have to go to work tomorrow and pretend to be a waitress. I have no idea what I'm doing. I need advice. It's urgent. All the pointers you can give me. Give me some lingo so I'll sound like I've done this before."

"OK," she said slowly. The connection to Connecticut was faint and liable to drop at any moment, but Trish's voice was calm and reassuring, her New England accent piercing the crackle. "Don't worry. I've slung hash, baby. I can help you."

I grabbed my pen, ready to take notes, as Trish began.

"The first thing you need to know," she said, "is whatever you do, don't fuck the cook."

"Um, I was thinking more along the lines of 'what's a four-top?' or what does '86 the bacon' mean?"

"Oh!" Trish said. "I can tell you all that, too. But this is really important. Because if you get involved with the cook, and it goes bad, then you're never gonna get your food. And then you're really screwed.

"Also, however they do things at your place, you tell them you did it *the other way* the last place you worked."

"Oh, that's good. Great. Thanks, Trish."

"You're welcome. And don't worry. You'll be fine. It's all about personality anyway."

Sunday morning I was at Skinny's in my Eagles T-shirt. Moe's new girlfriend was training me, which could have been a nightmare, but she was so busy bossing me around, telling me her way of doing things, I think maybe she didn't notice that I didn't have a way.

The menu was written on a surfboard and it was simple: mostly cheeseburgers, chilidogs, and mahi fish sandwiches. Skinny's didn't do French fries or piña coladas. *No fryer, no blender, no appliance that ends in 'e-r'!* one of the waitresses would say. I looked up "refrigerator" just to be sure. If a customer asked what kind of wine we had, the answer was *red or white, served in the finest plastic!* If there was a special, it was scrawled in magic marker on the back of a paper plate and stapled up over the bar. If you didn't see it in print, we didn't have it. So don't ask. And don't ask how long it's going to take. Skinny's promised "Same Day Service!"

There were four cooks at Skinny's. Mississippi Mel could "wrestle, kill, skin, and cook the best gator you've ever tasted." The first shift we worked together he asked me to complain about him because he'd been trying for 13 years to get fired. James, a West Indian, pretended not to understand my orders. Surf, a musician from California, informed me that he could read minds. Oscar, "a Jewish kid from New Jersey who should have been a lawyer," instead became the black sheep of his family when he

decided he couldn't take one more minute of abysmal winter weather and skipped town.

Waitressing at Skinny's turned out to be mainly multi-tasking and dealing with difficult people—not so different from my old reporting job—with a little math thrown in. Besides, I am a quick learner. One thing I learned is telling customers you're new, it's your first day, you just chucked your real life to move to the islands, etc. is good for a $30 tip on a $16 check.

At the end of my first shift, Jazz came to pick me up. (Like Mom on the first day of school, she dropped me off in the morning, too.) She found me sitting at the bar with Oscar, having a beer and eating a bowl of clam chowder.

"How'd it go?" she asked.

"Good," I replied, and made the introductions. "Oscar, this is my roommate, Jazz. Jazz, this is Oscar. He made the chowder."

"I can't believe you!" Jazz admonished as we were heading home half an hour later.

"Your first day on the job, I walk in to pick you up, and what do I see? You're sitting at the bar, flirting with the cook. I'm calling Trish."

Behind Skinny's bar, assisting Mean Jean, were Anna Banana, Rum Runner Rick, and Nigel, an ex-roadie whose music and movie collection was what passed for a library in Coral Bay. Nigel believed everyone needed to watch the surf documentary *The Endless Summer* and lent out his prized possession as a public service. Then there was Erin, bartending, waitressing, cooking. She seemed to work everywhere in Coral Bay, one of those energetic 20-somethings constantly in the midst of some long string of double shifts and no-days-off. I'm not sure she ever went home. One night, working at Skinny's on her birthday, she started crying when a couple of friends came in to visit her. "I can't believe you came all this way!" she bawled. "They came from Rhode Island?" I asked. "No!" she said through tears. "They came all the way from Cruz Bay!"

I got my own shot behind the bar at Shipwreck. Turned out

Pat and Dennis needed help after all and the two women living up the hill were definitely convenient. My first day there I trained as a bartender while Jazz waited tables and Pat tracked our every move like a bird of prey. I had to learn to make Painkillers (Pusser's dark rum, pineapple juice, OJ, cream of coconut, ground nutmeg) and Bushwhackers (light and dark rum, vodka, amaretto, Kahlua, and Baileys—"A Grownup's Milkshake," the island menus called it). At one point I had three blenders going, muddling my way through an order for two Bushwhackers, two Painkillers, and a virgin strawberry-mango colada.

"First time behind the bar?" the boss asked, dryly.

Shipwreck had its own cast of characters. Bethany, the veteran waitress who trained me, spent about two minutes showing me how to run credit cards and half an hour explaining how to fill the ketchup bottles. Sweet Sarah and Sistah Blistah tended bar. Sarah was a Rubenesque, pale-skinned girl from Minnesota who immersed herself in West Indian culture and did her best to teach me the difference between sugar-apple and star fruit, soursop and genips. Sistah Blistah was wiry and compact with leathery skin and a bullshit barometer that saw right through us. When Jazz relieved Sistah Blistah after her shift, Sistah Blistah would sit at the bar, listen to the orders, and tell Jazz how to make the drinks.

Our favorite Shipwreck cook was Jungle George, a big bear of a guy who also grew up in Philly. George was a paradigm of island reinvention, an ex-marketing exec with anger management issues now living on a sailboat called *George of the Jungle* and commuting to work in a derelict blue Suzuki jeep with an old outboard motor strapped to the back. (People were so handy, I believed, for a while, it somehow powered the car.) We did "Philadelphia Sundays" with Jazz bartending, Jungle George whipping up cheesesteaks, and me out front waitressing, using our combined spin and schmooze talents to sell a substantial amount of Saturday night's soup by re-branding it "Pirate Stew."

One day I was working at Shipwreck when Moe from Skinny's stopped in. Was he coming in for lunch? No. He needed me

to work that night for someone who was out sick. He had tried to call, he said, but my phone wasn't working. Apparently I had moved to a place where if the boss wanted you for something, he just drove around town until he found you.

Both jobs had their low points. For me, it was refilling the condiment baskets at Skinny's. Every waitress I worked with filled me in on her educational background over this tedious chore. "I used to be the principal at a private school in Massachusetts," said Belle, a single mom raising her 10-year-old son on a boat in the harbor. "Now I'm stuffing mustard baskets." Taking out the trash stank, too, but a couple of my regular customers often did it for me so I couldn't really complain. When people asked me what I used to do for a living, I usually just told them it didn't involve wearing a crop top which, to be honest, probably accounted for the helpful trash men.

For Jazz, the worst was mopping the floor on Sundays. It was a dirty job but not so bad if you remembered to look up. Ship-wreck was an open-air restaurant, right on the coast. Instead of walls you saw sapphire sea, framed by swaying palm trees. Little yellow bananaquits—known as "sugar birds"— zoomed in and out. If you were a Disney fan you could channel your inner Cinderella, toiling away while little birdies tweeted in circles around your head. Skinny Legs, in contrast, had no view and, because of an aging septic system, sometimes smelled more like bathroom than burgers. People came for the food and the unadul-terated local atmosphere. Dinner and a show. The tips were great, though. We paid our first month's rent in cash. Plus, there was whatever food was left over at the end of the night. Jazz came home from one shift with $128 cash, four potatoes, and a lime.

Not long after I started, the Board of Health cited Skinny Legs for enough code violations to close the restaurant for a couple of days. Seems somebody complained about the stray dogs wandering among the tables and one of them, Rex, had the bad timing to walk in and sprawl out in the middle of the floor in the middle of the inspection. The closure prompted all the bar

owners in Coral Bay to demand up-to-date health cards, an until-then loosely enforced requirement for working in the restaurants. Procuring a government-issued food handler's card was a laborious exercise requiring a social security card (a U.S. passport did not qualify as sufficient identification) and a minimum of two days to negotiate the Byzantine bureaucracy. Most of the process involved sitting around a dingy, pale green, cinder-block waiting room, reminiscent of a '70s-era public school classroom, and ... waiting. On the plus side, I recognized almost everyone there, so it was a lot like being called to the principal's office on a particularly rowdy day at the junior high.

After returning to work for one day with the proper documentation, I then missed a week because I was hacking and sneezing with something that felt a lot like the flu but my neighbors assured me was really "The Tourist Bug." Blaming tourists for importing germs was a fringe benefit of island living. On the minus side, in my new vocation as part-time waitress, I didn't get paid if I stayed in bed.

On a typical high-season day at Skinny's, the bar would be jammed and the kitchen backed up. People waited in line for tables. Taxi drivers would come in with truckloads of starving tourists, the aroma of grilled meat meeting them up at the road. The locals came in, too. "Oh, you need to talk to so-and-so," people would say during those first few months, when we'd inquire about a mechanic, or a handyman. We never needed phone numbers or last names. Eventually—usually sooner rather than later, sometimes minutes after the conversation—the person in question would be sitting at Skinny's bar. People made perfectly timed entrances, sitcom-style. Rooney announced his arrival by emulating a braying donkey. Bob Who Drinks Coke came in every weekday at noon for his Coca Cola. Irie, a Rastafarian who told me his job was "coconut technician," had his own stool at the far end of the bar.

One night Moe was glued to the TV, cheering on his Patriots. He leaned over to tease me about the Eagles, who had just

won the NFC championship and were headed to the Super Bowl.

"I have a friend coming down from Boston," he said. "He's going to bring me some Patriots jerseys and pennants and maybe another banner. I'm going to try to get some Eagles stuff for the Super Bowl too. It's a big day here. A lot of fun. Oh, and next week, we're going to have a flamenco guitarist and a dancer."

I was sure I heard him wrong. It got noisy during a football game. But there we were the following Sunday, and the noise that night was clamorous applause for a husband-and-wife flamenco act, performing on the ramshackle stage behind the horseshoe pit. How did they end up at Skinny's? Turns out Laura, the prep cook, was an aficionado. She had seen the duo when she was working in St. Thomas—she and Buccaneer Barbara had dinghied over to the Bottoms Up bar to catch the act—and thought they'd be great entertainment for the off-week in the NFL schedule. The locals dubbed it "culture night" in Coral Bay, with reaction ranging from curious to downright confused. One bartender had to quick get on the phone to his friends at JJ's in Cruz Bay after erroneously informing them over beers at breakfast that they should bring their dollar bills to Skinny's that night because there was going to be belly dancing. Moe observed that nobody was buying drinks during the performance but said that was OK because it meant his customers were enjoying the show.

And he really did care about his customers. The following week he had a health mobile coming in to offer free medical screenings. Lots—maybe most—of Skinny's regulars were uninsured. Moe figured Skinny's was a Pretty OK Place for just about anything: Weather reports. Veterinary care. A potluck to raise money for a neighbor in need.

Skinny's was the wacky community center where everyone congregated and it didn't take long to become my home base. If I heard about something at Skinny's, I signed up for it. I'm not a runner—kind of hate it, actually—but found myself in a road race from one end of the island to the other because, well, that's what

you did down there. 8 Tuff Miles started in Cruz Bay and ended in the ballfield right next to Skinny's. I came in second to last, besting a mother walking with two little kids. Then I shuffled over to Skinny's horseshoe pit for the "almost-annual" Pitch 'N' Bitch tournament. The name was a takeoff on "stitch and bitch" sewing and knitting circles. "We don't really have any quilters here," Moe said. "Our women are sailors and plumbers and painters and varnishers."

I hadn't tossed horseshoes since that time in my grandmother's South Jersey backyard when I was nine, so I was alarmed by the prospect of being paired up with one of the more ruthless sailors, plumbers, painters, or varnishers. My teammate was artist Billie, whose serene, New Age-y demeanor (I would later overhear her, at an international regatta, patiently try to explain to a befuddled Italian sailor with limited English skills that the opposite of *LOVE* was not, in fact, *hate,* but *FEAR*) evaporated the minute she took hold of the tiller on her sailboat. Horseshoes, thankfully, did not stoke New Age Billie's competitive soul like sailing did. She suggested a *more champagne!* strategy and I got to relax. We got eliminated in the first round.

Contenders for the 14th-Ever Pitch 'N' Bitch included sailing instructors Jenn and Vicki, Mollie from Connections, Nancy of Valley Doll Hot Sauce fame, Jill of Blind Betty Hot Sauce fame, and all the Skinny's waitresses: Erin, Belle, Fun Christina. Erin was up first, masterful at not hitting the chickens that kept running across the pit. Fun Christina upped the suspense level, performing Madonna-esque moves before every toss. Varnish Julie got the first ringer. Or at least the first one I remembered to write down.

And I was writing this down—all of it—often jotting surreptitious notes on the back of a guest check and stuffing it in my waitress apron for later. This was before smart phones and social media. A younger colleague had set up a blog for me before I left Philly, but I didn't know what that was, and it sounded like work. I did, however, have an email list and a small, but jealous, audience

back home. I had started sending short dispatches, detailing the conceits and characters of my new life in Coral Bay. Journalist friends stuck in the cold and living island life vicariously wrote back to offer encouragement (*DO Fuck the Cook!)* and accuse me of getting stoned and making shit up.

Too good to be true! they asserted.

Better than fiction! I'd retort.

St. John would make the real news when country music star Kenny Chesney got married. It was the first Saturday in May and in upscale Peter Bay, cases of Dom Perignon were being carried into Chesney's villa for the next day's top-secret celebrity wedding. But over in somewhat less exclusive Coral Bay, the event of the spring season was already underway: the Kentucky Derby Party at Skinny Legs.

Doug's ex-wife, who hailed from Louisville, presided over the free buffet of more than 100 pounds of ham and corn pudding and personally mixed the bourbon, sugar, and fresh mint to serve up the mint juleps. Partygoers embraced another Derby tradition, donning fabulous hats adorned with ribbons, toy horses, and tropical blooms. Some of the women wore dresses but most just added the hat to the preferred getup of shorts, T-shirt, and Reef sandals and called it a day. My own effort was a black straw hat with shiny, fake black flowers. Someone tucked bright pink bougainvillea into the band, adding the obligatory local flair.

Moe acted as bookie. He locked himself inside Connections and gamblers lined up outside the window to place their bets. Rules were clearly posted:

Number One: Tell us your name. (Even if we know you.)

The only person who didn't already know everybody there was me. I hung around the betting line, hoping to catch a few names.

Kentucky-bred revelers included Shipwreck bartender School Bus Kathy and her mom, from Lexington, and a retired couple from Paducah who had been cruising the Caribbean for a year and unwittingly sailed into Coral Bay just in time to stand with the crowd at Churchill Downs and sing "My Old Kentucky Home." Then it was post time and they were off! For the two minutes and two seconds it took Giacomo to win the 131st Run for the Roses, no drinks were served at Skinny Legs, which just might have set a record, even if the horse did not.

"I've been wondering, *What is it about this place?*" another waitress confessed one night. "It's an OK burger shack with a limited menu, an out-of-the-way location, and no view. It stinks when the sewage system acts up. But I've finally figured it out. It's Doug and Moe."

She was right. Tourists loved it because one time—last year, or eight years ago, or on their honeymoon—they came in for lunch, ordered a mahi sandwich with "the works"—grilled mushrooms and onions—and talked to Doug or Moe for five minutes. So they came back. And as they came back, year after year, they made Skinny Legs an island institution.

Moe was a consistent presence throughout my tenure but Doug made only an occasional appearance. The first time I worked with him was a Saturday night in high season and I was the only waitress on duty. Doug was helping me out, taking drink orders and adding up my tickets. He didn't know how much anything cost. He'd sidle up next to me at the waitress station. "Hey, honey. How much is fish?" he'd inquire in his gravelly voice. ($8.00.) "What about chicken?" (Ditto.) It cracked me up that he—the owner!—was asking me.

"She has a nice smile," I would hear Doug tell customers, perhaps a stab at justifying hiring a waitress with no waitressing experience. I tried to compensate by working hard, serving up attitude with the cheddar burgers and rum swizzles. "We guarantee Same Day Service," I'd shrug, as I walked away from a table, no intention whatsoever of following through on my promise to go ask the kitchen "what's taking so long."

Skinny Legs marked the seasons. The Halloween party was always a blowout. St. Patrick's Day too. Doug, the Italian, cooked the corned beef and cabbage. Moe plated it up. "Tell them a

Polack is dishing it out, that's why it's taking so long this time," Moe quipped.

Seriously, everybody went to Skinny's. That health inspector who cited Skinny Legs for code violations? I could have sworn I heard him order a burger, medium well with American cheese and the works—to go—before shutting the place down. And when the hurricanes came, Skinny's was the literal refuge from the storm. When Hurricane Marilyn clobbered St. John—a decade before my arrival—it was at Skinny Legs that the Red Cross set up shop with disaster relief. Of course it was. Coral Bay surviving a hurricane without Skinny's as a balm was inconceivable.

3

THANKSPIGGING
(THANKSGIVING, 2004)

Before landing in the Virgin Islands, sailing capital of the New World, I had been on a sailboat exactly once. My mother had rented a little Sunfish on a vacation in Florida when I was a kid. We sat under the baking sun on a lake with no wind, bored and motionless, and when the hour was up, that was that. So when Oscar, one of the cooks at Skinny Legs, invited me to join his crew for the Thanksgiving regatta everybody was talking about, I was thrilled. Sailing was obviously a big deal in Coral Bay—*boats boats boats!*—and now I had an in.

The Saturday after Thanksgiving, I was standing on the Dinghy Dock waiting for my ride out to the boat and willing the butterflies in my stomach to stay ashore. I had three goals that day: Don't get seasick. Don't get hit by the boom (whatever that is). Don't get in the way.

Oscar's sailboat, *At Last,* was a type of classic boat called a Cowhorn. She was all wood with a lavender hull. As the little powerboat taking us out to her mooring got closer, I could see she was also in a bit of disrepair.

And, I learned after boarding, she had never been at sea with Captain Oscar at the helm.

There were nine people aboard, including a few who knew

what they were doing, plus Grouch, Oscar's mutt. We all got crew hats with the name of the boat embroidered on the front and the date on the back: September 26. It wasn't a mistake. That was supposed to be *At Last's* maiden voyage, but she didn't quite make it.

After a little trouble getting off the mooring, we headed toward the start line and, in a spectacular display of seamanship, ran right over one of the markers, sinking the buoy and tangling the line in our propeller. A race committee boat sped over and next thing I knew, everybody was yelling, the dog was barking like mad, and two men were in the water. One dove off our boat holding a 12-inch serrated kitchen knife to cut the line. It was all very James Bond-like. I had no idea sailing was this exciting.

Because of the mishap, we were disqualified (DQ) before the race even started. Someone joked that instead of DQ or DNF (Did Not Finish) we might have just earned a DOA. Nevertheless, we forged on, got the sails up, turned the motor off and, finally, were sailing.

Toward land.

More shouting and scrambling ensued. One of the veteran crewmembers, rushing to adjust rigging, almost fell overboard. His girlfriend, who was at the tiller, laughed so hard I thought she would be next. We skirted the shore and turned back toward open water.

Captain Oscar had three goals too: Get his boat "off the hook," meaning off his mooring. Don't hit anything. Finish the course. Two out of three's not bad, and he would have finished the race, too, if he hadn't promised to have his passengers to work on time. We sailed our own course, cheering on other boats in the regatta and stopping in Hurricane Hole for lunch before heading back to harbor. The crew pronounced the voyage a success and the captain, a self-described grump, was caught smiling.

With good cause. It was majestic to sit on deck and see those sails rise into a piercing blue sky, to watch a crew work in tandem to harness the wind until we were gliding through water, sun on our skin, spray coming over the bow.

After the sail, I rushed back to Skinny Legs for my shift and was in the center of the action for the post-regatta celebration. Rum-happy sailors partied long past dark, some of them talking about setting off for an overnight sail to St. Martin. On a whim? Just like that? It all sounded so exotic.

Forty-five boats raced in the Coral Bay Yacht Club's 23rd annual Thanksgiving Regatta, their names as familiar as any resident's: *Rob Roy, Willful,* and *Osprey. Wallyworld. For Pete's Sake. Snap.* Friendly, but competitive, rivals *Reality Switch* and *Windshift, Tiger Maru* and *Trinka.* Sloops and yawls and multi-hulls. Big traditional boats like the custom-built *Ushuaia,* and *Liberty,* a classic built in 1924, in the glory days of yachting. Gaff-riggers like the schooner *Penelope,* built on Hassel Island off St. Thomas, and *Calabreeze,* one of the half dozen "Cowhorns" built on the beach in Coral Bay in the late-'70s and early-'80s.

The history of the Thanksgiving regatta is tied in with the Cowhorns and goes something like this: Augie Hollen—a guy who hailed from the prairie and may or may not have spent time in the CIA before landing in Coral Bay—built the first Cowhorn in the Virgin Islands. It was made from the same type of wood the Caribs used for their dugout canoes and modeled after the sturdy, double-ended workboats that originated in Block Island in the 1600s, designed to withstand the rough New England waters. Double-enders have bows and sterns with similar lines that, viewed from the side, look a little like horns. Thus the name. Augie's Cowhorn was called *Taurus.* Next, Les Anderson, the artist, built *Penelope* from the same wood in a similar fashion. Then it had to be determined who was faster. The first contest— held at Foxy's on Jost Van Dyke in the British Virgin Islands—was winner-take-all. Augie was the victor, sailing home to St. John with the girl from Les's boat.

Sometime after that, Augie sold *Taurus* to Tommy No Legs, who lost both his legs in a helicopter crash in Vietnam. Tommy

thought maybe he'd call it *Foot Loose*. The boat was refitted for
Tommy and renamed *Sea Legs*, along with the captain. Tommy
Sea Legs couldn't walk but boy could he sail. Then Augie and
Sylvia—the girl he won over in that first race—built another
Cowhorn called *Violet*, this time from a mold, which begat five
more identical boats, which begat the Coral Bay Yacht Club,
formed by the small band of folks building their own boats from
Augie's mold, plus another handful of wayward travelers who
sailed into Coral Bay or otherwise washed ashore on her beaches
and decided to stay. With a whole fleet now, a regatta was in order.
Thanksgiving weekend was the only free date on the calendar.

I know all this because by my second week on St. John, I was a
reporter again. So much for taking a break from my old life.
Wherever you go, there you are! one of the tourist T-shirts taunted.

I wrote a story about my big regatta debut for the second
edition of the new *St. John Sun Times*. I had met the editor,
named—wait for it—Tom Paine, on the beach near the
Cliffhanger the week before. Another Tom. After Jazz blew my
cover ("She's got Emmys!"), Tom Paine asked me to write for his
fledgling newspaper. I said no.

Don't get me wrong. I liked the paper and its woo-woo edito-
rial stance: *We believe St. John is a magical place, one that shares its
secrets only with people with the right vibe, people who are totally
open.* The inaugural edition the month before was smart and edgy.
But, I explained to Tom Paine, I was on sabbatical (a word my
mother had advised me to use, suggesting it sounded better than
"I'm just going to drop out of life for a while ...") St. John was my
tabula rasa. I didn't want to report on it. I wanted to be like the
former accountants and schoolteachers and Wall Street guys who
were tending bar or captaining charter boats or caretaking villas.
Work had defined me for too long. I wanted to know who I was if
I wasn't a journalist. Tom Paine said he completely understood.
Then he refused to go away.

A whirlwind of thoughts and energy, Tom Paine spewed zeal,
and it was infectious. And, like many of the characters who popu-

lated my new island home, he seemed to appear everywhere I went, each time trying to tempt me by promising to pay me 50 bucks to write about anything I wanted. I countered by telling him I earned more than that in tips in one lunch hour at Skinny Legs. When the money lure didn't work, he changed tack, tricking me into further discussion by asking if I had any good ideas for feature stories.

Was he kidding?

There was some shoeless old guy who hung out at Skinny's every day dressed like an honest-to-God pirate. What was his deal?

Some captain the locals called Jaybird with a powerboat named *Lloyds of London* had recently starred in an amphibious high-speed chase to reclaim *Lloyds of London* when the guy who sold him the boat hijacked it back because Jaybird still owed him $600.

There was allegedly an undercover hiker blazing unauthorized trails through Virgin Islands National Park.

Skinny's had run out of burgers one day, throwing the whole east end of the island into an uproar. During one of my shifts, a lifelong vegetarian on vacation fell off the wagon because Skinny's burgers were just that good.

I had just overheard a tableful of locals engage in a rum-fueled debate about whether Coral Bay was a village, a hamlet, or a burg. (There was no consensus.)

If I were back in the newsroom, I couldn't write fast enough. The place was a gold mine.

I looked at Tom Paine and said nothing.

Come on, he cajoled, as if reading my mind. *Wasn't I writing emails or letters to somebody back home, telling them about my new life here?* He could just print those and pay me $50 for that.

The man was persistent. Tom Paine wore me down. There's a common-sense joke in here somewhere, but suffice it to say, I caved.

Maybe I needed a news fix. I had had some misguided vision of starting Caribbean mornings at dawn on my deck with a strong cup of Puerto Rican coffee and the newspaper, but there was no newspaper delivery. You could get a copy of *The Virgin Islands Daily News* down at Connections, but it rarely had any news about St. John. You could also get the Sunday *New York Times* and try to make it last all week, but it cost $14.50, and you had to drive to the posh Caneel Bay resort on the other side of the island to get it. On Monday.

So how did we know what was going on? The Coconut Telegraph. Word of mouth so efficient it hardly mattered that the phones never worked. Gossip counted as news, stories were apocryphal, and it was all likely to be reported like this: Fun Christina, your co-worker from Skinny Legs, drops by on her way to work and announces, "Guess who's pregnant? And guess who made the dinghy ride of shame this morning? And it's not the same person. And there's pepper jack cheese on the menu today. And bacon! It's going to be busy."

One day when I was waitressing, Plumber Kathy—the Bostonian behind "fotty-two-shades-of-blue"—interrupted as I was taking a lunch order to give me an update on the Cliffhanger's cistern woes. By the time my shift ended, I had three offers to go to other people's houses to shower.

While everyone seemed to know my business, my new gig as freelance Lois Lane gave me license to reciprocate. Writing for the *Sun Times* let me pry into the lives of my island neighbors. That they still spoke to me—or served me drinks, or sold me mangos, or otherwise consented to interact with me—after the stories ran, I considered proof that I got it mostly right.

In my old job I interviewed future presidents and tracked down mob bosses. In my new job, I was assigned to write a profile on Pirate Bill who requested, pre-interview, that we stop first at the Calabash Boom minimarket for a beer run. He emerged with a six-pack of Elephant. No grog for this guy.

Aside from the imported beer, and the fact that I had never seen him near a boat, Pirate Bill looked the part. He was wearing his trademark bandanna covering long, yellowish-white hair. His beard hung down to his upper chest, stopping short of his necklace, which boasted three large silver coins. Blue eyes shone from a weathered face. He was barefoot, as always. Gave up shoes in the '70s, he told me.

In true Coral Bay fashion, he wouldn't tell me his last name. "Bill," he replied, when I asked. "My first name is Pirate."

He was soft-spoken, which caught me off guard, surrounded as we were by alleged grown men who, in lieu of actually sailing the seven seas, were living out their Captain Jack Sparrow fantasies by flying the Jolly Roger from their boats, swaggering about, and bellowing AAARRRRGHHHH! (A fantasy not exclusive to the tropics. When I told a Philly friend I was writing this story, he dramatically recited for me his one line from a college production of *The Pirates of Penzance.* "We are rough men! AAARRRRGHHHH!" he shouted into the phone.)

Pirate Bill was a regular at Skinny's. A few nights earlier, he had been playing horseshoes in the backyard and I pointed him out to a little boy eating dinner with his family. The four-year-old shyly approached the intriguing man, shook his gnarled hand, then ran back to the table, wide-eyed: "He said his name was Pirate Bill! He said he had to dive down to get the treasure!"

Now I was in my Suzuki Sidekick, driving toward Johnson Bay, with Pirate Bill beside me, talking about that treasure. Real treasure. The treasure he helped salvage off the *Atocha,* the famed Spanish galleon that sank off the Florida Keys in 1622, doomed by a hurricane that proved far more deadly than marauding privateers.

Pirate Bill directed me to pull off to the side of the road. We got out of the car, squeezed through a half-open gate, and walked down a little path toward the water. We came to a clearing nestled among mangroves and sea grapes that was furnished with two ratty lawn chairs, a chaise longue, a beautifully crafted table, and a hammock. Coral, driftwood, and some old fishing net decorated the space, along with assorted flotsam and jetsam from Hurricane

Marilyn and who knows how many other disasters at sea. It had an unobstructed ocean view.

"Nice spot," I said.

"Pirate's Beach Club," Pirate Bill replied, inviting me to sit down.

He cracked open two Elephants, handed me one, and leaned forward to give me a closer view of the small chain of gold links dangling from his left ear.

"This is the first gold we discovered," he explained, recounting the thrill of recovering an eight-foot gold chain draped over a barrel sponge in about 40 feet of water off the coast of Key West.

Pirate Bill learned to dive in Las Vegas in the mid-'60s, putting him among the first generation of scuba divers. He never intended to go treasure hunting. He moved to Key West to buy a sailboat, with the goal of impressing "little hippie girls" and maybe doing some bootlegging. He got his boat, a 30-foot motor/sailboat named *Evasion* ("A good smuggling ship," he confided), and wound up connecting with the legendary shipwreck hunter Mel Fisher.

We talked about the early days of the hunt, in the '70s, when there wasn't much money, or faith, in the expedition. When they could afford gas, they'd go out looking. When they couldn't, they didn't. Then, in 1985, more than 350 years after the *Atocha*'s demise, Fisher's team uncovered the mother lode. 250,000 pieces of eight. 47 tons of silver. 150,000 gold coins and bars. Thousands of uncut emeralds, some of them golf-ball sized. Not just the King's Loot, to use Pirate Bill's term for the treasure duly recorded on the manifest, but tons of illicit loot, too, stuffed in cannons and lockers by the plundering crew.

"We were hauling up so much treasure that we were offloading onto other boats."

And back then, it was finders keepers. So that silver around his neck? Real treasure. Spanish coins. A piece of one, a piece of two. And a piece of eight from the *Atocha*.

Pirate Bill grew up in Detroit, his closest pirate connection being his father, described by Bill as a math genius who, naturally, became a bookie. Dad got rich, with a little help from the mob, and his son got what Bill called a "charmed life," a life that, before St. John, included running coin-operated pool tables in Vegas, some time in the Army ("hated every minute of it"), and a stint working for the L.A. County roads department. He left the Keys when they started getting overdeveloped, bought a $45 plane ticket to St. Croix, and soon after ended up in Coral Bay.

"I've been retired pretty much all my life," he said. "I was an only-child spoiled brat who could do no wrong. But I was raised well."

He said he didn't really like to read or write or watch TV. He described himself as a loner, who liked to think.

"Do you still go diving?" I asked. "Sailing? Swimming?"

He shook his head. "No." Then he made a real confession: "I'm not much of a water person."

So to recap, I was interviewing a real seafaring treasure-hunter. Which, one could argue, made him a real pirate. Except his biggest haul was legit. And he didn't like the ocean.

An image of a frigate bird flashed through my mind. The split-tailed birds soar high over the sea, hunting for fish to steal from other birds since their vast wingspans make landing on the water unsafe. A seabird that doesn't like the water.

I asked Pirate Bill what it was about the pirate life he found appealing.

"The pirates of the Caribbean were the first democracy on earth," he said, launching into some background on pirate codes and constitutions. They elected leaders. Divvied up the booty. Offered a form of workmen's comp. "It's pretty well document-ed," he informed the reporter.

Dusk had turned to dark, and the no-see-ums were biting with purpose.

"I've had an excellent life," Pirate Bill concluded. "I'm able to do what I want to do, and I'm responsible for my own actions, and if I go out with other people I have to give them a vote."

I remember thinking that he had just summed up what might have been the prevailing code of the island. So many people professed to feel a freedom to, if not exactly control their destiny, at least live by their own rules.

I wasn't sure I would ever feel that way. But I liked being in a pirate's secret hideout, sitting in silence, and watching the sun go down with a really good beer.

My first official assignment for the *Sun Times* was covering "Thankspigging," Coral Bay's annual potluck Thanksgiving pig roast. I had first heard about this peculiar event on my second day as a resident of St. John, in the place where I was getting most of my information: the bar at Skinny Legs. Mixing up drinks for Jazz and me, Anna Banana asked if we had any family in Coral Bay. When we told her no, she proclaimed, "Well! Then you are cordially invited to Thankspigging!"

Thankspigging? The name alone conjured up all sorts of intrigue. Wild, drunken revelry? Or perhaps some esoteric, West Indian custom? Definitely not my grandmother's traditional turkey dinner. And how nice to have somewhere to go on a day we might be feeling a tad homesick.

We arrived at the festive, 200-strong gathering at Skinny Legs Thanksgiving afternoon just in time to see a gigantic roasted pig being sliced down the middle, stem to stern. Jazz snapped a few photos while I pulled out my notebook and pen. And here's what happens when you're the new girl in the village/hamlet/burg and you walk around a party asking questions: Nobody talks to you.

The burly, bearded guy doing what appeared to be skillful pig-carving refused to give me his name. The next person I approached didn't want to be interviewed. One man who deigned to speak with me wouldn't let me take his picture. I had never experienced people so reluctant to be identified for what we used to call "positive news," but this crowd was patently uncomfortable with the nosy stranger asking too many questions. Were they really going to make me write what should be a straightforward holiday story with off-the-record conversations?

Who did they think I was, Woodward and Bernstein? This was a test.

By 5 p.m. the party was in full swing. Guests mingled or watched football on the TV screens above the bar, the entire length of which had been transformed into a buffet, brimming with food. The restaurant was festooned with Thanksgiving-themed swag, including a turkey made out of a painted basketball and a flying (paper) pig with wings, suspended from the rafters.

The mastermind of this "Un-KEN-ventional Coral Bay" soirée was Architect Ken, aka Long-Haired Ken, who took pity on me and agreed to give me some quotes and pose for a photo—as long as I took the picture from behind and didn't show his face. He had a deal.

Ken started Thankspigging four years prior for "people who had no place to go." As a newcomer to the island a few years before that, he knew what it was like to spend Thanksgiving alone. The first Thankspigging, in 2001, was held in Ken's home. He provided the pig, mashed potatoes, and beer and asked the guests to bring the rest. The main dish was pig instead of turkey because it was cheap and could feed a lot of people. Good thing. Eighty showed up.

The next year 120 people came to dinner. After Thankspigging outgrew Ken's home, it moved into Skinny Legs. The restaurant, officially closed for the day, donated the drinks and the space. The feast had grown, too. In addition to the turkeys, pounds of potatoes, stuffing, cranberry relish, sweet potato casseroles, and pumpkin pies crowding the bar, there was sushi, deep fried turkey, and two huge pigs instead of one. Oh, also alligator. "Ten pounds of gator tail! I'm a Florida boy," Ken said, explaining how alligator made its way onto the menu. "Swamp cabbage. It's gator, all three kinds of peppers—green, yellow, and red—BBQ onions, and garlic."

Ken still provided the pigs and potatoes, and guests did the rest. Caroline from Colorful Corner was helping with the turkeys, walking around with a meat thermometer in her pocket.

St. Croix Tom barely got through the door—that's an expression, by the way; there's no actual "door" at Skinny Legs—before people started grabbing his jalapeño poppers. A man from Georgia, who had been living on island for only three weeks, made his grandma's turkey dressing, and was thankful to have a place to be. Everybody was asked to bring a dish, but no one was turned away. The meal was free for all who wanted to eat.

"That's Coral Bay. We're very tight here," one guest told me, clearly uneasy about the controversial nature of his comment. "Don't quote me on that," he added.

The line for dinner snaked all through Skinny Legs and out into the parking lot. The sushi and swamp cabbage were the first to go. Diners were mostly familiar faces (to each other, anyway)— single folks, whole families, some dogs, even a few tourists (at least everyone assumed they were tourists since no one knew who they were). Some locals who weren't able to contribute in past years arrived with food. Seeing that, Ken said, was one of the best parts. There were never any leftovers, and everyone helped clean up. After dinner there was music.

Late Thanksgiving night I stopped at the Love City Mini Mart on my way back to the Cliffhanger. A man checking out said he had dropped off three types of cornbread at Thankspigging but hadn't had any dinner himself. He called food "the best barrier breaker" and said he was just happy to help out. He figured he'd go home and make a salami sandwich. He declined to give me his name.

I did my best, writing up copy with the few quotes I was able to get. I filed the story and fretted until it was published. I honestly had no idea how my new neighbors would react to what I'd written about them.

The day the *Sun Times* came out, my stomach was in knots. I reported for my shift at Skinny's, scurrying past the fresh stack of newspapers that had been dropped on the table by the book swap shelf. As I began taking drink orders, one of the regulars approached me.

"You wrote that story about Thankspigging?" he asked.

I hesitated.

"Yes."

"It was really good."

"Thanks," I said, relieved.

"Yeah, you're an excellent writer. How come you're a waitress?"

Most people knew nothing about my background. I hadn't tried to keep it a secret, it just didn't come up much, what with Coral Bay's don't ask, don't tell protocol. It would be well over a year before I got "outed" when a former television colleague showed up at Skinny's with a handful of my old publicity photos. I wasn't working that day and it was an act creepy enough to ensure nobody would tell him where I was. Even a newbie was entitled to some protection. I could almost hear the guys at the bar interrogating the hapless cameraman: *Are you a cop? Are you from the IRS? Does she owe you money?*

Nobody gave up my whereabouts, but that wasn't the end of it. Someone gleefully swiped one of the 8 x 10 glossies, plastered my smiling face up on Skinny's wall, and scribbled "Manager on Duty" underneath.

"Hey!" said Moe, my boss of 16 months, genuinely surprised, when he saw the anchor photo. "You used to be on TV?"

Tourists always wanted to know how I got to Skinny's and what I did before. The locals didn't care.

"Good for you for getting out, kid," one of the old-timers at the bar, ever-present Betty Ford Clinic cap perched on his head, rasped after my headshot went up. "Even if you win the rat race, you're still a rat."

Moe could be forgiven for not knowing. His newest waitress certainly didn't look like she had ever been on TV. Never having to think about hair and makeup was just one perk of being an island "reporter." I wore flip-flops to work and did my job over a couple of cocktails. At long last, a chance to test my theory that a glass of wine or two might make me a better writer! I interviewed

Santa Claus—off-duty—at the bar at Island Blues. Santa drank vodka and soda with a splash of cranberry.

Refrigerator George was a dead ringer for St. Nick. He was featured in that December's issue of *Caribbean Travel & Life,* in an ad for the magazine depicting a barefoot Santa in shades, sack full of gifts on his back, stepping off a 15-foot skiff into crystal-clear blue sea, palm trees in the foreground. Textbook Caribbean Christmas. Nothing white to sing about except the sand and Santa's hair.

Refrigerator George sailed into Coral Bay to ride out Hurricane Hugo in 1989 and never left. Shortly thereafter he "got the color change in life," he chuckled, winking and pointing to his beard. A veteran of the U.S. Navy and the Coast Guard, he was recruited again to dress up in a Santa suit and entertain at Cruz Bay Lumberyard's annual Christmas party. He didn't quite know what to expect, being a Midwesterner in a new culture, but he discovered that "kids are kids," even if these kids had never seen snow. His first gig was a smash. The Lumberyard owners told him to keep the suit.

George was looking forward to "rafting up" on Christmas with sailor friends who decorated their boats with lights, then lashed the vessels together to create one big floating party. But his blue eyes twinkled the most when he talked about what, for him, was the true spirit of Santa: Kids and the Sea (KATS), Coral Bay's volunteer program that taught young people how to sail. KATS was created after three Boy Scouts drowned in a boating accident in the Virgin Islands in 1986. In the decades since, countless kids had learned everything from basic water safety to competitive racing. Many of the instructors didn't have children of their own; they had the KATS kids. George got roped in one Saturday morning and ended up hooked. His KATS commitment, he said, was as close as he got to Church.

I asked George if he had any untold stories about himself that his neighbors might be interested to hear. He shook his head, stating what should have been obvious: Everybody already knew

everything. "Santa knows if everybody's been bad or good," George said. "It's easy for Santa around here."

The holiday season was a low-key affair on St. John. No mall. No Christmas decorations going up the day after Halloween. One of the few signs that Christmas "soon come" was the radio promo running over and over on Mongoose 104.9, wishing listeners a blessed Christmas, praying for the safety of our troops in Iraq, and giving thanks that we were not hit by hurricanes that season like our brothers and sisters in Grenada, or Haiti—where Hurricane Jeanne left over 3,000 dead.

Black Friday was day one of the regatta in Coral Bay, when the single-handed racers competed. Nobody cared about shopping. They cared about sailing. Besides, gift-giving was simple. You needed less down there, which, eventually, morphed into wanting less, an enlightened state partially achieved by the exhausting nature of the sheer feats of procurement prowess required to actually acquire anything. My family that Christmas all got T-shirts from Skinny Legs, procured after one of my shifts.

When it was time for Refrigerator George to dress in full Santa regalia, Jazz and I donned red and green bikinis and lined up with the kids to get our picture taken with him under the palm trees at Mongoose Junction in Cruz Bay. We emailed our photo greeting to Philly friends, who wrote back with subject lines like "I Hate You" and "You Bitch!" This did nothing to deter our holiday spirit. We found a Charlie Brown-style tree and, in lieu of garland, hung a "Surrender the Booty" skull and crossbones pirate flag on the wall above.

Christmas Day it was 85 degrees with a view that stretched for miles. We went to the beach, snorkeled in Lameshur Bay, and saw a spotted eagle ray with a four-foot wingspan leap out of the sea, airborne. We threw a party, inviting everyone we knew. It was a perfect Caribbean night, stars out, an almost-full moon, Christmas Winds—the brisk, northeast winds prevalent that time of year—cooling the crowd gathered on the Cliffhanger's deck. Guests ranged from all the cooks at the two restaurants where we

worked to a few of the regulars who sat at the bar drinking all day. The cops came, a kid's hair caught on fire, and our local mechanic arrived wearing a collared shirt for the first time in 11 years. Dirt Digger Darlene from downstairs reiterated her disbelief that we knew that many people after living on St. John just six weeks.

I, moreover, had taken full advantage of meeting Santa and when it was my turn to sit on his lap, knew exactly what to ask for. I leaned in close and whispered in his ear:

Sailing lessons!

4

ATLANTIC STANDARD TIME

Here are some things that, after about three months, started to feel normal: Thinking three cars waiting to make a turn through an intersection is a traffic jam. Not thinking twice when you have to slam on your brakes for an iguana sunning itself in the center of the road, or chickens darting in front of your car, or a tourist taking pictures of a donkey. Reserving an entire day to go grocery shopping. Stopping at scenic overlooks on the drive home. Seeing 12 people you know in the first five minutes after you leave the house. Still not knowing any of their last names. Working with people who, when their shifts are over, dinghy home. Turning the water off in the middle of your shower. Washing your hair while a gecko, hanging in a window screen, observes. Having friends come over to use your shower because they live on boats, or in shacks constructed on property worth millions, with no running water. Not knowing when those friends are coming because they don't have phones, and even if they do, the service is probably out. Coming home to discover you have no running water either. Or propane. Or electricity. Or phone service. Paying a guy to come to your house every couple of weeks, drag a five-inch fire hose through your front door, and dump 4,400 gallons of water into your cistern

through a hole in the living room floor. Having all that water and still not flushing for number one. Talking about how bad the next hurricane season was going to be, even though it was still several months away.

The storms were always there, lurking behind the sunny skies and tropical breezes. Danger menaced from the edges. Not just hurricanes but bulldozers, too, twin threats to a fragile ecosystem. Fresh cuts in the luxuriant green hillsides appeared regularly, each new home that went up marring the landscape just a little bit more.

It was a new year, although the precise arrival of it had been a bit fuzzy. Instead of spending December 31 in tears, as I had the year before, I worked the New Year's Eve party at Skinny Legs, where the unadvertised festivities—New York City band, free champagne, and surf & turf—drew a lively local crowd with revelers dressed in everything from average-Friday-night casual to black-tie. Virgin Islanders live in Atlantic Standard Time, an hour ahead of the East Coast, so there was no Times Square ball drop for prompting. As twelve o'clock drew near, the bartenders donned sequined tiaras and began pouring the bubbly. "Happy New Year!" they toasted, every couple of minutes. Cardboard top hats, plastic leis, and noisemakers were passed around. 2004 was slipping away but Work of Art was mid-song and the dance floor was jamming. Would they stop for a countdown?

Nope.

The music rocked on while dancers did their own count-downs to 2005. Kissing, hugging, and horn blowing marked the arrival of midnight—give or take a minute. A cook chased me around, trying to score a midnight-ish kiss, but I outmaneuvered him. A girl asked me to go home with her. I politely declined. An hour (or so) later, someone suggested turning on Dick Clark to ring in the East Coast New Year. By the time the channel was changed, they were already playing "Auld Lang Syne."

In some mysterious, cosmic twist, all of my watches went on strike when I took up residence on St. John. Not one kept time.

Not the silver Anne Klein that I used to wear to work every day. Not the Dora the Explorer wind-up with the green plastic wristband purchased on Canal Street by a New York friend as a gag gift. Not even the Movado I got as a Christmas present the year before instead of the diamond I so desperately wanted.

Not that I needed a watch. Even with my three jobs, the pace was unhurried, so different from what I had left behind. Daily life bordered on the atemporal. I wrote for a newspaper whose editors didn't have a clock in their home or office. My second month writing for the *Sun Times,* I almost missed a deadline. Understand that in my entire career, I had never, ever, missed a deadline. But it was a perfect beach day. I mean, every day was a perfect beach day but this one was more perfect than normal. Turned out the editors decided to go to the beach, too. The paper came out a day late. Readers didn't seem to mind. Or even notice.

That posse debating whether Coral Bay was a village, a hamlet, or a burg? They once spent the better part of an afternoon arguing about what day it was. Too bad they weren't at the Soggy Dollar in the British Virgin Islands—where you had to swim to shore from your boat, cash tucked into the elastic of your bathing suit. The clock at the bar there only pointed to days of the week. At Connections in Cruz Bay, there was a row of clocks —like you'd find in an international hotel—showing the time in New York, Singapore, Istanbul. The first clock, for Coral Bay, had no hands at all.

Sometime that January I got an email from a friend in Colorado who did an Oscar contest every year. Glancing down the ballot, I realized I hadn't seen any of the movies. There was no movie theater on St. John. Jazz and I sometimes spent entire evenings on the Cliffhanger deck with friends, watching the moon shimmer on the water as it rose out of the sea and interpreting the shapes of the clouds. Who needed the silver screen for entertainment when you had the sky in all its widescreen, Technicolor glory? We lived in a place where the quotidian was exalted. The sun came up every day, and wasn't that extraordinary?

Besides, if you paid attention to the moon, at least you'd know when a month had gone by. Or, in my case, three months.

One of the best places to catch the lunar show was the full moon party and pig roast at Miss Lucy's. It was there, watching the moon rise over Coral Bay, that it dawned on me how fast the time was going.

I had been sitting under the sea grapes at the water's edge, listening to the band make its way through the moon repertoire —"Fly Me to the Moon," "Moondance," "Blue Moon"—when I first saw the famous hostess nodding in time to the music. There was a glimmer of gold between her two front teeth when she smiled.

Miss Lucy was presiding over a feast: grilled wahoo with mango chipotle salsa, fungi, rice and peas, sweet potato with raisins, callaloo soup, and, the highlight, succulent roast pork. The 400–500-pound pigs were raised on Miss Lucy's farm, right next to the little restaurant. The pigs, I'd heard, shared names with the kitchen staff.

Obviously, I needed to know: Who were we eating? Chef Ronald? Sal? Maybe Fernando. But more than that, I wanted to know who this island icon was. Writing about the idiosyncrasies of Coral Bay was entertaining, but it wasn't enough. I wasn't a one-week-vacation-er, not hanging around long enough to learn anything about the local culture. Nor was I any longer a general assignment news reporter, guilty of similar tactics: Drop into a place, become an expert for a day, then move on. Whatever happened to those people I did stories on? The family who lost their home in a flood? The parents whose lives were upended by tragedy? I never knew. I was a jack of all trades, master of nothing. Now I had no excuses. Now I had time.

One lazy afternoon after the party, I was sitting with the grande dame of Coral Bay in her yard. Miss Lucy's house—modest, bearing no resemblance to the mega villas the island was becoming famous for—was too big, she said. She preferred to be outdoors where she could keep an eye on her cherished goats.

"No more 'Little St. John,'" she sighed. "This is Big City St. John."

Miss Lucy's head was covered with a purple bandanna, and she wore a close-fitting hat. With her frayed, white button-down cardigan—buttoned all the way up on that warm, Caribbean day —the grande dame looked grandmotherly.

"Hippie!"

Miss Lucy called to the herd and a goat with a mangled front hoof rose and hobbled toward her voice. I had asked about the pigs, but she wanted to talk about the goats. This Hippie was her favorite, one she nursed back to health after a run-in with a barbed wire fence when he was just a kid.

"He knows everything that I tell him," she said. "They cannot speak but they have their own language. You know everything that they are telling you.

"Kids today ..." she continued, and I wasn't sure if she was referring to goats or children. Maybe both.

Lucy Matthias Smith Prince had a lot to say about the way things were on "Little St. John." She was entitled. "Born here" as they say on the island, she had lived on it a long time, though how long, exactly, she refused to say.

"Sweet 16!" she replied, when I asked. "I never tell nobody my age."

I did a few calculations. She had married and raised three children. Her husband died young, but she managed to put her son through college. Then she gave me a hint, mentioning that she remarried. At age 80.

"I've had a good life," she said. "Almighty God knows it, sweetheart. I'm ready for my good Lord."

Nigel, the bartender at Skinny's, had described Miss Lucy as "as close to royalty as you can get on the island."

"Oh, gracious!" she cried, when I told her this. "I was a taxi driver!"

Miss Lucy spent years driving a taxi, meeting people from all over the world. Tourists would come back year after year and ask

the unforgettable lady cab driver if she remembered them. "How the hell am I going to remember you, and all of you look alike?" she would joke, always getting a laugh.

"All the people who come here—white, yellow, blue, black—it's no trouble to me," she said.

Cab driving supported her real love: cooking. She would prepare meals at home and taxi over to Cinnamon Bay where she'd finish up her day, sometimes serving a hundred hungry beachgoers.

When we spoke, she had been operating her restaurant in one form or another for 30 years, years that had brought so much change. Paved roads. More people. Bigger houses. But she embodied a bit of the past, living as she did in her simple home by the sea, surrounded by family and friends; her goats, chickens, and pigs; and the last remnants of how it used to be.

"My memory is mostly gone," she said, when I pressed her for more stories.

"Those days are gone, sweetheart," Miss Lucy said, shaking her head.

"Forget it."

I knew she was referring to her St. John but Miss Lucy's comments might as well have been directed to me. I had been struggling to understand where my old life had gone and spent far too much of each languid day dwelling on it, turmoil camouflaged between the lines of fun tropical tales. When you live in a place where no one wears watches, there is a lot of time to think.

Why had my relationship failed? I anguished over the details, doubting, in black moments of loneliness and insecurity, that what we had was ever real. Would I be alone forever? How could I trust my heart again? Who was I without the status of my old job? Had I blown things up for good? What was next?

These were questions better pondered while absorbing the unspoiled beauty around me. Usually I'd seek solace at Maho Bay. It was one of St. John's most popular beaches, but, in the early hours of the day, often a private oasis.

How many days did I sink into her waters and just ... *dissolve* ... into sea so salty you could float without trying, every muscle relaxing, loosening, until it surrendered to complete rest. Being immersed in that warm liquid—feeling subtle waves at the back of my neck, watching the palms sway as they stretched toward the sky where the birds soared—left my soul as buoyant as my body, no matter how sad or weighed down I felt when I waded in.

Sometimes while floating I would close my eyes—basking in long stretches of soothing silence, no sound but the faint rustling of palm fronds caressed by wind—and when I opened them again, I would find myself surrounded by pelicans, floating along-side me, barely an arms-length away.

The Elixir.

I had ended up in this incredible place, on an enviable adventure, because I didn't get what I wanted. Was I supposed to be there?

When you make a career of asking questions, it's maddening when you can't get the answers that matter most. Some days I felt like I was just drifting, unsure of anything except the color of the water. I had a sense that something fundamental was shifting. To what, I didn't know. But when you wake up every morning and it's 80 degrees and sunny, you go with it.

I MIGHT NOT HAVE KNOWN what I was doing with the rest of my life, but I knew I wanted to learn to sail. But here's another thing that, after about three months, you discover is normal: Locals may talk about *boats boats boats* all day long, but they don't get in the water in the winter. For one thing, they're busy. It's high season. The island is overrun with tourists fleeing the frigid north. The real problem, however, is that 78-degree seawater. Tourists—and newcomers, like me—think it feels like a bathtub. The locals think it's cold.

Jazz wanted lessons, too, and sometime after Christmas we

targeted Jenn and Vicki, the instructors who ran the KATS sailing program. We pestered them every time we saw them at Skinny's, or anywhere around Coral Bay, to put us on the short list for the next ANTS (Adults and the Sea) class, but there was no class scheduled, and no list. I knew Refrigerator George had an in with KATS and I bugged him, too, whenever I'd catch him at the bar with his vodka cran, but to no avail. The women were in charge. Even Santa was powerless to get them in the water until March.

I would have to bide my time. But I had plenty of other invitations.

On one of my days off, Fun Christina, who had quickly become my closest compadre at Skinny's, called and asked if I wanted to "do something." Christina was a blonde bombshell, another 20-something trying to figure out what she wanted to be when she grew up. She wore a *Slacker* ball cap when we waitressed together. She lived on a sailboat called *Kalik* with one of the *boats boats boats* guys and wanted to be home in time to cook him dinner, so the plan was to hit the beach for an hour, pick up a few groceries in town, and head back to Coral Bay. This was back when I was still making plans, before I figured out that "island planning" was as oxymoronic as Coral Bay couture.

Christina picked me up at the Cliffhanger and we drove out North Shore Road, stopping in between two of the most-visited National Park beaches. We took a 10-minute hike down a wooded path and emerged onto a gorgeous spit of sand. We were the only ones there. The beach was a locals' favorite, a place I'd only recently heard about.

"Don't tell anyone," Christina said in a conspiratorial whisper. "It's a secret."

We spent the afternoon swimming, then headed to Cruz Bay, agreeing to stop first at the Beach Bar for just one Bushwhacker, which turned into two. We saw a lot of people we knew, including one of our bosses. Christina bought him a Heineken and he agreed to clean Skinny's bathrooms for us the next morning. By this time it was too late for grocery shopping. The boyfriend would have to fend for himself. We were just about to order dinner at the bar when Christina spotted her friends Ron and Amy, who ran a private yacht for a couple of rich folks who were scarcely on board. Next thing we knew, we were dinghying out to this right-out-of-Hollywood, 67-foot, all-teak, fully stocked sailboat for cocktails at sunset.

Not bad for a Monday.

Another day, while I was working at Skinny's, James, one of the cooks, called out my name.

"Margie!"

When James said my name with his thick West Indian accent, it sounded like MAH-JEE.

"Otis-wan-know-you-gon-play-dahts-wid-dem-Wednesday? You-gon-play-wid-all-ah-we?"

I had a little trouble understanding James's island syntax, and I suspected he sometimes talked fast on purpose. I was often tempted to reply, "HOW-YOU-MEAN?"—defined for me as a regional equivalent of "HUH?"—but as I was still relatively new, I usually chickened out and just tried to get the gist of the conversation. This was dangerous because by the end of any chat, I was never quite sure what I had just agreed to.

James was at the bar having a beer with Mr. Otis, whom I had recently met at Voyages. It was a Wednesday, sushi night, and James and some friends were playing darts. I was reluctant to join in because the guys looked serious, but raw eel was not my thing, so what the hell. I was on Mr. Otis's team. He was a good coach, and I had beginner's luck. Next thing I knew, I was being recruited to play in THE TOURNAMENT. This invitation did not come with a date or time. It did, however, mean that for the next few weeks, every time James saw me walking around Coral Bay, he would screech his Suzuki to a halt, lean out the window, and yell: "MAH-JEE! YOU-GON-PLAY-IN-DEH-TAHNA-MENT-WID-ALL-AH-WE?"

To further complicate the when-exactly-is-this-tournament issue, Voyages was shut down for a while, but the restaurant reopened in February. Then Mr. Otis offered to give me my own set of darts. That, I couldn't refuse. Plus, I figured I could get a story out of it.

The next Wednesday night I went to Voyages and found the same small group playing darts. The Tournament. Mr. Otis was nowhere in sight. James rushed over with a run-on explanation: Otis had been there but had to leave because he was having problems with his car and the guy with the part to fix the car had to get on the last ferry to St. Thomas so Otis had to get to the ferry before it left. Now I was on James's team.

James always wore a do-rag so I wore one, too, and despite our differences in height, build, and skin color, we decided we looked like twins. Jazz teamed up with Fancy Pants Stan who was wearing pants festooned with little tropical fish. Team number three was Crabby from Crabby's Watersports and Big Barney, who claimed to be the worst dart player in Coral Bay. Crabby disagreed, professing that he was the worst dart player in Coral Bay. Stan remarked that it was clear who had the worst pants in Coral Bay. The game resumed. My first throws missed the dartboard completely. Looked like I was a contender for worst dart player in Coral Bay.

I decided to start interviewing before I got kicked out of the league. I knew horseshoes was popular, but darts? I asked the competitors why they played.

"There's no golf course here, that's why," said Crabby. "There's nothing else to do."

Big Barney's explanation was even more compelling: "Crabby said let's go play and I said OK."

I was actually writing these quotes in my notebook.

Was there a West Indian dart connection? I asked James how he got involved.

"I just came in one day and saw this group playing and said let me try it," he said.

At this point, I needed a break, so I made my way to the bar to do some research for my big article—and by research, I mean ordering a drink and asking patrons about other pastimes. One of the bartenders said she wanted to host a poetry slam. Did anybody write poems? I was surprised by how many people said yes.

The crowd was starting to thin ("There's a new episode of *American Idol* on tonight," someone told me) so I got back to the dart business. Were there any good places to play darts on the other side of the island? Would there be a Coral Bay-Cruz Bay tournament? The group thought there might be people who played at the Quiet Mon pub, but they didn't really know.

"Put in the paper that we'd like to challenge them, though."

The gauntlet was thrown down. Except that's fencing. Which was also hot on St. John. I knew this because another Skinny's waitress invited me to join her fencing class, but I couldn't because I was spending all my time trying to figure out when I was supposed to be playing darts.

A few days later, I ran into Mr. Otis.

"I still have darts for you!" he said. "See you Wednesday?"

What's it like in paradise after the vacation ends? This was it. Life in Coral Bay was a *Seinfeld* episode: A show about nothing. And everybody tuning in to see what would happen next week.

AS THE SUN'S path moved northward, away from the winter solstice, we gradually got a better view of the sunrise, more sun on the Cliffhanger's deck during the day, more heat in the house. Even the bad weather was awe-inspiring. Some days an early-morning squall would shake the Cliffhanger with wind and thunder, shroud us in a downpour, and then poof! Gone. The skies turned bright and the day beckoned. I was still waking up every day not believing where I lived.

"How's your daughter doing down there?" a family friend asked my mother around that time. "Has she found herself yet?"

"I don't think she's looking," my mother replied.

The truth was, I hadn't completely committed to my new life.

I still had my Philadelphia apartment, sublet until March. It was my safety net, ready for me to return if I didn't like living on an island. But the lease was up for renewal. This was my window to bail. I had to decide. Did I like living on St. John? My heart wasn't sure it wanted its newfound freedom. My head said don't squander it. I let the lease expire.

I hadn't felt ready for a trip "home," the word itself fluid. It was too soon for a visit, but I had to finish cleaning out the apartment. On a hot February afternoon, I was back at the airport in St. Thomas, this time with a round-trip ticket to Philadelphia and back.

I was traveling alone, just two empty suitcases for company, but waiting to clear customs in Charlotte Amalie, I looked around and realized I recognized people in line: There was that family from Atlanta I waited on at Skinny's. And those two guys who brought four kids into Shipwreck on Sunday and had no clue how much food to order for them. The petite blondes must be their wives, who were at the spa that afternoon. I saw the couple from Philadelphia, more Skinny's customers, who had told me they'd be on my flight. I counted 14 people I'd interacted with in the previous week, and just as I was thinking that a few more looked familiar, the man in front of me turned around.

"Not working today?" he said.

Everybody really did know my business.

I arrived in Philadelphia after a snowstorm, on a full moon night. It must have been a month since the party at Miss Lucy's. Philly looked pretty, all white and glistening in the fresh dusting. I thought it might be strange to be back, but it felt normal pulling on boots, walking around in the cold, all bundled up in turtleneck sweater, coat, and gloves. I borrowed a friend's cushy Volvo to do my errands and had no trouble remembering to drive on the right. In a small nod to my island life, I kept forgetting to flush ... but blithely reacquainted myself with long showers, during which I never turned off the water.

Although I had given my notice weeks before, the physical act

of packing up for good had been looming—this was for real now! —but everything went without a hitch. On the last day of the month, the laid-back dudes from Mambo Movers, a moving company run by urban artists, whisked through my studio in a low-key, island-esque way, and loaded the last of my possessions onto their truck. I followed them across town to Self Storage Philadelphia (*Making Room for Life!*) and watched as they stowed everything in a small underground locker. Just as the last box was being carried off the truck, it started to snow again. I locked the unit and paid the movers. I schlepped a couple of boxes to the post office, mailed them off to St. John, and by noon, I was done. I no longer had a Philadelphia address.

That trip was my ideal winter: Seven days. Two snowfalls. One ticket back to the Caribbean.

Leaving was still hard. It was a frigid morning when I hugged my mom goodbye. Both of us were teary as we waved and my taxi pulled away, headed off to the airport. The cab had barely gone two blocks when the melancholy was shattered by the loud jingle of a cell phone. It took a moment to realize it was mine. I don't think I had ever heard my island cell phone ring.

"Hello?"

"Margie! It's Jazz! I'm on the deck and there are sharks in our water! Black tip sharks!"

I laughed. "It's 28 degrees here."

"Well not here, Sister. Have a safe trip home. I'll see you this afternoon. Can you believe there are *sharks* in front of the Cliffhanger? Ciao!"

My flight was on time and uneventful. When the plane touched down and the doors opened, that wonderfully oppressive equatorial air flooded the cabin. I walked down the stairway and onto the tarmac, relishing the mid-afternoon heat. I was poised to make the 4 p.m. ferry to St. John until my two bags, now full of favorite things from home, failed to appear on the carousel. US Air had lost my luggage.

The young woman behind the lost baggage counter never

lifted her head as she asked for my name, phone number, and flight information. She made a few clicks on her keyboard and, finally looking up, announced, "OK."

OK? OK what?

"OK?" I asked.

"OK," she repeated.

"That's it?"

"Yes."

"OK. Well, what do I do now?"

"Now? Now you just hope that your bags come."

I started to tense up, then reminded myself that I had just chosen to simplify my life. If the luggage never made it, so be it. I dashed for the taxi stand. If I could persuade a driver to hurry (oh, just a little!) I could still make the four o'clock boat. The driver did not hurry, but he did yell out to his friend on the crew, so they held the ferry while I ran to board.

I climbed to the top deck to take in the view, feel the breeze, and soak up what was left of the day's warm sunshine. The last time I made this trip I had been saddled with two suitcases and a ton of stress. This time, with just my carry-on, I felt free.

Back on St. John, Jazz met me at the dock.

"Where's your luggage?" she asked.

"US Air lost it all."

"Huh."

I shrugged.

"Oh well," she said. "Wanna go to the Beach Bar for happy hour?"

After the Beach Bar we headed back to Coral Bay. At the bar at Skinny Legs, we ordered cheeseburgers—blue cheese, medium rare, for me; medium cheddar for Jazz—and surveyed the scene. Some of the guys were hitting on a waitress whom I did not recognize.

"Who's that?" I asked.

"New girl."

"Huh."

"Yeah," said Jazz, "I have a theory that we're in Phase Two now. It's been four months. We're old news."

We left Skinny's and stopped down at Shipwreck where Sistah Blistah, the bartender, called out, "Hey, Margie! Wow! You look good. Did you get laid?"

I laughed. "Nope. Not recently."

"Yeah, you look like you got hit with the love stick," said an artist who was sitting at a nearby table. "You look great. You must be in love."

"Definitely not in love. But thanks for the compliment."

We talked for a while, with Sistah Blistah continuing to eye me suspiciously. I could tell she was only half listening.

"You got your tits done, didn't you!" she blurted.

"No!" I shot back. "Same tits I've always had. You like them?"

"Well, something's different," Sistah Blistah protested. "What did you do while you were away?"

"I just went home to Philadelphia to tie up some loose ends, ship down a few more of my things, and put the rest of my junk in storage."

"That's it!" Sistah Blistah exclaimed.

I looked at her, perplexed.

"That's it!" she shouted again. "You dumped your baggage! It shows all over your face!" She chuckled, satisfied. "I knew there was something different. You went home and got rid of your baggage while you were there, didn't you?"

I hadn't really thought about it like that, but maybe she was on to something.

"I guess you could say that," I conceded. "Yeah. Something like that."

"Well, good for you, girl. Whatever it is, you sure look good."

"Thanks, Sistah Blistah."

"You're welcome. Oh, and welcome home."

5

FIGHTING LADY YELLOW

The blow knocked the wind out of me. Thank God for the life jacket, keeping my head above water so I could breathe. I was flailing about in Coral Harbor, next to a little sailboat that had just capsized. With me on it. I needed to get the boat upright. I pushed with all my might on the centerboard, which should have given me some leverage, but the boat wouldn't budge. No matter how much I shoved or grunted, I could not lift the sail out of the water.

Nearby, KATS Jenn, the sailing instructor, floated calmly and watched me struggle. Eventually she righted the boat, with no help from me, and we clambered back on.

"Did you get hit in the head with the boom?" she asked.

"Yes," I sputtered.

"Hard?"

"Yes."

"Get used to it."

It was week two of ANTS, the Adults and the Sea sailing class. The water had finally warmed up enough for the instructors to get in, and they had a lot of confidence in their students. We had rigged the boats—14-foot Lasers—and taken them out just once so far, but on this day, they had optimistically set up a course for

us. One of them held up a chart and said something like this: "OK, you're going to start down here at this point, head upwind to the first buoy, of course you'll have to tack a few times to get there, then you'll sail past the committee boat to the second marker, pass through the no-go zone and come about for a nice run down to the third mark where you can either tack or jibe to complete the course and race around again. Who's ready to try this without an instructor?"

Were they kidding? I was still trying to figure out which direction the wind was coming from.

My brain rifled through the terms I'd been trying to memorize.

True Wind: The actual direction of the wind over land and sea. Felt only while at rest.

Apparent Wind: Wind generated by movement in combination with the true wind. The direction of the wind when the boat is in motion.

I raised my hand.

"Jenn? I need to practice stopping and starting."

"All right, Margie. That's OK, too."

ANTS met on Saturday afternoons around a picnic table near the Dinghy Dock, gateway to all Coral Bay sailing adventures. The morning of my first class I had watched from the Cliffhanger deck as the KATS kids sailed out, in flawless formation, and instantly had second thoughts, intimidated by what I perceived to be a group of 10-year-old sailing geniuses. (Not wrongly. At least one of them would go on to compete in the Olympics.) Most of the adult students were also experienced sailors who wanted to learn how to handle ANTS's sexy little racing boats. Lasers are small, with one mainsail and simple rigging, so they're good for teaching, but they're also tippy and designed to move fast, ideally with just one person on board.

Jazz and I, the pushy novices, had no business being in this class, as our neighbor Crabby would point out later. He liked the story I wrote about learning to sail, he would tell me, but he'd

been meaning to ask: How did Jazz and I get into the ANTS class? Because he'd been trying for two years to get into that class. Pushy is the operative word. Crabby was not pushy. He wasn't really even crabby, except maybe about ANTS.

The classes were led by volunteers, mostly women. They explained points of sail and proper rigging. They taught us how to tie knots: hitches, figure eights, and that mainstay of sailing, the bowline. We learned the terminology, so when I was sitting on my boat not going anywhere, at least I knew I was "in irons," even if I didn't know how to get out of it.

For us rookies, an instructor was always on board to coach and coax. I sailed with Jenn, the inexhaustible mother hen, who never ran out of patience even though I kept forgetting which way to push the tiller to steer where I wanted to go. I sailed with Vicki, the master competitor, who taught me to "hike out"—meaning lean out as far as I dared over the water so my bodyweight would help balance out the Laser when the wind was causing it to tip— or "heel"—in the other direction. I sailed with Jason, an easygoing 20-something *boats boats boats* guy, who let me get perilously close to messing up before suggesting I might want to try a different strategy if I didn't want to capsize—again.

Each week after class I would help de-rig the boats, dump a gallon of fresh water out of a plastic jug over my head in the parking lot, change into dry clothes in the shed where equipment was stored, and head directly to my job at Skinny's where the instructors would be congregating for their hard-earned drinks. Since I'd been waitressing about as long as I'd been sailing, I often bungled their order. But I made really good tips on those Saturday nights, probably because I couldn't stop grinning and jabbering about my day as a sailor.

On the final day of class, Jazz and I braved it together. We didn't single-hand the Lasers like our more talented fellow students, but we sailed without an instructor. We got the boat out of the harbor, navigated back in, and executed two hours of real sailing in between. Mostly we sailed in circles near the mouth of the harbor, the Cliffhanger pasted on the rocks above us. But ANTS had made sailors out of us.

I immediately offered to volunteer at the beginner KATS class, Rowing and Seamanship. Jenn said they could always use the help, even from a neophyte, but I suspect she thought I could use the practice. Teaching knot-tying and man-overboard drills to a bunch of kids, I'd have to keep up. There's no faking it when an eight-year-old looks you straight in the eye and asks for help tying his bowline.

After that I sailed as much as possible, often in a basic one-sail Sunfish, leisurely practicing tacks and jibes after a morning at KATS. One afternoon I rigged up a little boat and sailed all the way across the harbor to Hurricane Hole. Afterward, I hit Skinny's and told anyone who cared, and lots of folks who didn't, how proud I was of myself. There was something about those sails, with nobody telling me what to do—which way to point the tiller or how tight to pull the ropes—or reminding me to call the ropes "the sheets." Those few minutes of quiet gave me time to figure it out. So what if I sat going nowhere for a bit?

Other times I sailed in the Coral Bay Yacht Club's Wednesday night races, in the bigger boats, with anyone willing to take on extra crew. Artist Les, who lost the girl in that first Cowhorn race at Foxy's, took Jazz and me out in his lovely *Penelope*, giving each of us a turn at the tiller. Jungle George, the Philly chef, let me helm *George of the Jungle* for almost an entire race and didn't even care that we came in DFL (Dead Fucking Last).

The Coral Bay Yacht Club, it should be explained, was not what I pictured when I heard the words "yacht club." It bore no resemblance to the exclusive sailing institutions I had seen on the East Coast, or in the movies. It was certainly no New York Yacht Club or Royal Yacht Squadron. We're not talking America's Cup territory here. There wasn't even a clubhouse. Meetings were held at Skinny's. If you wanted to crew in a race, you hung out at the bar or loitered at the Dinghy Dock. Members thought blue blazers were pickups built by Chevy, quipped St. John author and

raconteur Cap'n Fatty Goodlander. Miss a meeting and they might make you commodore. There was no white linen, no preppy Top-Siders. No shoes at all, really. Most people sailed barefoot. Many Coral Bay Yacht Club members lived on their boats full-time and when I say boats, I mean boats. These were definitely not yachts.

My first overnight sailing trip was on a perfect example of a Coral Bay Yacht Club vessel: Puerto Rican Pete's *For Pete's Sake*, a 42-foot floating bachelor pad whose hailing port was listed, in her owner's grandiose way, as Planet Earth. We were headed to Jost Van Dyke, a laid-back island in the British Virgins where the Coral Bay crowd liked to go to "get away from it all." Jazz, a press gang of one, had shanghaied Pete to get us there.

Pete was a scallywag, always on the brink of big trouble (but, as he would point out years later in giving me permission to write about him, not WANTED for anything. Yet.) Rumor had it that he sailed naked. The rumors were true.

The captain set *For Pete's Sake* on course, turned on the automatic pilot, and disappeared down below where I presumed he stowed the hooch. A few minutes later, Pete popped back up into the companionway, cocktail in one hand, a fistful of papers in the other, and a joint dangling from his lips. Back then, recreational marijuana wasn't legal anywhere in the U.S.—including the Virgin Islands—but it was everywhere, passed around as freely as hors d'oeuvres at a catered party. Except for the fact that he was drinking vodka from a dirty glass instead of swigging rum from a bottle, he looked like a pirate—from the waist up. A red bandanna covered his head. Hoop earrings and diamond studs cascaded down his left ear. He was shirtless, and as he hoisted himself into the cockpit, his untied pink polka dot swim trunks slipped a little further down his ass. The next time I looked, the trunks were gone and Pete was settled in at the helm, quaffing his Stoli and reading from the papers, which turned out to be jokes printed out from the internet.

I wanted to put some space between us, maybe sit up on the

deck, but *For Pete's Sake* didn't have any lifelines. If the boat started heeling, there'd be nothing to grab onto. Pete explained that he was in the process of replacing them—along with the life jackets, also missing—and attempted to reassure me that this was SOP.

"Don't worry about falling off," he said in the everything's-under-control tone of voice most boat captains use to relay safety instructions. "If you fall overboard, it's no big deal. We'll just come back and get you. It happens all the time."

Really? It happens all the time? Even I knew that wasn't true.

Captain Pete would not have passed Coast Guard muster, but his insouciance was opportunity. He was relaxed ("not quite stoned yet," I kept telling myself) and more than willing to let the swabbies help out. Jazz was at the wheel for most of the trip. Pete showed me how to pull the sheets to manipulate the sails. He was patient. He never yelled. He was a surprisingly good teacher. For all its potential hazards, it was a glorious, four-hour sail.

We dropped anchor in Jost's sparkling White Bay, then hopped in Pete's dinghy to motor one alcove over to the renowned Foxy's for conch fritters, fresh grilled mahi, and live music. Afterward, the ride back to the boat was magical. A big moon hung low, casting twinkling reflections in the ocean and illuminating puffy clouds that strolled across the sky. Our little dinghy zipped around the harbor, past scores of big, beautiful sailboats and yachts. It was like Paris—a City of Light—on water. I crashed on the deck of *For Pete's Sake* and rocked to sleep under the stars, water lapping gently against the hull, tree frogs singing in the distance.

The spell must have broken sometime after a clock somewhere struck twelve.

I woke at first light, smelling the new day before seeing it when I caught a whiff of something funky. Realizing it was the comforter I had wrapped myself in, I threw it off and tried to move but I was stiff from sleeping curled up in a spot where I couldn't stretch my legs. When I finally stood, careful to avoid the

glass bottles and dozens of CDs that were scattered around the cockpit, I banged my ankle on an unsecured scuba tank that had rolled across the deck.

I was craving coffee. I wondered if Pete had any on board and started rummaging through the galley, but then remembered that we had emptied the cooler and the icebox the night before, not only of the alcohol, but also the potable water. I gazed enviously at the man on the next boat over, enjoying the sunrise while sipping java from a steaming, oversized mug. Then I noticed another boat with an actual table, set for breakfast. The smell of bacon drifted my way.

A bleary-eyed Jazz was up next and decided a refreshing swim would cure what ailed her. She dove overboard, took a two-minute dip, then spent the next 15 minutes trying to claw her way back on board because Pete's boat had no ladder.

When Pete finally got up, we headed to shore in search of caffeine and a meal. The dinghy's engine stalled three times. Then we hit the beach and while there were easily half a dozen places to get a Heineken at 9:30 a.m., no one was cooking. We settled in at one of the bars. Reggae music wafted out, competing with the roosters, crowing like it was dawn.

"Fuckin' chickens," Pete griped. "They never know what time it is."

Pete didn't want to give up his spot for that night's party on Jost so after "breakfast" he announced that he'd take us home in the dinghy. He wheedled a quart of oil from the boat anchored next to us (the one that had the coffee), got the motor running, and we set out across the ocean. As in The Atlantic. Remember, on the way over, this was a four-hour sail on a 42-foot vessel. Now we were tooling across open water in a 10-foot dinghy, pounding the waves with head-splitting force.

Pete gave us the old heave-ho at Maho Bay. He couldn't turn the motor off because it might not start again, so he had to idle a few feet from shore. Grasping our possessions, we jumped overboard into chest-high water. Tourists gawked at the waterlogged

women wading to the beach, a fitting end to our misbegotten overnighter. Pete, ever the gentleman, had called his friend Big Steve to come get us. We climbed into the back of Big Steve's pickup truck for the ride home to Coral Bay. Puerto Rican Pete dinghied back out to sea.

If you were serious about sailing, you stuck with the women.

I knew a sailor in Coral Bay who had been officially dead for seven years. She came home one evening after a bad day at work and, sorting through her mail, was greeted by income tax forms. "I was so annoyed," she told me, "I wrote DECEASED in big black letters across the form and sent it back to them. I didn't even owe any money that year. They owed ME money. I was just tired of dealing with them. I never heard from Uncle Sam again."

Similar, shall we say, *independent-minded* women—albeit not all with such a tenuous relationship with the law—existed in inordinately high numbers in Coral Bay. Circumnavigators. Competitive racers. A submarine captain. Women of relentless vigor who were unafraid to get dirty. Who became boat owners without knowing how to sail, buying first, asking questions later. These women were like the tide. You could set your clock to them. They would come flood your harbor, right on schedule, to get you floating again. And if you were still stuck in the mud, they would grab some line, tie a damn fine knot, and tow you out. The men in Coral Bay would stride about, spouting bluster, impersonating pirates, and attracting all the attention, but the one to watch out for was that unobtrusive woman sitting silently at the end of the bar.

One woman drove around in an old jeep with a bumper sticker that read "Eve Was Framed." A big seller at the Jolly Dog was the *Women Who Behave Rarely Make History* T-shirt. That one had an image of the swashbuckling Ann Bonny, whose own most-quoted remark, according to freebooting lore, was uttered in 1721 when she went to visit boyfriend and fellow plunderer "Calico Jack" Rackham in prison on the eve of his hanging. The

doomed Jack got no comfort. "Had you fought like a man, you need not have been hang'd like a dog," she spat.

Ann Bonny was also pictured on the commemorative T-shirt for the Virgins' Cup, a race in the British Virgin Islands from Road Town, Tortola, to Norman Island. Norman is the putative site of Stevenson's *Treasure Island*, but during my time in the tropics it was a favorite destination not so much because of the classic novel as for the good ship *William Thornton*, aka the "Willy T," a floating bar where the de rigueur activity was jumping buck naked into the water from the top of the ship's third-story deck. Free T-shirt for any woman who took the plunge. The lady pirate, Willy T tattoo inked on her inner thigh, was a fitting mascot for the race because in the Virgins' Cup all the skippers are women.

I knew I had crossed some kind of threshold when Belle, a Skinny Legs waitress who had more or less denied my existence for months, invited me to join her crew. Belle was the sailing doyenne of Coral Bay—co-commodore of the yacht club, self-assured, and an avid racer with the proverbial mouth of a sailor. She didn't— her words—give a fuck what anybody thought of her.

When Belle sailed her first regatta, her boat got dismasted in high wind. She was seven. She and three other young, cold, wet crewmates were stranded for hours. It was dark before someone figured out the kids were missing and sent out the chase boat to rescue them. After that, Belle decided there wasn't much she couldn't handle at sea.

Belle owned and lived on a sleek 33-foot racing boat named *O'dege,* which, she said, meant "over the edge" in "bastardized French." *O'dege* was painted "Fighting Lady Yellow," a color chosen for the name, and the fact that one could pee off the stern —something at which Belle was impressively adept—and not interfere with the paint job.

Captain Belle sailed with a rotating crew of Coral Bay women, all accomplished sailors: Fun Christina. Erin. Ivy League Abby. The Virgins' Cup would be an all-Skinny's crew as well.

Race weekend began Friday in Johnson Bay on St. John where we spent the morning scraping barnacles and other crud off the bottom of the boat. It was an unglamorous job but Kayleigh, Skinny's waitress and skilled snorkeler, made it look sexy by diving under the hull with a metal scraper tucked delicately in her scanty green bikini.

We set sail for Tortola in the early afternoon, dropped anchor in Road Town a few hours later, and, after clearing customs, had just enough time to change into dresses before dinghying over to the captains meeting at the Royal British Virgin Islands Yacht Club. Belle insisted that everyone wear a dress and kept a collection of extras on board. It was astonishing how many articles of clothing, of any type, she could pull out of the cubbyholes of a 33-foot sailboat. We piled into the dinghy and headed ashore. Halfway there, it started raining. We made our entrance soaking wet, raindrops running down our noses and landing on our spaghetti straps.

The name notwithstanding, the queen wasn't likely to make an appearance at the Royal BVI Yacht Club anytime soon. Still, it was an indisputable notch above the Coral Bay Yacht Club with, if not exactly a dress code, a dress awareness, and a party in full swing. One of the first partiers we met was Louise, a British captain who had already registered her boat, *Mermaid,* and was busy recruiting her (all-male) crew at the bar. I asked one of the men about to be pressed into service to take a picture of our team before Belle went off to argue with the race officials about *O'dege*'s PHRF (Performance Handicap Racing Formula) rating, something akin to a golf handicap. Friends would later dub the photo "The Drenched Wenches."

Saturday was race day. The Virgins' Cup rules require only that a woman be at the helm, and we appeared to be the only all-female crew. We also had outfits: matching neon orange Skinny Legs T-shirts with *O'dege* stenciled on the back. Belle hoisted the mainsail wearing her lucky racing skirt—a short, pink, flowered number with crinolines underneath.

There were 17 boats in the harbor, tacking back and forth, waiting for the start. We seemed to be passing awfully close to each other. My stomach did backflips. This was a much bigger deal than the informal Wednesday night races in Coral Bay. Belle was at *O'dege*'s helm, Kayleigh was on the foredeck, and Fun Christina and I were manning the port and starboard winches. At 11 a.m. sharp, the air horn blew. We were off.

The wind was light but not compared to the dead calm we had been trying to practice in over the previous weeks. With *O'dege*'s newly cleaned bottom, we were moving at a respectable clip. Now we were getting ready to tack—turn the boat from one side of the wind to the other—and it was my job to pull in the jib, the smaller sail on the bow of the boat. The jib and the mainsail both had to move to the other side of the boat as we turned. I wrapped the sheet connected to the jib around the starboard winch and cranked with all my might, but I was not very strong, or fast. We lost momentum.

"Good job," Belle reassured me. "That wasn't your fault. The wind shifted."

The next tack was perfect, with Christina and Kayleigh working side by side to trim the sail just right, and with great speed.

"Woo hoo!" Christina cheered. "We kicked your ass!" she shouted at me.

"I'm on your team, you idiot!" I yelled back.

"Oops!" she giggled. "Sorry! I'm a little competitive!"

So it went until, after a while, we were far away from all the other boats. Were we ahead or behind? Nobody cared. We had music. Fun Christina, whose fingers were bleeding too much to yank in any more sail, was singing, using the winch handle as a microphone. When she got bored of that, she stood on the bow nude and did yoga poses, giving *O'dege* a real live figurehead. Kayleigh was down below, mixing up a gallon jug of Painkillers. Belle was working the tiller alternately with her feet and her rear end, always leaving her hands free for her Becks. Belle could do any job on her boat without putting down her beer. What's that famous sailing axiom? *One hand for the boat, one hand for the beer?* Or something like that.

We came about at a chunk of rock called Dead Chest and, for the downwind run to Norman Island, Belle decided to put up the spinnaker. The handsome sail was all black with an enormous yellow sun that was, without a doubt, a lady: Blushing orange cheeks. Fiery red lips. Mona Lisa smile. We were thoroughly slowed down by our efforts to get the girl flying, but she was too gorgeous to keep down on deck. We waved to the crew of *Glass Slipper* as they overtook *O'dege*, snapping photos of our fantastic accessory. Then the boys on *Mermaid* sailed by—with no sign of Captain Louise—striking bodybuilder poses and mooning us. Refusing to be outdone, Belle flashed her tits and ordered her crew to do the same.

At this point it appeared that all other boats had passed us. And it began to rain. We voted not to turn on the motor. We'd be disqualified if we did, and we had come too far for that. Then the wind died. We held a recount.

By the time we finally approached the broad harbor of Norman Island known simply as The Bight, it was pouring.

"Where's the finish line?" Belle demanded, squinting into the rain.

"I think they quit doing that," Kayleigh hollered over the near gale-force wind.

Christina and Kayleigh were struggling to pull down the main. Belle was in the cockpit, trying to steer her way through the deluge. I had the camera, to capture our photo finish. The rain was blinding and I could barely see, but I managed to look up just as we rounded the Willy T to see crowds of racers—all of whom beat us there—cheering from the deck. We ended as we began: Drenched wenches.

We never saw the official results but pretty clearly finished DFL. So fucking what, Belle would say. Blame the squall. We spent the evening celebrating with the competition. Two of us crashed early and headed back to the boat to dry off and dry out and two of us stayed and closed the place (who knew the Willy T closed?) but not before giving Belle the titles of Best Captain and Most Fun. We voted ourselves Best Dressed.

It was somewhere in here that I turned 40.

I had been "almost 40" for at least a year and a half. Maybe two. Turning 40 had been an obsession for so long that it was a huge relief when I woke up one morning and realized that the next fall, the next New Year's Eve, the next spring, I would still be *only* 40.

My birthday began with an email from Ellen, who had finally found her own new job in Philly.

From: Ellen
Subject: Happiest

… of Happy Birthdays. It's 10:28 on Sunday, and I know I'm a bit early, but I was afraid to get tied up with my boss, the Demon Seed, tomorrow and forget.

40 ain't so bad. We all know it's better than the alternative, but more than that, there's a certain je ne sais quoi that you just can't have at 20 or 30. In the end, who wants to know somebody with a boatload of kids but no je ne sais quoi? I ask you, WHO?

Happy beginning of life. Love you lots and lots and wish I could be there to get really loaded with you and sleep next to you and tell you how fabulous your ass is.

Love, Ellen XXXXXXXXXXXXXXXXXXXXXXXXXXXXXXXXX

I turned 40 on a Monday in May. It was an 80-80-80 day.

80-80-80 is a term used to describe perfect diving conditions: 80-degree air temperature. 80-degree water temperature. 80 feet of visibility under water.

80-80-80 meant perfect weather for the day's agenda: an all-day boat trip featuring two high-speed powerboats and 15 women from Coral Bay. Captains Rum Runner Rick and Jarhead Bert raced us between the velvet green hills and white sand beaches of the U.S. and British Virgin Islands. We floated in the crystal blue waters off Jost Van Dyke, danced on the bar flourishing tambourines and bongo drums at Ivan's Stress-Free Hangout, and drank Painkillers at the Soggy Dollar, swimming back to the boats with cocktails held aloft. Lunch was at the new Foxy's Taboo. While we waited for our pizza, we hiked to the bubbly pool, dodging goats and poisonous manchineel trees to arrive at the secluded little beach where, on a good windy day, the surf squeezes through a set of towering rocks and crashes into the shallow, sandy bowl carved out by nature, creating a frothy, swirling, spa-like pool.

I love these women who welcomed me into their world with such big-hearted gusto. They are smart. Fun. Tough. I love that every last one of them—and they come in all shapes and sizes—was comfortable in her bikini, with nary a mention of weight or hips. I love how they appreciated the wonders of their home. At some point Erin looked around at our beautiful surroundings and said, simply: *We live here.*

With these women, turning 40 was practically an act of defiance. "After you turn 40, you don't have to be nice," one of them said. "You don't have to be good. And you sure as hell don't have to give a damn."

The last stop, the big finale, was the Willy T, where there were enough frozen margaritas to ensure everyone stripped to earn her T-shirt. *(I Came. I Saw. I Jumped.)* I got two. And even though I knew to jump with bathing suit firmly in hand so as not to lose it on the way down, I distinctly remember deciding not to bother putting it back on before emerging from the water the second time. The women were right. I didn't have to give a damn. I sashayed in my birthday suit all the way up the dock and back to our boat, where Captain Bert was waiting with a towel.

By the time I was back at work at Skinny's, the boat trip had become big news. Gertrude, the quiet woman who swept the floors in the mornings, surprised me by advising me not to worry about the sound of my biological clock ticking (or anything else). "Margie! You have plenty of time to have a baby," she sang. "Just find yourself a younger man!"

The excess of the celebration was measured in battle scars as the injury report trickled in: Fun Christina sprained her ankle (not sure how, but snapshots of her signature Madonna moves on the aft deck of the Willy T provide some clues). Anna Banana cut her foot and bled all the way back to Foxy's after losing her flip-flops on the way to (or from) the bubbly pool. Plumber Kathy would be out of work for a day (at least) because her knee had given out.

I, however, had never felt better. I wallowed in the attention. I served beers to the 20-something sailing instructor I had developed a crush on, who wanted to know if I really got my belly button pierced or if that was just a wild rumor going around and, by the way, what time did I get off?

The week ended with a new edition of the *St. John Sun Times*. Beneath my latest story, Tom Paine had placed a banner ad:

HAPPY BIRTHDAY MARGIE!
THE BIG 3-0!!

Team Skinny Legs reconvened for the Sweethearts of the Caribbean classic boat regatta where, once again, we were the only all-female (also all-blonde) crew. I jumped at any chance to sail with Belle on *O'dege* because she wasn't a control freak, so you got to do stuff—that is to say I, the inexperienced one, got to do stuff. Rounding out the crew were Fun Christina and Evie who, while neither a waitress at Skinny's nor an experienced racer, proved a willing stand-in when Erin, an excellent sailor, literally missed the boat.

It was windy. Three boats lost their mainsails before the race even began. *O'dege,* however, was built for strong wind. When the air horn sounded, she flew over the start line, heeling dramatically as gusts of air filled her sails. We charged out of the harbor with a brisk wind on our beam, rails in the whitecaps, spindrift prancing across the bow. Blonde tresses blew everywhere. We skated across the deck, cranking winches and pooling our weight to pull in the jib on the tacks.

Captain Belle was sailing fast, using every ounce of her five-foot-four, 115-pound frame for leverage.

"I feel indestructible in this boat!" she said.

Belle had *O'dege* gliding across the water. An hour into the race and we were doing well. So well that, after coming around the second mark at Flanagan Island, our captain stood up and—apparently deciding that she had earned a break—made an announcement. It was a little hard to hear over the wind from my position on the foredeck, but it sounded like she said, "Take. Nap. Now."

"Uh, what did she just say?"

"She said she wanted to take a nap."

"What! When?"

We watched Belle leave the helm and walk to the bow where she spread out, face down, on the deck.

Christina grabbed the tiller.

The captain barked two more orders from her prone position. "Head up a little!" "Stop! Now you're pinching, sweetie!" Then she fell sound asleep.

Christina and I sent Evie below to pick out music while we tried to figure out what to do. I took the helm next so Christina could trim the sails.

"Should we let the main out a little?"

"I couldn't tell you if my life depended on it."

"Go ahead and try it. See what happens."

The music came on. Evie had chosen the Police: "Sending out an S.O.S."

But we were sailing. We were even sailing in the right direction. No one was yelling or freaking out. So far, so good.

"Should we try to go a little faster?"

"OK. But don't heel over too much. We don't want the captain to fall overboard."

Maybe Belle was exaggerating her fatigue to test our mettle. Forced to take control, we did. We found the right balance, staying competitive without tipping our captain off her boat. We sailed with confidence. Until a schooner passed a little too close for comfort and we remembered we didn't know what the hell we were doing.

"What's the signal you're supposed to give when the captain's incapacitated?" I asked.

"Red over red, the captain's dead!"

We'd had enough. We rousted the skipper from her slumber. She looked around to see where we were.

"You guys did great!" she praised, walking back to her position at the helm. Everything was back to normal. We were heading toward the finish line. And then the jib blew out.

I didn't see it tear. It happened so fast. Suddenly this massive sail was thrusting horizontally from the masthead, overpowered by wind and thrashing out of control. The sheets were striking at the deck, lashing through the air like whips. It was dangerous. And exciting.

In an instant, Belle was on the foredeck, yanking on the halyard to pull the monster down. Christina sprang into action, snatching at sail and line. I swear I saw Evie fly over the lifelines, suspended in mid-air, clinging to a piece of sail. For a split second I wished for a few big, burly men, then jumped in to help. After what seemed like an eternity, we got our break. With each woman's weight pulling on some piece of the jib, it finally gave. Sail and bodies collapsed in a heap in the cockpit.

Unfortunately, to bring in the sail we had to turn on the engine. We were disqualified. We motored back into the harbor, defeated. "Well, that was a real hootenanny!" said Christina, as she hooked the mooring ball and secured the lines.

Back on land at Tortola's Jolly Roger Inn, fellow racers greeted us. "Hey! It sure took a while to bring that jib down!"

Belle, dog-tired but adrenaline racing, responded with a stream of obscenities saltier than seawater.

The man backed away. Most people, I noticed, were keeping back a good 20 feet. Could have been the attitude. Or maybe because none of us had showered in three days.

At the crowded bar, a man relinquished his stool to Belle and lifted his glass to "Women, divine." The toast turned into a poem; the man turned out to be Foxy, proprietor of the most illustrious bar and restaurant in the British Virgin Islands. A couple of cheeseburgers and a few cocktails later, the ladies of Team Skinny Legs were again approachable. Our captain was the Belle of the Buccaneers' Ball. She may not have finished the race but she got a prize—a gift certificate for sail repair. And we all got coveted Mount Gay Rum red hats—the mark of a true Caribbean racer.

I wore my new prized possession the next time I waitressed. At least two Skinny's customers offered good money for it—you can't buy the red racing hats. But I had earned mine and it was not for sale.

One guy, humblebragging about doing "a little sailboat racing up north" while I was trying to take his order, pointed to my cap.

"So, what was your position on the crew?" he asked. "I'll bet it was decoration, right?"

"Excuse me?" I said, eyebrows arched.

"You were decoration on the boat, right?" he repeated.

"Decoration?" I said the word slowly, with all the malice I could muster.

Moral of this story: Never underestimate an all-girl crew. Do not assume your waitress was "decoration" on the boat. Unless you want to wait a really long time for your beers.

I don't know what a midlife crisis is supposed to feel like. After the Sweethearts Regatta, my body was in pain. My shoulders ached, my back hurt, my legs were black and blue. I could barely lift my arms. I was sore in muscles I did not know I had. I wasn't sure if this made me a bad sailor or a good one. But the more bruised I got, the more competent I felt.

During all of those sails, every now and then, something would click. I'd feel a brief but intuitive flash of wind and water and sail all coming together, just right. For a few moments I'd be "in the groove." And not just on the water. My first months on island I'd been "luffing," to use the lexicon—sail flapping wildly in the wind, making a lot of noise, but not moving forward. Now, waters tested a bit, I was starting to "reach." The wind was coming directly across the beam, creating ideal sailing conditions. I could seize the helm and plot a course—if only I knew where I wanted to go.

6

THE WORST-CASE SCENARIO
(HURRICANE SEASON, 2005)

The Atlantic hurricane season officially runs from June 1 to November 30. Three weeks of spring, the entire summer, and most of the fall. Six full months.

Aren't you worried about hurricanes? people back home kept asking. My answer was still no. Not the kind of thing you dwell on when you've made a leap of faith. Besides, that leap had landed me in the alleged Land of No Worries. People liked to focus on the positive.

A good example of this was Julia, a vivacious Southerner with humidity-defying chestnut hair. She lived in Cruz Bay and was my liaison to all things "town." We met when I did a story on the Middle Age Majorettes, whose only worry seemed to be getting even with the five-year-old baton-twirlers who beat them in the previous year's Carnival parade. Ask Julia what she did for a living and you'd get her stock reply: "As little as possible." She actually did a lot. Raised money for non-profits. Helped the homeless. Volunteered for everything. She never saw a problem she couldn't fix.

One Sunday in hurricane season, I had a friend visiting. We met up with Julia in town, en route to a snorkel at Honeymoon Beach. Jungle George wanted to go, too, after his shift was over.

Of course somebody's phone, or quite possibly everybody's phone, wasn't working, and after a convoluted half hour of failed calls, static-y lines, and total lack of clarity about what time George got off work (one of his stock phrases was "clocks were not involved"), Julia announced that the rest of us should just go to the beach and trust that George would eventually either amble down the path and find us or wait for us at one of the bars at Mongoose Junction.

"Worst-case scenario," she drawled, "we'll just meet up at Margarita Phil's and have nachos."

"Let me get this straight," said my guest, who had been quietly taking in our attempt to forge an island "plan." "Drinking margaritas and eating nachos at some place called Margarita Phil's is your *worst-case scenario?*"

One December day our house shook violently. There was a low rumble, then a crash, like something fell on the roof. The Cliffhanger sits below the road. Was it a water truck toppling over? If the cistern was making that noise, we were in trouble. It was an earthquake. Magnitude 5.1 and centered 20 miles north. But that was just a little afternoon excitement, not the deadly 9.1 Indian Ocean earthquake and tsunami that had wiped out entire towns and killed a quarter-million people the day after Christmas.

Earthquakes were not uncommon. Another way to find St. John on the map is to look for the Puerto Rico Trench, the deepest part of the Atlantic Ocean and the boundary between the Caribbean and North Atlantic plates. The Virgin Islands are nestled just below this 27,000-foot-deep abyss. Fault lines and massive tectonic plates grinding into each other was another thing I didn't dwell on. Again, when making a leap of faith, the only shifting tectonic plates you want to think about are the metaphorical ones.

The 2005 hurricane season, though, was looking like it might be a real worst-case scenario. It had been hot since March—an early indicator of an active season. The water was unusually warm. As summer approached, the weather grew more oppressive. Air temperature was above normal, with highs averaging 89 degrees and lows around 80. It was sticky and humid. People who never wasted water by doing too much laundry complained about "three T-shirt days."

NOAA, the National Oceanic and Atmospheric Administration, confirmed the collective bad feeling by predicting more than a dozen tropical storms and several major hurricanes. A worse-than-normal season.

I had been on the hunt for my next *Sun Times* story, and this was it. What did people think about the forecast?

No one wanted to talk about it.

Many of my Coral Bay neighbors had lived through Marilyn in 1995 and Hugo in 1989, the two worst hurricanes to hit the Virgin Islands in modern memory. It had been 10 years since Marilyn. I didn't understand then, seeing only a thriving island, how vividly the terror of a storm could be relived years later.

"Hugo and Marilyn were both really scary," Mean Jean said.

Marilyn had hit on September 15, her birthday. There had been some mix-up in the weather report. No one was concerned about anything except losing power. Skinny's stayed open, giving away free ice cream before it melted.

"They told us Marilyn had passed and it wasn't that bad," Mean Jean said. "That's why nobody believes it when they tell you stuff!"

Because she had a concrete house, she had about a dozen people seeking shelter at her hurricane party. ("Hurricane parties are really not the smartest idea," she said. "To drink everything you can? Rum makes you dumb.") Even before the winds started gusting at 129 miles an hour, and the house started to flood, the tension had her "guests" grating on each other's nerves. One of them, "sick of everybody," walked out in the middle of the storm.

When it was over, everyone was rattled, but alive. Mean Jean crawled over and under downed trees to get to the road where she saw *Silver Cloud*, a 90-ton schooner and one of the flagships of Coral Bay, dumped ashore. Marilyn's 10-foot storm surge had

plucked the steel boat right out of the water and tossed it on land. She made it down to Pickles, another Coral Bay institution that had been shuttered when I lived there, and joined other dazed survivors. She was doing OK, she thought. Until somebody noticed the bear. Someone had given her a teddy bear for her birthday, which she held onto during the storm. She was still clutching it, pushing the stuffing out with her death grip.

"This is my new bear. I love my bear. Don't take my bear!" she remembered thinking. She hadn't realized she'd been clawing at it. "Someone had to pry it out of my hands and sew it back up."

No one talked about PTSD back then.

"I still sleep with the bear," she added.

After that, Mean Jean started celebrating her birthday stateside. But she had a ritual before leaving. She'd do a little circle, thank all of her stuff, say goodbye to her house. In case she never saw it again.

Jazz and I had been doing our due diligence, prepping for disaster. We'd contacted Coconut Charlie about the Cliffhanger's hurricane shutters. We'd informed our friends with the most desirable villas/bunkers that we might show up on their doorsteps in case of emergency. We had a trip to St. Thomas scheduled to stock up on water and canned tuna and flashlight batteries at Kmart. We must have been missing something, though. What else did we need?

On this subject, my willful neighbors had plenty to say. Here were their suggestions, starting with the most mentioned: Valium. Drugs of some sort. Intimate company. Rum. Beer. Plenty of booze. Monopoly. Scrabble. Cards. Good books. Bug spray, aka Caribbean cologne. Citronella candles. Mosquito netting. Battery-operated fan. Toilet paper. Tampax. Baby wipes. A Bible. A purpose.

"You need something to do. You have to stay active, so you don't get depressed. Help the community," said one lifelong resident, who had seen despair.

What about the names? *Arlene. Bret. Cindy. Dennis.* Any

predictions? I thought *Gert, Ophelia,* and *Wilma* sounded particularly ominous. There was also one called *Katrina.*

Don't make light of the names, I was reprimanded. "There are a lot of superstitions about hurricanes," one resident warned. Don't joke about it. Not at this latitude.

TROPICAL STORM ARLENE was named on June 9, nine days into hurricane season. She came and went, and two days later Chef Harry from Shipwreck married Kelly, a ranger at Virgin Islands National Park, on the beach at Hawksnest. The ceremony was attended by the entire staff of Shipwreck and many of the Coral Bay residents who seemed to live at Shipwreck's bar. The bride wore a white gown and pearl flip-flops. The groom wore shorts and a tropical shirt designed by Billabong. It was a blistering 90 degrees. Guests in bathing suits floated on purple Styrofoam noodles in the crystal blue Caribbean. Unlike the Kenny Chesney affair a month earlier, there were no paparazzi. The only wedding crasher was a young park ranger, recently relocated to St. John from somewhere else, who strode onto the beach ready to issue a fine for the illegal consumption of alcoholic beverages in the water. He retreated when he realized the bride was his boss. Islanders who should have known better swam or stood neck-deep in the water for hours without sunscreen. Everyone went home with sunburn.

The island wedding was a happy ending I envied. I continued to harbor Hollywood fantasies that my ex would show up, cop to his terrible mistake, and profess his love for both me and my newfound home. That's what would have happened in the movie version, but my life, though it sometimes seemed like one, wasn't a movie. I wasn't exactly swabbing the decks when I finally heard from him—or, rather, about him—but close. I was wiping down dirty tables at Skinny's when the email came in from Philly. The subject line was Didja Hear?

"He won a Pulitzer," it read. "For his photos of the war in Iraq."

"How do you feel?" asked a friend in another email. "Bitter? Proud? Empty? Hurt?"

I didn't know how to feel. All of the above was probably the answer, but I didn't want to latch on to the wrong emotion. My gut instinct was to contact him, but that didn't feel right either. I felt detached.

I shared the news at work.

"So what?" said Jungle George. "You have Emmys."

"It's not even close to the same thing," I said.

I went about my business, and was doing all right until Bob Who Drinks Coke came in.

Bob was an older gentleman, around 80, spry and flirtatious. He was also a photographer. And a scuba diver. A sailor. A fisherman. One day he came into Skinny's with a 14-pound lobster he had just caught. He let all the kids hold it and get their pictures taken. He was also a minister and married couples on the beach. There was no doubt more, but that's what I knew about him. Bob came in every day for his Coca-Cola. He always made me smile.

He sidled up to me.

"Why aren't you smiling today?"

"My ex-boyfriend who decided to take a job in Baghdad last year instead of marrying me just won a Pulitzer."

"Wow. That's tremendous."

"Hey! You're supposed to take my side."

"I am on your side, sweetheart. But it's a big deal. Not too many people win the Pulitzer Prize."

"I know, Bob."

He whistled. "That is something. That doesn't mean he's not a dummy, though. Did you congratulate him?"

"We're not in touch anymore."

"Well, it would not be inappropriate to reach out and congratulate him. You should be proud."

I swallowed. "I am proud," I told him, my voice cracking. "But I was proud of him before all this, and it wasn't enough."

I started to cry.

"But I meant that you should be proud of yourself, too," Bob said, "because whatever happened before he went over there, you helped him get there."

I couldn't speak. I just nodded.

Bob pulled his Yankees cap off his head and plopped it down on mine. I yanked the brim down over my eyes and dashed off to the bathroom to blow my nose. I would have splashed some water on my face but this was one of those island days when there was no goddamn running water in the sink.

When I came back, Bob was gone.

"Bob's right, you know," said Laura, the prep cook. "Send him a note and say congratulations. Take the high road. You are part of this."

She handed me an overflowing plastic cup with a salty rim. If I knew then what I know now, I would have toasted blessings in disguise, but I wasn't ready for that. There would be a lot of tequila in the hours that followed.

In the end, I sent the note. It was short. It was sincere. There was so much it didn't say.

He did not respond. I would not hear from him again.

MID-SUMMER IS one of the best-kept secrets in the Caribbean. Yes, it's hurricane season, but the worst storms seem to lie in wait until September. Hurricane season is also off-season which, back then, meant fewer tourists, a less-hectic work schedule. Locals went to the beach. The water was warm. The flamboyant trees were in riotous orange and red bloom, exploding like fireworks, one-upping even the showy bougainvillea, all magenta, yellow, and coral. The weather was an even bigger drama queen, thrilling when she wasn't threatening. One morning I woke up to driving

rain and fog so thick I couldn't see a thing outside. Five minutes later, I was standing on the deck in a light drizzle, watching the storm move west, breathing in the fresh smell of rain. The sky didn't look real. The harbor was still obscured, but to the east it was perfectly clear and blue. The sun rose over this split screen, a theatrical opening act to my day. And at night, stellar Scorpio crawled along the zodiac, the sprawling constellation entirely visible, skimming the edge of the horizon.

I used my down time to explore more of St. John, checking out some of the wonders that had taken a back seat to getting acclimated. My sailing preoccupation meant I hadn't done a whole lot of hiking, at least not beyond the requisites. I'd been down the Reef Bay Trail to see the Petroglyphs, the cryptic rock carvings archaeologists believe to be sacred symbols, carved by the Taíno 1,000 years ago. I had traipsed around Drunk Bay, where beachgoers leave behind whimsical—and anatomically correct—figures fashioned out of shells and coral. And I loved the easy Lind Point Trail to Salomon Beach. A 15-minute hike—more of a walk, really—down a rocky, wooded path deposited you on a secluded stretch of sandy beach where, if you were lucky, you could snag a shady spot under one of the low-slung palms. The trees reached down toward the water, fronds providing a bright green, un-thatched, canopy roof. If you were really lucky, you'd be the only one there.

That summer, hiking became a regular thing on Fridays because Jen—an energetic mother of two little girls—banged on the door at 7:30 a.m. raring to go, ready to point out century plants and lignum vitae and cacti, quick with her lessons about the local vegetation, from the lushness of Bordeaux to the arid, desert-like terrain around Salt Pond. Jen was also well-versed in toxic plants, trail hazards, and surviving other worst-case scenarios. Several years earlier, an erupting volcano had forced her to flee her home on Montserrat. More than half of the little island 200 miles south of St. John is uninhabitable today.

One Friday we were not far from the well-trodden path to

Ram Head, but our trail was nowhere to be found on the hiking guide distributed by the National Park Service. We trekked around Lameshur Bay Beach, "scrambling over rock outcrops," as instructed by our map, and turning left at, well, a tree. We climbed up to see, as promised, "great views of the sea below" and eventually intersected with a trail marked as the Tektite Trail. We peered down the vertical drop to the cove concealing the Navy's old underwater laboratory and, as I recall, ventured down just a few feet before deciding the climb back up might be too much for the day. Jen gives us more credit, remembering going down the cliff at least halfway before turning around.

The Lameshur Bay Beach Trail and the Tektite Trail were hikes #29 and #30 in *The Trail Bandit Guide*—a glossy hiking brochure that began appearing in shops around St. John that year. *The Trail Bandit Guide* had color maps, elegant graphics, and water-resistant paper. It sure beat the poorly photocopied, hard-to-read hiking "guides" available at the National Park office. And here's the kicker: *The Trail Bandit* map boasted 34 trails. The official park map had only 20.

Where did this map come from?

I had visions of a masked, machete-wielding trailblazer, clearing paths through the scrub on moonlit nights like the one that had just passed. Was he out there that week? Or did he do his work on moonless nights to avoid detection? Hoping to exploit the St. John phenomenon of pretty much everybody knowing at least a little something about pretty much everybody else, I started asking around to see what people knew about the Trail Bandit.

"No one knows who he is!" I kept hearing. "It's all very mysterious."

Really? I could have sworn I saw his name and contact info right there on the map.

I looked again and, sure enough, there they were. The Trail Bandit proved easy to reach. He had no qualms about his identity being revealed, but in the interest of preserving an aura of mystery

—and the magic that people like to associate with St. John—we'll just call him Bob.

We were conducting our interview, like most of my off-island communication those days, by email. I couldn't hear his tone but imagined him laughing when he read my description of his Zorro-like alter ego. It was "a little too romantic," he wrote. "Yes, there is the machete, but no mask, and if I start early in the day, I am usually pooped by 2 p.m."

Bob was a "mostly retired" guy from New Hampshire who had been visiting St. John since 1965. His metamorphosis from tourist/hiker into Trail Bandit/cartographer began with a hike down a path parallel to the Reef Bay Trail. Marked "Jeep Road" on the U.S. Geological Survey (USGS) map of St. John, the trail was hard to find on foot, and definitely not passable by jeep. Bob spent many days, over several visits, with a machete and hand saw, cutting enough brush to start down the road. There was a lot to see out there. Beautiful views of Fish Bay and Reef Bay. Thriving wild pineapple. A bay rum forest. A lone baobab tree, likely transported to St. John from Africa as seed in the pocket of a human in chains.

When the trail seemed to disappear completely, Bob purchased USGS aerial photographs from 1954, on which the road was very visible. With a handheld GPS and a mapping program called Fugawi (as in, *Where the Fug-are-we?*) he was able to locate the road and cut through to the end of the trail. But those aerial photographs led to another discovery: more trails, lost due to lack of use or maintenance. Bob, now in full Trail Bandit mode, hiked the more prominent ones, clearing as he went. Then he made his own map.

Task complete, the Trail Bandit visited National Park headquarters in Cruz Bay and offered up his information, suggesting the Park update its own guides. When he got little interest, he published the map himself.

(At this point, traditional journalism would dictate that I include some response from the National Park Service, but in my

Sun Times newspaper world, my editor told me I didn't have to. Still, old habits die hard, so I tried. The ranger with the most knowledge on these issues, I was told, was on vacation for a month. The superintendent didn't return my calls.)

The Trail Bandit said he did not create any new trails, but simply located and maintained existing ones. He didn't want to destroy park property. He just wanted to preserve what was there so future generations could enjoy St. John's exceptional hiking. He wasn't making any money. He saw his map as a public service. Lots of people were hiking the "new" trails with brush cutters and saws. Just having many feet walking the trails made a difference.

"St. John is a rugged, beautiful island," he wrote. "The network of trails gives access to many parts of the island that the busses and taxis don't get to, where you can see the beautiful views in relative peace and quiet. A good half-day hike here gives enough physical exercise that you really enjoy and deserve having a beer under your favorite palm tree ... Thanks for helping get the word out to all hikers. And Happy Hiking."

Years later Bob will describe himself as "sort of a protected terrorist" who could have been arrested at any time. The Park Service will eventually credit his work. Trail Bandit maps will still be for sale on the island, but the baobab tree will be gone.

BY MID-JULY we were on our fifth named storm of the season: Emily. I was at the bar at Skinny's where it seemed all of Coral Bay had gathered, waiting for the Weather Channel's Tropical Update at eight minutes before the hour. When the hurricane warnings were posted for Grenada, Barbados, St. Vincent, and St. Lucia, a cheer went up. "Go Grenada!" one sailor yelled. It appeared Emily would pass us, but boaters moved their vessels into Water Creek or Princess Bay—all parts of Hurricane Hole—just in case.

The Caribbean used to be one blue and green blur on the map to me—an enticing yet nebulous Vacation Spot somewhere south of Florida—but I had learned to identify what islands were where and, more to the point, where the Virgin Islands were in relation to all the hurricane-warning red on the TV weather maps. (Remember? We're the tiny group of islands just to the right of the pretty big Puerto Rico, which is just to the right of the really big Hispaniola and the even bigger Cuba.) Tropical Storm Brett and Hurricane Cindy had both kicked around the Gulf of Mexico, and if you don't still have your map out, I'll just tell you, that's far away. Hurricane Dennis, however, dumped torrential rain on St. John and knocked out power, reminding Jazz and me that our final storm preparations were overdue.

We went to Kmart with our trusty list, always tacked up on the refrigerator. Here's a sample:

KMART Shopping List
Toilet paper
Toothbrush
Sunscreen
Water
Cat Food
Coffee
Purses
Beach Chairs
Tire
Toilet Bowl Cleaner (1000 Flushes, etc.)

By summer we had Kmart down to a science and could purchase a month's necessities in half an hour, leaving time to peruse what was new in women's clothing. Paradise was hell for fashion. Eight months after transplanting my once ready-for-prime-time self in the tropics, most of my garments were amorphous, stretched out beyond the boundaries of any recognizable trend. My colors were faded and my whites were gray. I don't know if it was the cistern water, the washing machine, or the sun, but nothing, skin and hair included, escaped unscathed. The last guy who cut my hair also ran a business delivering beach snacks out of a powerboat.

It took me three minutes to get ready for work. I had come to think that being required to wear sleeves and closed-toe shoes was a hardship. My closet contained 13 pairs of flip-flops—including a fleece-lined pair that Trish sent after I complained about the cold when it dropped to 65 degrees—and one pair of sneakers. I cried the day I lost my second pair of sneakers when, after literally kicking off my shoes after work, one sneaker went hurtling over the Cliffhanger's balcony. I believed dumpster diving was a perfectly acceptable way to furnish your closet. I had purchased my entire last new outfit (cabana pants, tank top, flip-flop pair #13) for $15 at the Mumbo Jumbo Crazy $5 Sale. I was starting to believe my Malibu Barbie—another gag gift from a friend back home—with her do-rag, hooded black mesh vest, and ultra-mini board shorts—had a terrific sense of style. In August, I would think the April issue of *Vogue* was current. I had used my 618-page, special holiday edition of *In Style* magazine to obliterate a three-inch cockroach. The only makeup I wore was lip gloss and toenail polish. On the plus side, it was Chanel. All the Skinny's waitresses had Chanel lip gloss and nail polish because I had waited on a guy who worked for Chanel, and he actually followed through on his promise to send me a box of all the hottest new colors. Now that was a good tip.

I think we did a commendable job assimilating to island life. There were, however, a few concessions Jazz refused to make. When her watch broke, she had a meltdown. Friends suggested she just *try* going without it. She made it three days. She'd blow dry her hair before work. I hadn't seen my blow-dryer in months. As a TV dropout, I was more than happy to give that up. Friends who wondered if I'd changed down there—*Yes!* I'd tell them. *I look like I did when I was 13.* A writer for the *Philadelphia Inquirer* walked into Skinny's for lunch one day with her family. I would get a shout-out in her next column: *Our waitress is Margie Smith, a recovering Philadelphia publicist and TV reporter, her hair now untamed by salt water.* She was being kind. And yet, stripped down, I felt more like myself than ever.

On the day we went to buy hurricane supplies, so, too, apparently, did half the denizens from the bar at Skinny's, who seemed weirdly out of place browsing the aisles of Kmart. Irie, the "coconut technician," took one look in my basket and shook his head.

"Not that one," he said, pointing to my choice of flashlight. "You need something that you can drop over and over into the water and it will still shine."

Irie escorted me back to hardware. "You need this one. I have three of them," he said, presenting me with the industrial-sized flashlight he deemed "best for when hurricane come." I put it in the cart with the Martha Stewart candles and the Chef Boyardee.

In the midst of this interaction, my phone rang. My phone at that point was held together with duct tape, but I got fantastic reception at Kmart. It was Fun Christina, calling to let me know that she had just broken up with her boyfriend. I promised to help move her stuff off his boat when I got home. She, in exchange, would provide an on-the-spot storm-prep consultation.

"What did you get so far?"

"I've got flashlights, a battery-operated radio, water, bug spray," I replied, ever the Girl Scout. "Wait, here comes Jazz. Let me see what's in her cart."

I assessed my roomie's selections. "Jazz has an ink jet printer and a three-foot standing electric fan," I reported.

"Better tell Jazz to buy a generator," Christina advised.

We checked out and rushed to the dock for the five o'clock ferry. The boat wasn't running. We'd have to take the seven. We ordered takeout Chinese for the ride, then climbed the two flights of stairs to SopChoppy's bar to wait with a view of the water. A couple of Heinekens later, our Suzuki was squeezed onto the last barge of the day. We sat on the top deck and ate cold pan-fried dumplings for dinner. We drove home in the dark. Our shopping trip had consumed an entire day. Back at the

Cliffhanger, while unpacking our haul, we discovered we had no running water.

"Good thing we bought this," Jazz said, holding up the 2,000 Flushes toilet bowl cleaner. "In this place, it'll last the rest of our lives."

2005 WAS one of the worst hurricane seasons ever. There were 28 storms—so many, they ran out of names. Fifteen were full-fledged hurricanes, three so powerful, they still top the list of most intense Atlantic hurricanes. Five were so deadly, or destructive, or both, they retired their names: Dennis. Katrina. Rita. Stan. Wilma.

But in St. John, it was mercifully calm.

That September, at the height of hurricane season, I did what a lot of islanders do and left for a while. I spent three weeks in the States, most of it in Philadelphia where, despite the marvelous fall weather, I froze my ass off because everywhere I went, the air conditioning was cranked up to full blast. Why didn't anybody just open a window?

I had not had three weeks off since entering the full-time working world right after college. Being away from my job that long was a new concept. So was the concept that when you don't work, you don't get paid. I had to go home—to St. John—because I ran out of cash and needed more. I worried I'd been away so long I wouldn't remember how to do my waitressing job. I couldn't even remember what time I was supposed to show up. This was disorienting. These feelings would have been 100 percent foreign to the woman who moved there the previous November. She was no slacker. She knew how to do her job and certainly would have known what time to be in. Her only worry would have been returning to work to discover she'd been replaced. She, come to think of it, would have spent most of her vacation worrying about that.

THE WORST-CASE SCENARIO • III

"No worries!" said Fun Christina, when she picked me up at the ferry dock in muggy heat and promptly suggested we go have dinner at ZoZo's, one of the priciest places on the island. "It's been quiet. Work will be easy."

If winter was High Season and summer was Low/Slow Season, September was No Season. Tourists were gone. Places shut down. At Skinny's they joked that there was a two-drink minimum. For the staff.

"Oh, and I almost forgot," Christina continued. "Saturday night there's a benefit for the Katrina victims. So everyone's giving their tips to the Red Cross."

My initial reaction was dismay. My first night back at work and I'd be going home with pockets still empty. Then I felt ashamed. I was no victim. I had plenty.

While our community proper had been spared, it was not unaffected. Mississippi-born Mel, the Skinny's cook, had been talking incessantly about his planned five-week vacation roaming around the States. He left Coral Bay the same day I did and got as far as his first stop, Biloxi, where he remained, helping his mother repair her roof. Bethany, the Shipwreck waitress, was still on island, waiting for the all-clear to fly home to New Orleans, destroyed by Katrina. Traveling was nearly impossible and, frankly, there was nowhere for her to go once she got there. Lisa, a bartender at Island Blues with no ties to the Gulf Coast, had just spent a week in Houston, volunteering to help refugees, simply because she felt moved to do something.

Saturday's fundraiser brought in all the locals, effusive in their greetings: *You're back! Welcome home! How was Philly?* As usual, everyone knew where I had been. A few months earlier, I had found this disconcerting, even irritating. But I had come to accept the interest as genuine. Most people, I believed, were truly sincere, even if unnervingly over-informed. They always seemed to know when you'd been sleeping (and with whom) and when you were awake. Are all small towns like this?

"Every time I go to the States, my visits get shorter and short-er," said one local. "I can't take it up there for very long anymore."

"Could you see the sky where you were?" asked another. "I always miss the sky."

Ah, my free-spirited neighbors. Do I idealize them when I write about them? Maybe. But I give them credit for espousing a simpler way of life. For placing importance in, as one sailor friend always said, *las cosas pequeñas*. The little things. You're not supposed to live this way? "Says who?" they'd reply. They loved their beaches and their boats, their sublime surroundings, and their autonomy. "No worries" wasn't just a phrase—it was a philosophy. People didn't sweat the small stuff, not when there was big stuff to worry about: Drug and alcohol abuse. Domestic violence. Gentrification. Racial tension. Are all small towns like this? Aren't all big towns like this? Seems to me it's the same everywhere, just more exposed here, better camouflaged there.

"How long are you and Jazz going to stay down there?" friends up north had started asking. "Is it a forever thing?"

I had absolutely no idea. "But in the movie version," we used to say—again with the movies—"one of us meets a millionaire and sails back to The City on a big yacht, and the other lives happily-ever-after in paradise."

I had, however, decided to stay another season. I still wasn't sure what I was trying to accomplish, but I knew I wasn't done. I definitely wanted to sail more. Maybe I'd read *Anna Karenina* or something else from that stack of books I had shipped down the previous fall and hadn't touched.

This did not appease the Greek chorus back home.

"Don't worry about me," I had to reassure my mother at lunch on my last day in Philadelphia. "I am happy where I am."

Was it where I thought I would be?

No.

But that was OK.

I played defense again at the airport when a reporter friend called just as I was getting ready to board.

"So," she launched right in. "What are you going to do now?"

"I'm going to get on the plane to St. Thomas."

"No!" she scolded. "I mean what are you going to do *next*? With your life? What's your plan?"

Plans were so big where we came from.

And then there was the email from a colleague.

From: A Conscientious Objector
Subject: Flip-Flop

I enjoy your stories immensely. You have a real gift. I have to wonder though, are you planning on living island life forever? Maybe it's my Protestant work ethic but you're bright and talented. Do you have a cricket on your shoulder urging you to do something more ... meaningful?

That one really got under my skin. Yes, I wanted to do something "meaningful." Of course I did. In fact, I thought I had. But in my master plan, I was also "supposed" to be married with kids by 40. When that vision didn't materialize, there I was, thinking, is this where I want to be standing a year from now? Five years from now? Ten? Or worse, blaming somebody else because I didn't like where I was standing? Still with that "meaningful" job, nice apartment, good shoes, and ... what else? Wasn't there something else? In the absence of anything more substantial, would I fill up the empty space with work?

I took time off thinking I just needed to step back, ruminate, get a little perspective, but in the process, I had discovered there are non-traditional ways to live a life that is happy and productive. Meaningful. I wasn't convinced "non-traditional" was my way forward but in the short term I had latched onto it like a fugitive from the wrong life. A fish that had been out of water too long. My body craved the sunshine and the rare air, and I couldn't believe how free my mind felt.

Maybe I didn't know what I really wanted. Maybe that was why I didn't have it yet.

And in the Land of No Worries, I worried.

I worried that my choices would preclude my ever having a "normal" life. I worried that I'd never fall in love again. I worried about money. I worried about not being able to find a job if I returned to my old world. (Although Fun Christina told me not to worry about that since, because I have restaurant skills now, I can always waitress until I'm 83.)

I was even starting to worry about hurricanes.

But I never worried that it was the wrong decision to move to Coral Bay.

Back in Philly, friends had been telling me about all the meetings in their respective places of work about how to help the victims of Hurricane Katrina. Lots of talk, not as much action. Skinny Legs didn't have meetings. Owners Doug and Moe just picked a day, booked a band, and gave the entire night's take to charity. No worries.

The benefit was a success. Skinny Legs reprised its role as a center of hurricane relief. Moe was proud of his efforts to be a source of aid, and relieved not to be the recipient of it. To have survived another season.

"The Red Cross helped us out when we got hit," Moe said.

The unspoken second part of this sentence was that next time, it could be "us" again.

———

FUN CHRISTINA WAS ANIMATED, talking about the movie she had seen the night before, *What the Bleep Do We Know!?* The meaning-of-life cult documentary had recently arrived at the K2 Video store, dividing Coral Bay into two camps: those who thought it was profound and couldn't wait to see it again, and those whose eyes glazed over at the mention of the words "quantum physics." Christina was category one; her ex, she lamented, was category two.

"I miss talking about philosophy," she complained. "I feel like I don't use my brain at all here."

"Really?" I said. "I'm just the opposite." Now that my brain wasn't cluttered up with all the mundane work stuff I used to worry about, I had creative energy that I hadn't felt in years.

We were at work at Skinny's and it was raining. It had been raining for three days straight. When I say rain, I don't mean the hooray!-it's-raining, listen-to-the-cisterns-fill, wash-your-rugs-and-car, take-a-long-shower rain, I mean ceaseless, pelting, wash-out-the-roads, everything-is-dripping, is-it-ever-going-to-stop? downpours. It was all-day gray except when heavy fog created white-outs. Humid doesn't begin to cover it. The air was soup.

Island roofing tends to leak and against an assault like this, even the most solid structures withered, never mind Skinny's old sail "roof." Everything was damp—T-shirts, napkins, your hair, your underwear. It was impossible to dry out. Tourists were whining because the weather was bad. Didn't they know it was hurricane season when they booked their off-season-prices vacation? The locals, i.e., me, were wearing jeans and long sleeves because we were cold. And wet. Did I mention wet? But it was not a hurricane.

It was, however, Columbus Day, and while the explorer is one of the most contentious figures associated with the Caribbean, as the catalyst for yet another federal holiday, the Admiral of the Ocean Sea was wholeheartedly embraced. Between the government workers with a day off and the construction guys who were out of work again because of the weather, the bar at Skinny Legs was full even before it officially opened.

Christina was bartending and I was waitressing. We were wearing feathers in our hair because we thought it looked Spanish. We considered doing Columbus trivia but were off to an unpromising start as no one seemed to know who Ferdinand and Isabella were.

Christina opted instead for a joke:

Q: If April showers bring May flowers, what do Mayflowers bring?

A: Pilgrims.

OK, so the connection between the Pilgrims's transatlantic crossing in the 17th century and Columbus's 1492 expedition to the New World is tenuous, but any six-year-old knows the answer to this riddle. Nevertheless, Christina had completely bamboozled the 10 a.m. crowd at Skinny's.

I, meanwhile, was about to commence an uncertain voyage of my own.

In late fall, opulent sailboats move from their summer playgrounds in New England or the Mediterranean to their winter haunts in the Caribbean. These trips, called deliveries, often require extra crew because of the time and distance involved. Thanks to some string-pulling from Vicki, the KATS instructor, I had finagled my way onto the crew for one of these yachts sailing from Rhode Island to St. John.

The trip would be entirely offshore, meaning we would not see land. I was thrilled. Also—what's the word? (Consulting my thesaurus, here...) Oh yes. Scared. Apprehensive. Nervous. Anxious. Uneasy. Stressed. Tense. Intimidated. Agitated. Panic-stricken. Petrified. Freaked out. Did I mention scared? Name a *holy crap!* emotion and I was probably internalizing it, aided and abetted by the good sailors of Coral Bay who, as word spread that I would be making my first delivery, had been eager to share the (horror) stories of their own (mis)adventures at sea. These stories included descriptions like *blown off course in a gale* and *hurricane-force winds* and *the time we had to heave-to for three days to wait out weather.* I had no idea what they were talking about half the time, but it sounded terrifying. Was heaving-to the same as heaving? Because I was definitely worried about that. Puking for two weeks straight.

I blame Fun Christina. Like Jazz disapproving of my plan to battle heartache with work, Christina thought I set my sights too low. When I told her I planned to visit Trish and her new baby in New England when I was up north the previous month, I mentioned wanting to stop and see the yacht Vicki was working on up there. Christina suggested instead of merely aspiring to look AT the boat, I try to get ON the boat.

That's the thing about Coral Bay. One minute you're standing on a dock, admiring some big, beautiful boat. Next thing you know you're on the boat, embarking on a 1,500-mile seafaring journey.

I would spend the one-year anniversary of my move to St. John somewhere in the Atlantic Ocean, no land in sight.

TRUE WIND

7

CAPTAIN KID

One day near the beginning of my second year on St. John I was answering one of the recurrent "How'd you end up here?" questions from a woman I waited on at Skinny's. By the time I got to the part where I had just decided to stay another season, she was practically jumping out of her chair.

"You have to stay until whatever is supposed to happen to you happens!" she squealed. *"Make sure you stay until whatever is supposed to happen happens!"*

It would have been hard to believe back then how much more would still happen.

So much had already happened. My first long-distance sail, for example.

We didn't get blown off course or sail into a hurricane, but it was a rough ride. We left Rhode Island in a gale with 40-knot sustained winds that flogged the ocean into mighty rollers. I had never seen waves that big. I was dumbstruck. And seasick. When I was finally able to write—48 hours into the trip—I wanted to be careful not to embellish. "10-to-12-foot seas," I wrote in my logbook, recording the captain's observations.

"But that's from sea level," corrected one of my crewmates. "So you can double it, crest to trough."

The crew had reacted with such sangfroid, I assumed it was normal. Only afterward did they fess up.

"Make sure you write that the breakers were on the beam," said one, meaning the waves were slamming the entire length of our boat, broadside.

"And that you were looking up at some of them," added another.

"Yeah," chuckled the first. "That was definitely baptism by fire for you."

The boat was a 76-foot yacht, and I joined her crew at the Newport Shipyard, the blue-chip boatyard where at least one America's Cup yacht was docked. *That* was what I pictured when I heard the phrase "yacht club." I was a long way from Coral Bay.

I had flown north the week before we set sail: St. Thomas to Puerto Rico to Philadelphia to Providence, all one-way. Up in the clouds, on each leg, I looked out the airplane window and down at the blue. All that blue I was flying over in a matter of hours would take nine days to sail back down.

The extra crew on a long passage help maintain a 24-hour watch schedule so the boat doesn't hit anything. At any given time, there were two people on watch. Everyone got four hours on and eight hours off. My watch was 8-12, a.m. and p.m., and I was "on duty" the same time as the captain, meaning I didn't really have to do anything except stay upright and learn—about longitude, and reading the compass, and how to stop the boat and blow the horn to alert the others if the captain fell overboard, which he kept assuring me he wouldn't, even though he seemed to be constantly tinkering precariously close to the edge.

For two days everything I ate came back up. Before each shift I'd grope my way to the toilet and vomit or dry-heave before bundling up in foul-weather gear, buckling up my safety harness, and staggering up to the cockpit, but I never missed a watch. My partner brought me dry toast and chicken soup. I was pretty sure the captain wasn't supposed to be making me breakfast, but I was in no position to argue. When my stomach settled, he taught me how to spot boats and how to determine whether they were coming toward us or moving away.

The voyage was a barrage on the senses. My body resisted the unnatural tilt of the boat. Making tea, a simple task, became an ordeal because it required pouring boiling liquid while balancing in a rocking vessel. The dramatic heel meant my berth was on an angle, something like 40 degrees. I discovered what a lee cloth was, and how to tie it up to keep from falling out of bed. *Learn your knots!* I could hear the KATS instructors preach.

How far were we from land? Approximately 600 miles from Cape Hatteras, North Carolina, I had written at one point. Or 2.9 miles "if you can hold your breath," said one of the crew, pointing to the bottom of the ocean floor.

One night there was a lightning storm. There were blinding flashes of light, followed by jagged bolts that sliced the sky and shot down into the sea.

When the seas calmed and the seasickness subsided, the night watches turned pure magic. The constellations Orion and Taurus were rising in the sky as my shift began. I knew Orion's belt, but out there we could see the stars in his sword. There were billions of stars, their brightness eclipsed only by the bioluminescence, hockey-puck-sized diamonds shimmering atop the waves. Shooting stars plopped out of the sky with such regularity it was almost routine, but my childlike refrain of "(Gasp.) Wow! Did you see that one?" went on all night.

Come daylight I was able, gradually, to look around and take it all in. To absorb that there was absolutely nothing in sight except water and sky. I had been hearing about this "blue water" sailing since landing in Coral Bay and now here I was—*At Last!*

I remember one night in particular listening to Jungle George and other sailors rhapsodizing about their blue-water voyages with their 360-degree horizons, nothing to block the view of sun, moon, and stars. I'll never forget them describing how, when the moon was full, you could see the sun rise and the moon set at the exact same time. I was mesmerized. I wanted to see that.

We wouldn't have a full moon on my trip, but we had Impressionist sunsets and pods of dolphins as escorts.

"Dolphins!" someone yelled after dinner one night. "They're swimming along the bow!"

Everyone ran to the front of the boat. OK, everyone else ran. I, I don't know, what do you call it when you sort of half-crawl, half-shuffle, all the while clutching whatever person or piece of boat is within reach? A dozen or so dolphins were racing alongside us, diving back and forth under the boat. They executed spectacular leaps off to starboard, where the sinking sun was giving the water an effervescent pink glow. Then they swam off and I found myself out on the bow, paralyzed. With the light fading, it was time to get back to the safety of the cockpit but the foredeck separating us suddenly looked like the Serengeti. I was scared to move. *This is ridiculous,* I tried to reason with myself. *We aren't heeling or even rocking that much. You've done this before on other boats.* My feet—and eyes—weren't buying it. Looking out at all that ocean was utterly unnerving. *(Ah, yes. We're in the middle of the ocean. Maybe not so ridiculous?)* I took a deep breath and cautiously made my way back, one lily-livered step at a time.

Halfway home we made a stop in Bermuda, where the streets of spotless St. George's stretched out from the harbor like a maze of—what felt like—gently rolling docks. Feeling woozy on land, I was told, meant I was starting to get my sea legs.

Back underway, as we approached the Caribbean, the air warmed up and the colors of the water changed from the murky brown of the North Atlantic to various shades of blue, even violet. Continued calm emboldened me. The yacht had a little seat, just big enough for one, at the very front of the bow. On a splendid day near the end of the journey, I ventured out to the foredeck, alone, to try it out. Grasping the pulpit, I positioned my backside squarely on the thin slab of aluminum, straddling the rail in the foremost part of the boat with my legs dangling overboard, just like we dangled from the Cliffhanger's balcony, except this seat was in motion. The frisson of that movement—pitching up toward the sky, plunging down into the water—was like a carnival ride.

I can still feel it. The rhythm of the boat. The wind on my face. The splashes of seawater on my toes, feet, and legs. There is nothing in front of me, nothing on the horizon, nothing behind. Nothing for 360 degrees except ocean and sky. I think of that scene in *Titanic*. It's exactly like that. *I'm the king of the world!* It's exhilarating. I feel like I'm flying. I feel alive. Free.

WE SAILED BACK into Coral Bay in time for the Thanksgiving regatta. I raced with Belle on *O'dege*. The competitors were my friends: There was Colin, racing his lovingly restored Tahiti ketch, *Buxom*; and Jason, the KATS sailing instructor, on F-Stop; and Birdie in his beloved *Dolphin*. Was Anna Banana out there? She had put in weeks of grueling labor refurbishing her boat, *Dulcinea,* at a no-frills boatyard in St. Thomas the locals just called Independent. At the end of the day, if she wanted to get clean, she had to keep feeding quarters into the meager shower— 25-cents for each minute of water. Every time I took a shower at the Newport Shipyard, where the hot water blasted like a power wash in the spa-like ladies' locker room, I thought of Anna and her quarters. And no Coral Bay race would be complete without Puerto Rican Pete bringing up the rear in *For Pete's Sake,* and always looking like he was having more fun than anybody else.

Jazz and I went to Thankspigging where, to an outside eye, everything would have looked exactly the same as the year before, but everything had changed. That first holiday, two new girls taking pictures and asking questions had been met with suspicion. (I had since learned there was a rumor going around that we were Feds. Someone who had recently been to Philadelphia reported seeing a lot of federal buildings in the city. Conclusions were drawn.) At our second Thankspigging, everyone posed for photos. There we were with our fake tattoos—a turtle on Jazz's left breast, three tiny flowers on the back of my shoulder—mugging with Gino the tattoo artist; and Long-Haired Ken, who organized the event; and Jersey Tom, who carved the pig the year before and wouldn't tell me his name. On this Thanksgiving, I was thankful for the unqualified way in which my neighbors—always around to help out if necessary, but willing to leave me alone to do whatever it was I came there to do—had accepted me (once they were convinced I wasn't going to bust them for anything).

While I had committed to another season, it was a bittersweet holiday for Jazz, who, at the end of the year, left St. John for a new job, one that didn't involve mopping floors on Sunday mornings. As I drove her to the ferry for her final flight north, we reminisced about our countless beach days—immersed in the Elixir—at Salt Pond or Haulover, Maho or Francis. We tried to never take them for granted. Sometimes, if we were heading to the North Shore beaches, we'd pick up lunch at Colombo's Smoothie Stand *(FREE RUM in any Smoothie),* each time taking in that triangle of blue sea you saw driving down the mountain like we were seeing it for the first time, each time wondering anew how it could take that girl half an hour to make a sandwich. Every excursion into our saltwater world seemed to surpass the last: Swimming with the turtles and sergeant majors and parrotfish. Spotting a stingray or barracuda. Hovering over the yellow sponges, avoiding the black spiny sea urchins and fire coral. Peeking under rocks. Pausing, hypnotized, by a waving sea fan, fluorescent purple, or what must have been a whole galaxy of starfish, lounging over the reef at Waterlemon Cay. Recreational scuba divers always dive with a buddy and Jazz was the best, spotting the most interesting sights and always watching my back.

My gregarious roommate's generous spirit meant we often shared our space with the strays she'd bring home. One time it was a puppy (vetoed by our three cats) but usually it was people. I was never quite sure who or what I'd find sleeping on the couch in the morning. Looking for action can be an arduous task in a corner of the world with only four places to hang out, but Jazz could always find it, even if it meant she had to create it (sometimes on our deck at 2 a.m.). Without her, I might have gotten around to reading *Anna Karenina* but I wouldn't have had nearly as much to write about. Jazz, meanwhile, would say she will always remember the sound of St. John not as the coquis at dusk or the surf below our house but the tapping of my keyboard in the early morning hours out on the Cliffhanger's deck.

With Jazz gone and the lease on the Cliffhanger up, I moved in with Fun Christina who, newly single and therefore boat-less/homeless, had spent the fall setting up housekeeping in a plush vacation home owned by a friend we called Villa Guy. Since Villa Guy's place wasn't rented off-season, he agreed to quarter Christina until she found a new place to live. I noticed she wasn't looking very hard, but who was I to judge, lazing, as I was, by Villa Guy/Christina's infinity pool. By the time tourist season kicked back up into high gear, though, Christina was kicked out and we were living in a concrete, still-under-construction apartment— what the locals would refer to as a "shack-teau." Our stark studio had an unfinished bathroom and a million-dollar view. I'd taken the next step in my No Makeup, No Hair Dryer existence and now lived in a place with No Mirror. No kidding. Morning ablutions were a snap.

With all that extra time, I had developed a goal: I wanted to sail "down island"—another intriguing and seemingly far-flung place many of my Coral Bay neighbors had been—and go to Antigua for Antigua Classics, the splashy season-ending regatta the *boats boats boats* guys talked about incessantly at Skinny's. I rearranged my waitressing schedule so I could sail more, with whoever would have me, and during one of the Wednesday night races had my first sail on *Carina*.

Carina had become a bit of a celebrity since sailing into Coral Bay. She was a beauty: Thirty feet of graceful lines, gleaming varnish, and flawless, hand-crafted detail. "Seductive and full of strange promise and the hint of trouble," to quote from "The Sea and the Wind that Blows," E.B. White's song of praise to small-boat sailing. Lustrous and new, *Carina* was constructed in traditional style, like something from the 1800s. Her owner and captain, whom I had not met, built her himself.

Having admired the sweet little boat from afar, I was delighted when one of the regulars at Skinny's, who worked with *Carina*'s captain, arranged for us to crew on her. I figured he was trying to impress me with another dude's boat, but so what.

As race time approached, there was no sign of my buddy the wheeler-dealer. I scanned the happy hour crowd at Skinny's for unfamiliar faces—some burly, grizzled, weathered old salt who might be the shipwright—but didn't see anyone who looked the part. I started asking around: I was supposed to go sailing on that boat everybody's been talking about. Did anybody know this boat builder guy? Somebody pointed him out and I went over to introduce myself. No wonder I hadn't spotted him. He wasn't at all what I expected. He was lean, clean-shaven, and dark-haired, with no gray at all. He was 23 years old.

I followed Captain Kid down to the Dinghy Dock. Most of the tenders tied up in Coral Bay were plastic—rubber or PVC-coated inflatable rafts with outboard motors—but we stepped into a smart little wooden boat with oars. Captain Kid rowed us out to the moorings.

I would have sworn there were only two of us on board for that sail. Years later Captain Kid will tell me there was a third person, and when he says this, my memory glimpses another of our Coral Bay neighbors, an athletic older woman with a purple streak in her hair, standing on *Carina*'s deck. It must have been another race, I think. Captain Kid doesn't think there was another race. This contradiction will gnaw at me every time I tell a story, make me wonder how accurately I remember anything. But one thing that is not in dispute is this: There was an odd change in the weather that night.

At six o'clock, start time, it was nearly dead calm. With so little wind, Captain Kid wanted to know if it would be OK to just sail around instead of racing. Fine by me. But there was a good turnout. Then the wind picked up. As we were heading out of the harbor, the skipper changed his mind and decided to join the competition. He wanted to put up more sail. *Carina* essentially sailed herself, he assured me. Would I take the tiller?

I steered the entire race, even through a little squall, even when the wind shifted 180 degrees and started blowing, eerily, out of the west—the "wrong" direction, as anyone familiar with Coral Bay will tell you. With the big headsail up, we were completely overpowered when a strong gust hit. *Carina* heeled way over, but she was plenty sturdy, I held on, and Captain Kid never flinched. He never said much, either. He was preoccupied, nimbly climbing the mast, or dangling off the bowsprit, or making a minor adjustment in some other unsecure-looking location. I had to keep reminding him that maybe he should keep an eye on me since I had never sailed his boat before and, oh yeah, I was still pretty new at this helmsman stuff.

It was an exciting race, enhanced by the lovely boat and the mellow proficiency of her taciturn shipwright. After the sails were put away, we sat on deck with a couple of beers and made a few stabs at conversation.

To say that Captain Kid was reserved would be an understatement. He was altogether lacking in bravado, bordering on downright bashful. But I had heard the veteran sailors of Coral Bay talk about his boat, so I knew she was something special. Sure, they talked *boats boats boats* all day long, but this was different. They were in awe of this boat. This kid was not just another wannabe pirate with a second-rate boat and no clue what he was doing. This kid was serious.

How serious? For starters, *Carina* had oil lamps. That's how the crew of the *Pequod* sailed. Captain Kid modestly described *Carina* as "a traditional, 30-foot, all-wood, Lyle Hess-designed cutter, based on a 19th-century English workboat." But I think

Did you say 19th century? Isn't that Moby Dick *territory?* is more to the point.

"Traditional" meant *Carina* had no engine, no electricity, and no head. For the uninitiated, that's what you call the toilet on a boat—the head. This boat had no toilet. This is how serious Captain Kid was about tradition.

Instead of a motorized autopilot, *Carina* had a windvane (named Mona), a mechanical self-steering system powered by the wind. The windlass, used to haul up the anchor, cranked by hand. There were no fancy electronics. The "depth sounder" was 60 feet of rope with a weight attached ("because if it's deeper than 60 feet, it doesn't really matter," Captain Kid reasoned). Navigation was by chart. The running lights—the red and green lights displayed on the sides of a boat to indicate the direction it's traveling—were antique lanterns with colored glass, also fueled by oil. Where other boats have plastic, nylon, and snaps, *Carina* had wood, cloth, and rope. Her handsome interior and decks were teak, the mast was spruce. The frame, backbone, and hull were oak, cedar, and mahogany painted white with green trim. At the end of the day, when the halyard was secured and the hand-stitched sails furled, the sail cover went on, fastened with a row of uniform knots along the underside of the boom, all carefully tied by hand.

A native of Cape Cod, Captain Kid had the sea in his blood. His great-grandfather was a shipwright. His grandfather, a fisherman, helped him build his first boat when he was 11. He got a job in a boatyard and, at 17, began building the boat he would sail away in. It took him five years. He spent his last winter up north sleeping in an unfinished berth, the boat's hull frozen in the water at the dock where he worked, piles of blankets the only protection against the bitter New England cold.

That's how serious Captain Kid was about his boat.

Carina, which is Latin for "keel," was named for the main navigational star in the southern hemisphere, found in a constellation depicting the hull of the *Argo,* the mythical ship of Jason and the Argonauts. Captain Kid had never seen this constellation. He finished building his boat, christened her, and immediately set sail for the Caribbean, a place he had never been and knew no one. Friends accompanied him for the first part of the trip, but he sailed alone from Bermuda to the Virgin Islands. He eventually made his way to St. John, dropping anchor just after Thanksgiving in Coral Bay where he was instantly adopted by the local sailing community.

I would have to wait for most of this information. That first night, after the race, we barely managed small talk.

Captain Kid told me he planned to sail to Antigua for the classic yacht regatta, and then sail across the Atlantic. I told him I wanted to go to Antigua Classics as well.

"I'm looking for crew," he said.

"I'm looking for a bigger boat," I replied.

Captain Kid laughed. He rowed me back to shore in *Carina*'s little dinghy. I thanked him for the sail, said goodbye, and walked away. Or so I thought.

———

FOR THE NEXT SEVERAL NIGHTS, with the wind still blowing from the wrong place, I couldn't sleep. I couldn't stop thinking about that race, or that boat. I kept wondering: What gave this kid the idea that he could just build a boat and sail away in it instead of doing something more, I don't know, *normal*? Before moving to Coral Bay, I didn't know anybody who did anything like that. How do you grow up even thinking that this is an option and then, you know, actually do it? People in my old world thought I was living an unconventional life? I had nothing on this guy.

Maybe I could get those questions answered if I sailed to Antigua with Captain Kid. At the very least, I thought, I'd get a story. Then I'd remember the size of the boat. Thirty feet of vessel was nice for a sail around Coral Bay—but out in The Ocean? With nothing but a bucket for a bathroom?

"Are you afraid you're going to die?" asked New Age Billie after a sail a week later.

"No," I said. "Is that the only criteria?"

"It's mine," she replied.

Belle was more direct.

"You're a candy ass if you don't sail down on that boat," she said. "Why don't you watch my kid for a couple weeks and I'll go?"

I convinced myself I wanted to go. Captain Kid was too good a story to pass up, I rationalized. Island hopping down the Caribbean chain in a little boat was a once-in-a-lifetime opportunity. I would regret it if I chickened out. OK, maybe it was the candy ass comment. Being called a candy ass, it turns out, is a powerful motivator.

Whatever. I changed my mind about looking for a bigger boat and went out looking for Captain Kid. I kept hanging around the wood shop behind Skinny Legs until I finally caught up with him at work. The conversation that seals the deal is succinct. Here it is, verbatim:

Me: "Hey."

Him: "Hey."

Me: "Are you still looking for crew?"

Him: "Yeah."

Me: "I want to go."

Him: "OK."

———

THE UNLIKELY ALLIANCE between the quiet, winsome, dark-haired young sailor and the assertive, (slightly) older blonde who had only learned to sail the year before raised a few eyebrows around Coral Bay but by the time we left St. John a few weeks later, Captain Kid had acquired a(n) (age-appropriate) girlfriend. *Carina* embarked on her journey south with a crew of three, leaving the gossips ashore wondering who was sleeping where.

We hauled anchor early on a Thursday morning with great anticipation. We were going sailing, and not just on some frivolous cruise to the BVIs. We were headed for real foreign ports of call! We would have our passports stamped in multiple languages! I had sold my *Great Island Car!* and given my notice at Skinny's. None of us planned to return anytime soon. Off we went—sailing directly into a squall. With zero visibility, we were forced to turn around and drop anchor again. In Coral Bay.

"The weather's always better in the afternoon," Captain Kid shrugged, opening a beer and putting his feet up.

Sure enough, after noon the skies cleared. We weighed anchor again. Then the wind died. "Flat-ass calm," pronounced Charlotte, Captain Kid's chatty new girlfriend. In a sailboat with no engine, if there's no wind, you don't go anywhere.

As our neighbors watched us drift aimlessly around the harbor for three hours, we used the time to get to know each other. Charlotte informed us that she was once voted "The Person You'd Most Want to Be Stranded on a Desert Island With." Captain Kid told us about the time he accidentally sailed off his mooring without having the tiller in place. (You can't steer without it.) I told them that every time I told someone I was sailing to Antigua on a 30-foot boat, the almost universal reaction was to share some personal experience of a small-boat voyage-turned-nightmare. After one cautionary tale about horrendous weather and barbaric seas—from a couple I had just met—I lost it. "I don't want to hear this!" I blurted. "I am nervous enough as it is!"

"Oh. Well, don't worry, I'm sure it will be fine," was the response. "Most boats make it."

Captain Kid laughed.

By late afternoon the wind picked up and off we went. Our plan had been to start the trip island-hopping, spending at least the first night tucked safely in a BVI harbor. I didn't like the idea of sailing overnight, in the dark, in a little boat. But we no longer had enough time to make it to Virgin Gorda and anchor before we lost the light. Forced to choose between sailing through the night or turning around and going back to our starting point in Coral Bay yet again, we voted to head directly offshore. We sailed out Sir Francis Drake Channel and by nightfall we were out in the ocean, the British and U.S. Virgin Islands disappearing on the horizon behind us.

"How does it feel to be leaving St. John like this?" Captain Kid asked me.

Leaving.

I had been so busy in the weeks leading up to our departure—giving away more stuff, selling another car, downsizing yet again—and so busy worrying about being seasick on that little boat, I almost forgot the real news was that I was leaving St. John, ultimately destined for who knows where. The last of my belongings were crammed into an oversized red duffel bag, now stowed in *Carina*'s hold. I had some half-assed plan to look for a big yacht in Antigua and try to hitch a ride to Europe, but I was also prepared to go home to Philadelphia. Nothing was definite except that I was sailing away. How did it feel? It's that stupid question reporters are always asking people.

Extraordinary? Almost incomprehensible? Are those feelings? I'm not sure I answered. Moving *to* St. John was momentous. Now I was leaving. *In a sailboat.*

We lit the oil running lights and Captain Kid gave Charlotte and me a lesson in traditional navigation. Using charts—the nautical term for maps—and rulers and a little bit of math, we figured out the direction we needed to go and set our compass heading. We were sailing like Captain Cook, circumnavigating the globe with the first clock accurate enough to determine longitude. Like Captain Ahab, piloting toward the South Pacific on the prowl for the great white whale. I was lost in that little fantasy until we had to steer ourselves out of the way of the modern-day leviathan—the great white cruise ship. It was monstrous, a floating city disgorging more light than any island town and propelled by some obscene amount of fuel. Its captain was certainly not using pencils and dividers and paper maps to chart his course. *Carina* wasn't even half the size of the yacht I had sailed on from Newport the previous fall. We were so small.

Our renaissance captain cooked dinner. "Do you like to cook underway?" I asked, commencing what I hoped would be the first of many incisive conversations on the journey stretching before us. "I like to eat underway," he replied, using a fistful of dry spaghetti as a visual to demonstrate the advantages of *Carina*'s keel-stepped mast before dumping the pasta into a pot of boiling water and turning his attention back to the meal.

We set up an 8 p.m. to 8 a.m. watch schedule. Charlotte 8 to 10, Captain Kid 10 to 12, me 12 to 2, etc. until morning. After dinner, I went immediately below and slept until Captain Kid woke me for my midnight watch. He waited for me to get settled on deck, then was gone.

We were sailing beautifully. *Carina* was on autopilot, gliding through the water with Mona, the windvane, steering, but at that moment, I was at the helm. It was my job to look out for big ships, or other little boats, or anything else that might crash into us or run us over or otherwise threaten us and rouse the napping captain if anything seemed amiss. On my first offshore sail, there had always been an experienced partner on watch with me. Here, I was responsible for the safety of *Carina* and her crew. Here, in *Carina*'s little cockpit, we were so much more exposed to the elements. I could touch the ocean if I wanted to. It was *right there*.

Two hours flew by. I had done my first watch alone.

——————

FRIDAY MORNING STARTED out overcast and rainy. Captain Kid tried to explain how to interpret the weather, but I wasn't getting it. I thought we had avoided one line of storms when we saw an opening of blue sky ahead but Captain Kid, in his low-key way, suggested we take down the genoa, the big headsail that had given us such good speed overnight. I didn't understand why we were doing that but, wanting practice on the foredeck, readily obliged. We dropped the sail and just as we finished securing it on deck, the wind picked up dramatically and rain teemed down. We were suddenly in a powerful squall that Captain Kid would later describe as the second worst he'd ever sailed through. Winds gusted to 35 knots, visibility was nil, and the ocean had turned a shade of gray I hadn't seen before. The worst of it lasted over an hour, long enough for me to start feeling alarmed, but every time I looked, Captain Kid appeared completely at ease at the helm.

The storm passed, leaving behind more hours of flat-ass calm. We were—again—far from our next planned overnight stop in St. Martin so we would—again—stay offshore. We sailed slowly on through a tenacious drizzle, gradually getting more comfortable around each other. I tried—again—to solicit answers to some of those questions that had nagged me into signing on.

"Why did you choose to build an old-fashioned traditional boat, with no modern conveniences?" I asked.

Captain Kid said he never thought about doing it any other way. He would answer a question or two, then disappear below.

"Just so you know, Margie, our captain's taking another unannounced nap," Charlotte would say.

I had some experience with snoozing skippers. I knew it meant he trusted us. If we got nervous up on deck alone, we recited Charlotte's favorite mantra, from her days running high school track: *I am tough! I am strong!*

That night the lights of Anguilla, then St. Martin, twinkled in the distance. My watches flew by. When they were finished, I plopped into the narrow little starboard berth, or the double-sized port bunk, whichever was free, and rocked to sleep.

I BECAME A Real (Traditional Boat) Sailor on day three of the trip.

We were in St. Barts, anchored in ritzy Gustavia harbor amidst the private megayachts with helicopters, swimming pools, and deck space that could have stowed *Carina* next to the jet skis. Captain Kid and Charlotte were both down below, frying sausage and making pancakes on the tiny propane stove, but I could no longer wait for a moment of privacy. I brushed past them in the cramped galley space, made my way forward where we kept The Bucket, and, not 10 feet from where my two shipmates were cooking breakfast, did my business.

"That was a really nice piss, Margie," said Captain Kid, my friend of very few words, as I squeezed past them on my way back up to the cockpit.

———

BY THE TIME we set off again, the weather was perfect. Once at sea, we took turns posing on the bowsprit for pictures. Captain Kid and Charlotte each stood, triumphantly, on the very tip, suspended over the ocean some four feet from the front of the deck. Me? I sat, having scooched out on my ass about half as far as they did. But I look so happy in the photo.

We had the wind at our backs—not at all the rough, upwind conditions everyone warned we would encounter for the final leg of the trip. We even flew *Carina*'s brilliant red, blue, and orange striped spinnaker, a sail you only put up in downwind conditions. St. John sailors who have made the passage to Antigua will be dubious of this spinnaker claim, but three witnesses will swear that it's true and we have the pictures to prove it. Just like my very first sail on *Carina,* the wind was coming from the wrong direction, and it was a gift. Our reward for the rocky start.

We sailed past Saba, St. Eustatius, St. Kitts and Nevis. We could see—and smell—the volcano on Montserrat erupting in the distance. But our ride remained calm. Charlotte painted her toenails. Captain Kid fiddled with his new hammock. I pulled out my notebook again.

Captain Kid's first stop in the Caribbean had been Jost Van Dyke, in the British Virgin Islands. Why there? I wanted to know.

"Because it's the first land you hit," he said.

Charlotte helpfully added that our self-effacing shipwright was extremely proud of his boat's custom-modified bilge pump, and that I would be remiss not to write that down.

The captain, meanwhile, retreated to his hammock, finished stringing it up, and promptly fell asleep.

———

ADMIRAL LORD NELSON famously despised his time in Antigua, calling it an infernal hole. "English Harbour I hate the sight of," he wrote in a letter. For the present-day competitive sailor, however, the island where the British naval hero began his career is the Mecca of the Caribbean.

Two weeks of events mark the end of the Caribbean racing season. The final week, Antigua Sailing Week, is the testosterone-fueled set of serious races with the fast, modern boats. We were there for the first week, Antigua Classics, the "gentleman's regatta" for the vintage wooden sailboats. Picture the elegant yachts you see in movies about the 1920s, Gatsby-esque swells milling about the docks with gin cocktails. Or the marvelous sailboats from the heyday of the America's Cup when the yachts were piloted by men with names like Lipton and Vanderbilt. These are the kinds of boats—decades-old, meticulously preserved, restored, and maintained by a small subset of sailors with one foot in the past—that assemble for Antigua Classics.

We tacked into Antigua's Falmouth Harbor at sunrise on Monday, four days after leaving St. John. The captain sailed expertly in, weaving among the dozens of boats already populating the harbor, while Charlotte and I handled the sails, dousing the jib and main. Captain Kid used the piece-of-rope-and-a-weight "depth sounder" to find us a good spot, and we dropped anchor.

The Antigua Yacht Club was buzzing. The docks were lined with splendid old boats, conspicuously maintained. Officious (salaried) captains strode about as their spiffy, clean-cut (paid) crewmembers in matching (not to mention immaculate) polo shirts busied themselves swabbing, polishing, and tidying things that already looked well-swabbed, polished, and tidy. Captain Kid joked that the free Panerai shirts and hats handed out by the event's Italian watch company sponsor could be *Carina*'s uniform.

In the midst of this activity, we found a kindred spirit—our Coral Bay friend Speedy who owned *Gaucho*, a 1943 Argentinean classic on which he and his wife, Roni, raised two children. I asked them once about the boat's namesake—a South American plains cowboy? Must be a story there. But all I could find out was that Speedy had inherited the name when he bought the boat.

"You should be shot if you change the name of a boat," he told me.

"Hung, drawn, and quartered," Roni nodded.

"Made to walk the plank," Speedy added.

So, no story. But good dialogue.

Speedy, an old salt who looked the part with his bushy gray beard and leathery skin, was wearing his yacht regatta finest: Budget Marine baseball cap, sky-blue Crocs, and a stained and well-worn T-shirt from Le Select, the Skinny's of St. Barts. Captain Kid joined him at a small table overlooking the harbor and soon the two were hunched over, scrutinizing their registration paperwork. Speedy was rubbing his temples, trying to convert *Gaucho*'s dimensions into metric. As Captain Kid picked up a pen, a well-dressed lackey from some sophisticated crew marched briskly into the yacht club and dropped off a drafting tube containing, we assumed, neatly rolled blueprints of his employer's yacht. Captain Kid didn't have any official drawings showing *Carina*'s specs, so he started sketching the boat on the back of our application. Speedy, I think, gave up on the metric, figured the hell with it, and just signed his name to the forms.

My heart swells, picturing these two men on the dock that day. *Carina* and *Gaucho* were beauties, but in those environs, in the shadow of 100-plus-foot professionally maintained yachts, we were the ghetto crowd. We washed our dishes off the stern. We hung our dirty towels and wet clothes over the lifelines. We were "traditional" indeed.

What followed was four top-notch days of racing. One course was a 24-mile windward/leeward reach, up and back to the same mark twice. Smaller, slower boats like *Vilona May*, built in 1898, started first, followed by the bigger, faster ones, so by the second or third pass, dozens of boats of all sizes and speed—the 1931 gaff-rigged schooner *Altair*, the 162-foot classic replica *Eleonora*, the J-Class racing yacht *Ranger*—were passing by us and each other under glorious full sail. At the end of the race each day, a serene Captain Kid would steer *Carina* back to the dock, yielding to the large yachts that, despite their engines and practiced crews—which should have made docking a breeze—always seemed rife with tension. There was a lot of yelling around that time of day, but not on our boat. Our captain never wavered or lost his composure. Not once.

On the final night, the rum flowed endlessly as awards were given out behind the old Copper and Lumber Store in Nelson's Dockyard, a colonial relic surely haunted by the enslaved people who built it. *Carina* took second prize in her racing class, and also placed second in the Concours d'Elegance, a beauty contest for boats. I could have been a judge. In my two weeks aboard *Carina*, I had learned a lot about her painstaking detail. My respect and admiration for her enigmatic skipper had grown by the day. But I didn't get very far into his psyche.

My last day on the boat, I wrote Captain Kid a note gushing about my experience, while he signed my log. He sat with my brown faux suede-covered journal for what seemed like a thoughtful amount of time before handing it back. Then he rowed me to shore where we said goodbye. He and Charlotte and *Carina* were headed across the Atlantic. He wasn't exactly sure where they were going, but probably Falmouth, England. Because it's the first land you hit. I would be making a similar trip, but toward the Mediterranean, and on a sailing yacht four times *Carina*'s size.

As I stood, alone, in line at customs, waiting to transfer my name to the manifest of another ship, I opened my logbook, impatient to read what the prodigious sailor I had become so fond of had written. Perhaps some revealing nugget that would work well in my story. Some profound thought, unuttered, that would offer insight. I thumbed through the pages until I reached his entry.

Thanks for sailing and best of luck. Captain Kid.

8

THE KNIGHTS OF ST. JOHN

It was sometime during my second year on St. John that I hatched my plan to sail across the Atlantic. I have two versions of how that happened. The first is all mystical and involves a full-moon hike up Ram Head, during which I heard supernatural voices. In the second version, Fun Christina and I were sitting at the bar at Skinny's after our shift one afternoon and I said something like, "I really want to go to that classic boat regatta in Antigua next April." And she said something like "OK. And then when it's over, we'll hop on one of the big yachts and cross the Atlantic. Because how many people can say they've done that in their lives?" And it was settled. A few of Mean Jean's margaritas may also have been involved.

I might have been happy just sailing to that regatta with Captain Kid on his little boat. I might, afterward, have gone home to Philadelphia feeling pretty good about myself. It would have been a respectable ending to my whole St. John adventure. But instead, because once again I had aligned myself with Christina, who thought I didn't aim high enough, when I got to Antigua I walked the docks looking for a ship to carry me across the ocean.

I had told Captain Kid I was looking for a bigger boat and I found one: a 111-foot ketch called *Yellow Bird* with a crew of six, twin Rolls Royce engines, and flush toilets. Next thing I knew I was headed across the Atlantic Ocean toward the Mediterranean. I say "toward" because sailors are superstitious and believe that, at sea, you should never say you are sailing "to" a destination, only "toward" it, lest you tempt the fates. In other words, I loaded all my worldly goods onto a strange boat with people I didn't know and set off across the ocean not knowing where I was going.

Ten days and 2,200 miles later, we were in the Azores. The remote chain of nine islands is part of Portugal, but the European continent is still 1,000 miles away. Horta, on the island of Faial, is the port where many boats on transatlantic crossings stop to rest. Ships that pass through leave behind their names or logos painted brightly on the docks.

Yellow Bird docked on a Monday, the eve of my 41st birthday, and shortly thereafter, her crew was in the pub. Peter's Café Sport appeared to be the only game in town, catering to local fishermen and international yachties alike. I was jostling for a drink at the bar when I bumped into a stocky, boisterous seaman.

"And where are YOU from?" he demanded, five inches from my face. He bore a striking resemblance to Shrek.

"Philadelphia," I replied, taking a little step back. "By way of the U.S. Virgin Islands."

"PHILADELPHIA!" he bellowed in a broad Scottish accent. "I LOVE Philadelphia."

He asked my name and introduced me to a tall, fair-skinned man beside him. "MARGARET, this is the IRISHMAN!"

"Nice to meet you," I said.

The Irishman had blue-gray eyes. He took my right hand and inspected my Claddagh, the traditional Irish ring my grandmother had given me when I was a teenager.

"The heart is turned out," he said. He had a hint of a brogue. "Do you know what that means?"

"It means *free as a bird*," I said. "*Unattached to any love in your life.*"

The men worked on a tugboat that had also just arrived that

day. I had seen it when we sailed in, garish yellow with a dark Maltese cross on the side. Shrek was the cook and chief storyteller. He LOVED America and held forth on his travels—Indianapolis, Pascagoula, three trips to Graceland—while the Irishman listened, amused, and gazed at me. At midnight, Shrek led a rousing chorus of "Happy Birthday," waving his arms in grand gestures as the carousers around us sang.

The next night, *Yellow Bird*'s crew was back at Peter's Café for dinner. We sat beneath a map that showed the route taken by the first Portuguese—a fisherman from the Azores—to sail around the world alone. The tugboat guys showed up with gifts. Shrek presented me with a cheesecake (because Americans make the BEST CHEESECAKE) and a cookbook, signed by the crew. I thanked them, telling them I needed it since we all shared cooking duties on our boat.

"I'm a terrible cook. It's hard getting everything to come out just right."

"Margaret! There's nothing hard about COOKING," said an exasperated Shrek. "Nothing is HARD. The only thing that's hard is what's in YER HEAD." He invited me to come to the tug for a cooking lesson. What did I like to eat? Because he could cook ANYTHING. Chicken in black bean sauce? I asked. Because I'd been craving Chinese. He repeated that he could cook ANYTHING and scheduled my cooking lesson for Thursday, *Yellow Bird*'s last day in port.

The Irishman interrupted. He wanted to introduce me to someone, a Portuguese fisherman named Genuino. He was the local sailor whose circumnavigation was immortalized on the wall above us.

Genuino had sailed around the world in his 36-foot boat, *Hemingway*, named for the author who wrote his favorite book, *The Old Man and the Sea*. He told me that he still fished every day, and that he was getting ready to sail around the world again in October.

"Today I have arms. I have legs. I can work," he said, in broken English. "Today I can do it. Tomorrow it might not be possible."

"I understand," I said.

I understand, I tried to explain, because that was also the reason I was on my journey.

"I have the freedom to do this today," I said. "Tomorrow, I don't know. My mother could get sick. Or something else bad could happen. And then my chance would be gone."

Genuino nodded.

"Do not forget this," he said to me.

"I won't forget."

"*Saude!*" he toasted, and we drank.

The Irishman walked me back to *Yellow Bird*. When I complained that I was cold, he wrapped his fleece jacket around me.

"My blood is thin from living in the Caribbean," I said.

"Your blood is thin from too much alcohol," he said. Then he asked if I'd like to go to dinner the next night.

I spent the next day wandering Horta's cobblestone streets, steep inclines that dropped to the sea. The weather in the port town was like a damp, spring day in Philadelphia. The air was brisk. I climbed up to an immaculately manicured public garden, dripping with roses and lilac and other flowers I couldn't identify, but it smelled like heaven. A gazebo overlooked the harbor and its colorful boats. Pico, the nearest of the other Azores, rose in the background, its mountain peak draped in wispy cloud. I stopped in Faial's oldest cathedral, next to the town hall. It was a beautiful old church, so blissfully still I imagined even God was holding his breath so as not to disturb the pure peacefulness.

At sunset I met the Irishman at the docks. We dined at an intimate little restaurant where we cooked our own swordfish on steaming slabs of marble, washed down with bottles of Portuguese *vinho tinto*. And if it sounds like some romance novel trope to say two people from opposite sides of the ocean came to a place that

neither had ever been before on the very same day, met within hours
of arriving, and felt as if they had known each other for a very long
time, so be it. Because that is what happened. He told me about his
love for the sea, and his regrets about not seeing his son more often.
I told him about my newfound enchantment with sailing, how I fell
into it after my plans to get married and start a family didn't quite
work out. He was a great kisser and an even better listener and his
searching, blue-gray eyes never strayed from my face when I spoke.

After dinner we went to the tugboat where the crew was
lolling around the mess, listening to music. Shrek, unconcerned
that I had just feasted on an entire meal, made me macaroni and
cheese. Frank Sinatra sang. Then Elvis. The Everly Brothers.

"I love 'Let It Be Me,'" I said.

When you're a woman traveling alone, or even living alone,
you don't want to appear vulnerable. *I am tough! I am strong!* was
a good mantra. But I didn't always want to be tough and strong.
Frankly, I was getting sick and tired of feeling like I had to be
tough and strong. It was nice to be taken care of, even for a few
hours. For a little while, sitting in that mess, eating mac and
cheese and listening to Frank, it felt safe. I let my guard down, and
it felt good. It felt a lot like home. And just as I was thinking how
at ease I was around these characters, the Irishman asked, "Are
you comfortable, Maggie?"

"Yes," I replied.

"Then it was meant to be."

Later that night, we walked back to my boat in a cold drizzle.
When the wind whipped around, the rain started pelting sideways. I had to walk fast to keep up with the Irishman's stride, but
he had broad shoulders and I nestled in close with his arm around
me and I felt warm and dry, protected.

The water in the harbor was churned up. Waves spattered
against the bulkhead.

The only thing that's hard is what's in your head, I heard.

Restless boats were swaying back and forth, tugging on the
lines that restrained them at the water's edge. *It was meant to be,*

they protested. The docks creaked under the strain. It was an almost erotic sound.

The wind whistling through the rigging made a plaintive wail. *Do not forget this*... it whispered.

The next morning *Yellow Bird*'s captain made an announcement. He wanted to leave a day early. Be ready to sail in two hours.

I rushed back to the industrial dock. It was blocked off because a container ship had come in and heavy equipment was offloading cargo. The barriers—physical and language—made it difficult to maneuver, but I had to return a cake pan.

When I got to the tug, there was no one in sight. I stood on the dock and called out until the Irishman finally poked his head out. "We're leaving in an hour," I said.

We said goodbye. Maybe I'd go to Ireland while I was on that side of the Atlantic, I said. He would meet me there, he said.

"It is a promise," he said.

When we pulled out of port, I saw my Irishman with Shrek high up on the wall in front of Peter's Café Sport. They raised their glasses. An hour later, *Yellow Bird* was back out in the open Atlantic, under sail in 30 knots of wind, bearing away from the Azores. I sat on the aft deck, seeing Faial slowly get farther and farther away. I watched for a while but did not want to see it disappear completely. I took one last look as the sun set behind the island, then went below to sleep before my first watch.

I dreamt I was on a little yellow boat, sailing past the rolling green hills of what could only be the Emerald Isles. An old Portuguese fisherman was at the helm. "Do not forget this," he said, as he handed me a bowl of steaming chicken cooked in a fragrant, spicy black bean sauce.

WE SPENT 12 more days at sea. Across the Atlantic, through the Strait of Gibraltar, into the Mediterranean Sea—"The Med," the sailors called it—and, finally, toward land. Malta. Another speck in the middle of the ocean that, like St. John, no one can find on the map.

I didn't know anything about Malta. I thought any boat from Antigua would eventually dump me in Palma de Mallorca, Spain or Antibes, France. Some major yachting center where, I'd been told, it was easy to find summer crew positions. Valletta, Malta? No clue. But I had to learn fast because now that we were in port, I had to get off the boat. And I had nowhere to go.

Yellow Bird was required to pay for my repatriation. As crew on a one-way job, I was entitled to a plane ticket home or the cash equivalent. It all could have ended right there. Was my adventure over? To the extent that I had set out to "do" anything, hadn't I done it? If sailing away from St. John in a little boat was enough of an ending, I had doubled down by crossing the Atlantic. I could take that plane ticket and fly home, content. A heroine. But I could also take the cash and see what happened next.

What happens if you just ... keep going?

HERE BE DRAGONS says an ancient globe in the library where I'm writing this more than a decade later. *TERRA INCOGNITA* proclaim all those early maps. That's where I was. Uncharted territory. Neither here nor there.

My move to St. John had set in motion a series of remarkable events, but at each crossroad, in between each exploit where I got to sound so carefree and brave, I went through this little panicky thing. Sailing across the ocean wasn't the scary part. This was. I was paralyzed with indecision: What do I do now?

First, I did what every veteran journalist does when faced with an assignment and no deadline. I procrastinated. I made a cursory walk of the docks in neighborhoods with intriguing names—Ta' Xbiex, Sliema, Manoel Island—ostensibly looking for job leads, then plopped myself in an internet café where I wrote a bunch of emails trying to sound pithy and cool:

To: All
Subject: Land Ho!

So hey! I sailed across the Atlantic Ocean! 22 days at sea (plus two days on land in the Azores) and 4,400 miles. I'm in Malta, in the middle of the Mediterranean.

Not sure what my next move is. I should go to the south of France and look for a job … but I keep looking at the map and Sicily is *right there* and from there, well, you can practically *walk* to the southern coast of Italy, which I've always wanted to see. (Anybody have any family in Sicily?) And there's always Door Number Three, which is whatever turns up in Malta in the next couple days.

After telling everyone how fine I was, I checked my bank account online to see how fine I really was. I was sure I was going to run out of money. I browsed through some shops, admiring souvenirs I couldn't afford. I checked my email again, trying to figure out the time difference between Malta and the U.S. I tried not to be discouraged. (*I am tough! I am strong!*) I checked my email yet again. This time, there was a flood of responses:

From: South Philly Landlubber
Subject: Land Ho!

Margie! Me and the rest of the United States are chanting "SI-CI-LY!" Right now! We are united. We really want you to go. And send back photos. And eat well. Oh, and totally fuck the job.

My inbox was full of similar directives from Philadelphia to St. John, rooting for destinations, sending support from 4,000 miles away, throwing my little inspirational quotes back at me. (*If you risk nothing, you risk everything!* Blah, blah, blah!) But it was an impassioned email about Malta from a Philly friend that galvanized me.

From: A Landlocked Sailor
Subject: Malta!

Malta! Malta! Stay in Malta! Malta is the crown jewel of everything that is exotic and mysterious in the ancient history of Med sailing. Hang around and soak up the lore, then hop aboard anything going—east. You're on the most fantastic odyssey of your life.

Malta! Malta! Stay in Malta! became my rallying cry. Now that my travels had been upgraded to an ODYSSEY, there was a duty to uphold. I needed to explore *Malta!* I needed to get a grip. Something would turn up. Odysseus never collapsed in a puddle of panic.

The next morning a guy on the boat docked next to *Yellow Bird,* a sailboat called *Selkie,* said his boss might be looking for crew for an upcoming race. The one in Antibes? Next week? I asked. That was promising. I could hitch a ride to France, do the race, then look for a yacht job. The sailor wasn't sure. The boss wasn't around. Come back later.

I told *Yellow Bird*'s captain I'd be off the boat soon and tried to look industrious as I set off down the dock. The waterfront was brimming with multicolored fishing boats that I would soon learn dated to Phoenician times. Each boat had a pair of eyes painted on the prow to ward off evil spirits. I wanted to check out Valletta's cathedral, high atop the capital city. A wondrous sight, the church was a beacon when we sailed into port. I approached an elderly couple sitting on a bench and asked for directions.

"Why do you want to go to church?" the old woman demanded. "You want to pray for boyfriend?"

"Yes," I answered. "I think I do want to pray for a boyfriend."

She scowled.

"I also need to pray for a job. And a place to live."

This seemed to convince her to give up some information. She suggested a bus. Her husband suggested a different bus. They argued in Maltese. The woman offered to accompany me if I would give her three pounds. I reminded her I was going to church to pray for a job. Her husband laughed. He directed me to a bus across the street and wished me luck.

Valletta—a fortified, medieval city—is situated on a cliff that juts out into the Mediterranean. It was built in the late 16th century by the crusading Knights of Malta after their victorious battle against the Turks in the Great Siege of 1565. In the resplendent Co-Cathedral of St. John, every pillar is adorned with an eight-pointed Maltese cross, the knights' symbol. Caravaggio's gory masterpiece, *The Beheading of St. John the Baptist*, commands the oratory. Salome clutches her platter, expectant. The artist, a murderer himself, signed his name in the blood spilling from the dying prophet's throat. St. John the Baptist is the patron saint of the Knights of Malta. I had landed in a place founded by the Knights of the Order of ... St. John.

Blinded by a scorching midday sun, I bought a ticket to something called *The Malta Experience*. Seven thousand years of history in 40 minutes plus air conditioning. Malta, the film taught me, had played a pivotal role in the centuries-long fight for control of the Mediterranean, starting with those earliest of sailors, the Phoenicians, all the way through to the British, who ruled when the island was bombed by the Nazis. In between were the Knights of St. John—the Knights Hospitallers—a powerful military and religious order founded after the First Crusade to protect pilgrims visiting the Holy Land. After being expelled from Jerusalem, the knights landed in Cyprus, then Rhodes, then were homeless until 1530 when King Charles of Spain gave them the island of Malta for the ridiculous sum of one Maltese falcon a year.

I ambled down to Fort St. Elmo, a star fort with strategic views of the sea and named for the patron saint of sailors. Mariners of old who witnessed the strange weather phenomenon known as St. Elmo's Fire—which makes the top of a mast appear to be ablaze—took it as a good omen, a sign their guardian was near. My sailing guardian had apparently been working overtime. I had been deposited in a place that had been a sailor's destination since sailors had boats. A place where journeys converged. Where East met West.

I hopped on a bus to Vittoriosa, another medieval city with a modern marina where I might find a job. After walking the docks, again to no avail, I made my way into the heart of the old town, meandering up and down 500-year-old stone streets and winding alleyways, past the auberges—the residence inns—where the Knights of St. John lived during the Great Siege. The city, originally called Birgu, was dubbed Città Vittoriosa—the Victorious City—in honor of their victory.

I lost myself in Vittoriosa. Scarcely noticing that everything was closed up tight, European-style, for the afternoon, I walked for hours, oblivious to the time, or any sense of why I was there. There was something about the place. It was an enchanted forest without trees. Occasionally I glanced over my shoulder, thinking I heard footsteps and ... the clanking of chain mail? Was I in such a state of liminality I had ghost knights as companions?

I had a visceral reaction to the old neighborhood and wanted to linger. *Malta! Malta! Stay in Malta!* I heard in my head as my bus rumbled back to Ta' Xbiex and *Yellow Bird*. My mind was racing as I approached the marina—and saw the owner of *Selkie* sitting on his deck.

My first instinct was to dodge him. My interest in sailing to Antibes to look for charter boat work had vanished during the afternoon. I wanted to stay in *Malta!* Still, it seemed remiss not to talk to him. He was, indeed, looking for crew, he told me. But he wasn't leaving for several weeks.

"Isn't the Antibes race next weekend?" I asked.

The captain shook his head. "Not Antibes. Saint-Tropez."

Selkie, her owner explained, was going to compete in the Trophée Bailli de Suffren, a 12-day offshore regatta with ports of call in Saint-Tropez, France; Porto Rotondo, Sardinia; Palermo, Sicily; and back to Valletta in Malta.

Would I be interested?

The next morning, full of resolve, I hopped on a bus back to Vittoriosa. I remembered Shrek saying his friend owned a bar there. Maybe that was a lead on a place to stay. I followed my nose to a bakery, bought an almond pastry, and carried it to the square. There was one bar there—closed—so I ducked into a café and ordered a cappuccino. A table of old men drinking Cisk beer and smoking were arguing loudly in a language I didn't understand. A little girl with dark curls and a frilly orange jumper chased a dog around the chairs. She was backlit, a dancing ray of light in the dim restaurant.

I finished my coffee. Still no signs of life at the bar, so I wandered down toward the waterfront, getting lost in the maze of streets. I stumbled upon an old stone house with a Maltese cross over the door and a small sign that said 1565 Museum. A museum visit was not on my agenda, but a sprightly woman standing outside caught my eye and beckoned me over. Why didn't I come in and have something cold to drink?

In the next 10 minutes I learned that her name was Edith; she had first come to Malta in the '60s when her husband, Oliver, was stationed there with the British Army; they moved down permanently after they retired; but she'd been extremely busy acting as an extra in blockbuster movies like *Gladiator, Troy,* and Stephen Spielberg's *Munich,* all of which were filmed in Malta. Could I smell the oleander surrounding the museum? It's what she smelled stepping off the plane all those years ago into sweltering heat, dressed in her fake fur from damp and rainy England, her six children (and one on the way) in tow. She had fallen instantly in love with the island. Couldn't I feel the presence of the knights? The history was palpable.

I told my garrulous hostess I was looking for a place to stay for about two weeks before heading off on a sailing trip. She shook her head. There were no hotels in the old city, and she didn't know of any rooms to rent. But the tour guide was ready for me.

Each room in the museum featured life-size figures of armored knights and turbaned Turks depicting a scene from the Great Siege, a gruesome battle between the forces of Christianity and Islam. Suleiman the Magnificent nailing the bodies of his enemies to crosses and sending them drifting across the harbor. Grand Master Jean de la Vallette retaliating by decapitating prisoners and flinging the heads at their comrades. My guide insisted on taking my picture standing beside Vallette, the hero, and a knight preparing to catapult a severed head over the fortified walls at the retreating Ottoman armada. This round of the holy war went to the Christians. The guide placed his hand over a map of Vittoriosa and the adjacent peninsulas projecting into the water like fingers. "God's hand," he said reverently.

Back at the entrance, Edith announced that she had just called Oliver and he said if I didn't mind the four cats and the dog, they would be happy to move the boxes out of their spare bedroom and give me room and board for two weeks for the ridiculous sum of five Maltese lira (about $15 U.S.) a night.

Would I be interested?

"I believe in fate," Edith said.

Half an hour later I was back on the bus—headed to the marina to retrieve my red duffel off *Yellow Bird*—half unable to contain my glee at my good fortune and half unsure that everything I think just happened really happened.

A man stood up at the front of the bus, pulled a rosary out of his pocket, and said a prayer in Maltese. About three-quarters of the passengers responded, making the sign of the cross.

I looked out the window, daydreaming as neighborhoods blurred by.

When I snapped back to the present, I realized we had stopped. Dozens of people were getting off the bus, but we were not at the usual transfer station in Valletta. This place looked foreign. I rummaged through my bag, searching for my bus map and trying to appear nonchalant while I waited to see if everyone was disembarking. I didn't want to look like I was lost.

I felt a tap on my shoulder and turned around to see a little old man in a white fishing cap looking at me intently. Clearly he had noticed my confusion.

"Valletta," he said.

"Sorry?" I responded.

"You are going to Valletta, right?" he asked kindly.

"Yes."

He nodded reassuringly, gently pushing me back into my seat.

"Sit down," he said. "You are on the right bus."

HEY—IF you have any more of the fairy dust, could you spread some my way? wrote the Landlocked Sailor who christened my journey An Odyssey.

Was it, as Edith believed, fate? Was it serendipity? Synchronicity? Jung's "meaningful coincidence?" It couldn't just be random that I had alighted in a place protected by the Knights of St. John. Could it?

Edith would have made a great reporter. There wasn't a barrier she wouldn't walk around, no closed door she wouldn't try to open. For the next two weeks, my landlady squired me from one fascinating site in *Malta!* to another, admonishing me every time I gushed ineloquently. "Bloody hell! Can't you Americans think of anything better to say than 'That was SO AWESOME!'" she mimicked in her best bad American accent.

Then I sailed off on *Selkie* for the 12-day regatta from St. Tropez back to Valletta.

Then I just ... kept going.

My notebook and pen were my ticket onto a succession of vintage boats, each one more beautiful than the last. I crisscrossed the Mediterranean again. Malta to Sicily. The Aeolian Islands to Naples. The Balearics to the Italian Riviera. Genoa. Cannes.

Through the Strait of Messina, between Scylla and Charybdis. Literally Homeric waters.

The *Sun Times* ran my dispatches all summer. I still got $50 a story. Hardly enough to underwrite my charmed existence. Each time I could trade some boat work for a berth and board, my travels went a little farther.

Wherever I went, I taught myself how to say *Hello! I arrived in your country by sailboat!* An excellent icebreaker. I crewed with sexy Italian/French/Spanish sailors who assured me the best way to learn to speak Italian/French/Spanish was to get myself an Italian/French/Spanish boyfriend. My language skills improved.

Are you ever coming home, you globetrotting tart? wrote Ellen in an email.

This is not the normal me, I kept telling the new sailors I met. *This isn't who I really am, cavorting around, living like a vagabond, worrying about tomorrow tomorrow* I'd say, wondering, then, who it was I was describing. People would look at me funny, not comprehending. Because, of course, that's exactly who I was.

Life had been, imperceptibly, shifting. Malta was a watershed. I don't think I knew it at the time, couldn't have, really, but looking back now, I know that taking that plane ticket home—whether home to Philadelphia or home to St. John—was never an option.

I am not really sure whose life I am living, I wrote in my emails.

Baby, you are living your life! Came the replies. *HELLO? This is your life!*

Somewhere in there, I logged my 100th day at sea without even noticing.

Fall came. Another Caribbean hurricane season passed by. On St. John it was, again, mercifully calm. In the Mediterranean, sailing season was winding down. I was looking at my map again. And just as I was thinking I was running out of moves, I got this:

From: Captain Kid
Subject: Carina

Hi Margie this is your old friend from Carina. It sounds like you have been having quite an adventure since you left Antigua. Charlotte and I had a great time crossing the Atlantic. When we got to Ireland I had Carina hauled out in a boatyard and flew to California for Charlotte's friend's wedding. We had planned to spend the winter out there. Things did not work out very well, so now I am back on Cape Cod with no boat or girlfriend. I flew in a week ago with no plan at all. I started working for my brother building houses. The responsible thing to do would be to stick around for the winter and actually save some money. However I don't feel like I belong here right now and I miss my boat and the ocean. I have come up with a kind of long-shot plan involving flying back to Ireland in a few days then sailing south ultimately to the Caribbean by the end of December. Stops would probably be in Spain, Portugal, Madeira and the Canary Islands. The only problem that I have not come up with a solution for yet is finding a good crew. This is why I am writing my first email ever, to ask if you are interested in coming along.

9

SYZYGY

ack in Coral Bay, across from Skinny's, there used to be an art gallery called Syzygy. A syzygy is the alignment of three celestial bodies—the sun, moon, and earth during an eclipse, for example. St. John, some believe, is a magnet. A piece of paradise with its own gravitational pull. I can't explain all the divergent forces that lined up to send me to St. John in the first place. But two years later, when I was an ocean away, I got on a boat headed right back there.

Once again, I was alone on the deck of the lovely *Carina* while her devoted creator, my sole companion, napped below. There was a ring around the moon, a gossamer wreath of some astronomical substance or another. Were we in for some weather? I knew we were in for a time change soon.

We were—well, I didn't know precisely where we were—but we were in the middle of the Atlantic Ocean. We had a 360-degree view of it.

Water comprises about 60 percent of the adult human body, 75 percent of our brains, and, allegedly, 71 percent of the Earth's surface. But out there, science and figures and numbers were hollow. Seventy-one percent? That couldn't be right. There was nothing but water. This was Melville's watery world. Arthur Clarke's Planet Ocean.

We were a thousand miles from anywhere, somewhere between the beginning and the end of an estimated month-long, 2,800-mile transatlantic crossing. Yes, I had already sailed across the Atlantic once, but this was so much more intense. This was 2,800 miles in a little wooden boat, sailing as if from another time. Writing in my journal, I tried to summon the muses, to call on Calliope—wasn't she Homer's muse?—but could think of no epic-worthy way to say it.

Awesome.

In the old days, sailors would toss a log—attached to the stern by a length of rope—overboard, to calculate speed and distance, hence the word "logbook." We were not quite that primitive, but we bordered on the atavistic. We had one hand-held GPS, which we turned on once a day, at noon, to get our bearings and mark our position. It might have felt like nothing changed, but on the chart, our map, the tiny X's with circles around them slowly, but certainly, inched their way across the blue. We were plotting our course the old-fashioned way, with compass, dividers, and parallel ruler, the way sailors have done for centuries, the way Captain Kid taught me on our sail from St. John to Antigua the previous spring.

I hadn't seen or heard from Captain Kid since then. I was in Palma with Fun Christina when his first-email-ever popped up.

Christina had a job "boat-sitting" a lavish yacht called *Paraíso* while the crew was on vacation. Like Homer (Simpson, that is), Christina's biggest challenge was trying to stay awake. I would help her do a little work (yes, we were cleaning up *Paradise*), then take advantage of the marina's free Wi-Fi. I was sending off a resume for some PR job in New York when Captain Kid materialized in my inbox, a flutter of a butterfly's wings somewhere on Cape Cod causing a seismic shift on a boat in Spain. More chaos theory than syzygy.

"Listen to this," I said to Christina, reading the email out loud. "What do you think?"

"About sailing across the Atlantic on *Carina*?"

"Yes."

"It's still 30 feet, right?"

"Right."

Right.

I don't remember committing to anything, but my response must have been encouraging because Captain Kid did indeed fly to Europe and start readying *Carina* to sail home. A month or so later, I received what was, presumably, his second email ever:

From: Captain Kid
Subject: Hola

Carina y yo en Espana. No gente habla Ingles. Yo aprender Espanol rapido.

El pasaje de Irlanda muy tempestuoso. Yo estar de viaje sur a Madeira y Las Islas Canarias despues uno semana.
Hasta luego.

If my words were encouraging, his were not. You didn't have to be fluent in Spanish to pick the word *tempest* out of that little update. Captain Kid's sail from Ireland to Spain had been stormy. I didn't have time to think about it, though, because I was engrossed in a Spanish tempest of my own, a harmless flirtation at a regatta in Cannes having escalated into a full-on fling with a temperamental Argentine sailor who called me *Divina* and spoke only a handful of words in English, most of them expletives.

I had been slumming with the Argentine in the run-down Palma apartment where he resided when not at his job captaining a luxury yacht and thinking how great it was that we had a language barrier because it prevented us from quarreling over stupid things. If he said something in Spanish that sounded objectionable, I just figured I didn't understand—literally—and let it go. Then one night, out of the blue, he wanted to know what happened with my past relationship, and what was his name, and was I in love, and did I *suffer*, and—the crux of the inquisition, I suppose—what was I looking for now. I told him I wasn't looking for anything but hoped to find another Big Love in my life someday. And that's when my South American boyfriend said oh no, not him, he'd never been in love because he was a *puto perro callejero*—roughly translated, a son-of-a-bitch street dog—and street dogs *no tienen dueños.* They don't have owners. If, however, I wanted to stay with him and look for work in Palma—he thought swabbing the decks was a fine job—it would be no problem for him. As long as I remembered that he was allowed to get up in the morning and go wherever he wanted. Like to Barcelona.

I flashed back to an earlier exchange in which my paramour said relationships should be *sin compromiso,* which I thought meant *without compromise.* I had interpreted this to mean *not settling*—an ideal you cleave to if you've made it to 40 unattached. Turns out, though, *compromiso* doesn't mean compromise. It means commitment. While I was talking about the virtues of not settling, he was advocating for relationships without commitment. This made me think maybe I should hightail it back to Philly and try dating reputable, English-speaking lawyers again, but then I remembered that they don't commit either. Since Argentinian sailors have it all over Philadelphia lawyers in the ass-and-arms department, I rationalized, might as well continue shacking up. Maybe adding *fluent in Spanish* to my resume would balance out the fact that I didn't have an address. Or any job prospects.

My Spanish got quite good. I made friends in Palma. From one I learned to say that I was living *como una puta reina*—like a fucking queen. I watched the news in Spanish. One day the top story was that a popular Mallorcan pastry that came packaged in a wide, octagonal box had been banned as carry-on luggage and there was bedlam at the airport. The second story was the midterm elections in the United States. The last time I voted—for president—was two days before moving to St. John and it hit me: I had been away from Philadelphia for two years.

Perhaps it was this reflection on the passing of time that made me agree so wholeheartedly a few nights later when one of my new friends kept insisting that *one month* is not a very long time at all.

"And so I was thinking," she said in halting English, "of course you should sail home to America with your friend on that little boat. It will only take one month!"

And there was someone else at the table, nodding enthusiastically and seconding the emotion: *Yes! What is ONE MONTH out of your WHOLE LIFE?*

Maybe I had been lulled into a false sense of security. I had been spoiled by a summer of crisis-free sailing. It would certainly be an adventure.

A little concise persuasion from Coral Bay sealed the deal:

From: The Old Salt
Subject: Advice

It's a once in a lifetime trip. Downhill all the way. Big following sea. I am sure his boat would do fine.

I said goodbye to the Argentine. The reality was that I was the one with the privilege to get up in the morning and go wherever I wanted.

I kept saying I was scared, but by the time I met up with Captain Kid in the Canary Islands, I felt ready to go.

We left without fanfare. The first day of our "transatlantic crossing" we were well within sight of land all day, Tenerife on our starboard side, Grand Canary to port. Possibly to avoid the magnitude of it all, I fixated on the details. Mona, the windvane, making her squeaky noise. A stream of bioluminescence floating atop the water. A Cheshire cat smile of a moon prowling among the clouds. We sailed through the night and before long, land was out of sight. It was just us three: Me, Captain Kid, and *Carina.*

We had no concrete plan but thought we'd try to stop in Cape Verde, off the coast of Senegal, about 800 miles from our starting point. It would break up the crossing, give us a chance to rest. I also secretly hoped for one last chance to bail before the point of no return. There were deterrents, though, including a high crime rate. Since we weren't 100 percent sure it was safe, if the weather didn't cooperate we wouldn't push it. We left the Canaries prepared to sail straight through to Antigua.

"I love this boat!" I announced when I woke up on Day Two. I had forgotten how much I loved the boat—her rhythm; her lines; the sweet, deep sleep she induced. We were on port tack, heeled way over, perfect for snuggling into my bunk. Captain Kid ran his hand over his head and smiled his shy smile.

If we averaged 100 miles a day—about 3.5 knots or 4 miles an hour—the passage would take a month, although similar sized boats had done it in three weeks if they caught the prevailing easterlies—the trade winds—just right. Our compass heading was 240, then 230. We were heading a straight SW course. "The same one Columbus discovered," Captain Kid told me. The same one Vasco da Gama followed when he sailed around the Cape of Good Hope to India. The same one Magellan would take in the first circumnavigation of the globe. Thanks to the trade winds, Captain Kid liked to point out, it would be almost impossible not to reach our destination. A raft with a sheet for a sail would eventually make it to the other side. Probably.

About 72 hours in we got the trades. Twenty knots of wind behind us. Big swells. *Rough,* Captain Kid wrote in *Carina's* log. *Now sailing dead downwind in Force 5-6 Northeasterly. Steering and motion are not great but tolerable and safe so far. Seas up to around 10'.* Ten feet? The seas looked a lot bigger to me. But I liked it because I had that flying feeling again.

We were wing-on-wing, the sails spread in opposite directions. There were three reefs in the main—meaning the sail wasn't open to full capacity—to keep us from getting overpowered. The first day of the trade winds we covered 125 miles, hull creaking, sails luffing momentarily whenever the wind shifted, the wind itself whirring. Sometimes the sail filling with wind sounded like a zipper, a whoosh of air hitting our canvas and vaulting up to the sky.

On Day Six we had a storm.

The night before there had been a spectacular light show, billions of stars and shooting stars, and lightning in the distance. With the clouds, it looked otherworldly. And then the wind died down—the first hint of trouble.

We had a stalled day of sailing, our first under 100 miles. At nightfall, I helped Captain Kid set the sails and, as he had first watch, went to lie down.

Sleep was fitful. I tossed and turned but must have zonked out because next thing I remember, someone—or something—was banging on the door. BANG! BANG! An ominous, unremitting thud. BANG! Who was this relentless person, pounding with a heavy, blunt object on my bedroom door? Was I dreaming?

Groggy and disoriented, I rolled over, releasing a churning deep in my stomach. *Where am I?* I wondered, wiping sleep from my eyes. *What day is it?*

Another THUD and my body was thrown against the wall. Only it wasn't a wall, it was the hull of the boat. On the other side, a storm was seething.

I pressed my hand against the cool, dry teak. One and a quarter inches of wood was all that separated us from a turbulent, unmistakably violent sea.

Squeezing my eyes shut, I concentrated on getting my bearings, mentally grasping for something familiar, urging my brain to hurry and catch up. There was a gurgling in the bilge. Splashes of surf outside peppered what I can only describe as a persistent, electrifying—buzz. It was the low, menacing growl of the whole ocean.

I started to sit up but was smashed again into the hull as the loud BANG of another mighty wave broke against our tiny boat. How does water make this awful noise? I envisioned Poseidon personified, rising from the sea in a fury, wielding his trident like a club. CRACK! It smacked down upon us, testing the strength of the unknown vessel and the mettle of her crew. What did we do to conjure his wrath? Did we forget to show him proper respect?

Now I was awake. There were more jarring, vicious-sounding crashes. The sea was "confused," swells coming from the north, south, east, and west. Blinding flashes of light pierced the portholes over my bunk.

Captain Kid, the ship he built at the mercy of an angry ocean, stood in the narrow space between our berths. He couldn't feel calm, but that's what he exuded. He was keeping watch from below, having decided the danger of being struck by lightning outweighed the risk of hitting another vessel. We were far away from land.

Another ferocious blow reverberated through the core of the boat, shaking *Carina*'s timbers and rattling a dozen things on board: The forks in the silverware container. Our two coffee mugs in the sink. The top tray of the cooler. The handle of the teakettle. A loose can rolled around in the cupboard. The plastic box of baby wipes slid frantically back and forth over the navigation table, where the ship's log noted wind and sea state: Force nine winds. White, cresting waves. Rough conditions. What words describe the sound? Was that rumbling thunder? Or the roar of the Atlantic?

Every few minutes the captain slid open the hatch and looked around outside. Water and sky were indistinguishable, he reported. Both were pure white.

I imagined the tempest of my wildest nightmares: Bone-chilling, driving rain pelting down. An onslaught of waves, crashing over and over, flooding the deck. Fierce winds, lashing at our sails, howling through the rigging.

Above, the storm raged. Below, we were dry and, for the

moment, safe. We had done everything in our control. There was nothing else to do but hold on and wait for it to pass.

Which I did, mostly by sleeping.

It's not as unbelievable as it sounds. Captain Kid told me that on another of his most harrowing sails—when he had come much too close to lethal rocks while battling gusty winds in a gale—his sole crewmember that time dealt with it by cooking through it.

Even when I woke to see those lightning flashes through the portholes, our volatile, potentially fatal situation didn't fully register. No doubt I was in denial, but I don't remember being afraid. Because of Captain Kid, because of his unflappable demeanor, because of the sturdiness of the boat, some piece of me was convinced everything would be fine. I couldn't believe it was blowing over 40 knots because, as long as I was lying down, I was comfortable. Captain Kid, of course, would not sleep through a storm; our watch schedule was irrelevant in an emergency, when there was real sailing to be done. I did feel a little guilty for not getting up in moral support, but taking quick stock of the status quo I had discerned three very important things: 1) I was not seasick. 2) I was not freaked out. And 3) I did not have to pee. I knew Captain Kid would rouse my ass if he needed it. Until then it was *first, do no harm.* I stayed right where I was—in bed.

I slept on and off, restless sleep, with weird, vivid dreams. Awake, I was aware *Carina* was lurching, and there was loud thunder, and my skin was itchy, an odd thing to notice, but I noted it. Through it all, Captain Kid was coolheaded.

Once, I think, I woke to see him lying in his bunk, napping from fatigue, maybe, or submitting to the momentary powerlessness. But most every time I jolted out of sleep he was up and composed.

How bad was the storm? In the log, the understated captain wrote simply: *Large line of thunderstorms and squalls. First squall started at 20:00, and was very strong with gale force winds, heavy rain, severe lightning.* Years later, he will say it was the worst lightning he had ever seen, but his log entries are a model of brevity.

Carina had endured worse. Sailing from Ireland to Spain in an abusive storm with 50 knots of sustained wind and zero visibility, she had been hove-to—essentially stopped—in a busy shipping lane. Captain Kid said he could smell the exhaust from invisible ships passing by, that's how close he came to collision. It was so bad, at one point—unable to make a reasoned decision about what to do next—he actually flipped a coin.

I'm not cavalier about the dangers. Ships sink. Small boats disappear without a trace. Sailors do get washed overboard—drowning or dying of hypothermia, bodies never recovered—especially if on solo watch on a dark night. And some sailors revel in those cautionary tales, like campers telling ghost stories around the fire. You practice man-overboard drills in the most basic of boating classes but out there—outmatched, unaided—a rescue is an act of providence. Some weather is unsurvivable.

Then again, like that doomsayer back at Skinny's told me before my first sail on *Carina*: Most boats make it.

The next day, the seas were calm. We were on a starboard tack with warm sun and easy headwinds. I did all the watches and cooked while the captain slept. At least I was good for something. At noon I turned on the handheld GPS to get our coordinates. I found the latitude and longitude on our chart, marked our location with a little X, and drew a ring around it.

I was charting not only *Carina*'s journey, but also my own, one that had started over a year earlier on the summit at Ram Head, one of the highest points on St. John. That was the night I heard a call to sail away.

I had followed the trail but felt like the Trail Bandit, blazing my own path over the big smooth stones at the water's edge, finding my footing on rocks and tree roots long embedded in the dirt. There's one stretch up high where the trail narrows between two promontories and you feel suspended over the precipice, as if on a bridge designed to give a little in the wind, which blows extra hard at that spot. The trade winds. A few more minutes of climbing and you're at the top. On a full-moon night, if you begin the hike an hour before dusk you'll reach the peak in time to see, at the exact moment the sun is setting, the full moon rising out of the sea in the east.

That's where I was—at the end of the trail—standing as close as I dared to the edge of the cliff as the moon appeared, an enormous disk hovering over the Caribbean 200 feet below. It lit up the night as it rose, a spotlight casting long shadows across the rocks and cacti. Between the light and the altitude, you could see for miles, or forever. There was Norman, Peter, Salt, Cooper, Ginger—all those Virgin Islands I had sailed to from Coral Bay—but you could see far beyond them, too. What else was out there? What was just beyond? Africa, said someone.

There was something in the air, not just wind and shifting light in the dimming sky, but some supernatural energy. I felt a pull. Like in that song: Larger voices calling. I was overcome with a sense of wanting—needing, even—to be "out there." "There" being ... Here. In the middle of the ocean. After months of sailing in circles, I was ready to go somewhere.

Now here we were. Africa.

As we skirted—by sea—the western edge of the Sahara Desert, the sky grew thick with dust. I remembered St. Johnians talking about this mysterious Sahara Dust, blaming it for hazy days in the Caribbean. It was hard to fathom desert particles blowing 3,000 miles across the ocean but they do, and here they were, fresh from the source. The whole sea looked dusty.

Sahara Dust is exactly what it sounds like—minuscule bits of sand and soil from the Sahara Desert. When atmospheric conditions are just so, the wind scoops up African earth, carries it across the Atlantic, and dumps it on the other side. Tons and tons of the stuff make the journey. Sahara Dust dropped in South America feeds the Amazon rainforest, providing phosphorus-rich nutrients. In the Caribbean, thick, orange-y plumes invade the sky, aggravating the air quality, enhancing sunsets, and yes, ruining an otherwise perfect beach day.

We sailed through the dust and dropped anchor in Cape

Verde—a 10-island archipelago a few hundred miles from Dakar. It was Thanksgiving Day. We were greeted by a pair of entrepreneurs who sped up alongside us in a little skiff and offered to help with anything we needed—for a fee. In other words, we could pay them not to rob us. Minor extortion, however, was not going to prevent us from celebrating the first leg of our journey with a couple of local beers at whatever watering hole we could find.

On shore, I followed a woman carrying thick slabs of fresh tuna in a tub on her head and found a market where I bought fruit and some odd-looking vegetables. I washed the produce and myself, together, in the shower at a place called Club Nautico. It felt good to be clean.

Meanwhile, over at customs, Captain Kid witnessed the aftermath of a genuine mutiny. A group of young sailors had turned in their captain—who was being detained, handcuffed, in the customs office—for allegedly threatening them with a gun. Seriously. A mutiny.

The characters at Club Nautico would have looked right at home at Skinny's, but there was no Thankspigging, no turkey, no one who had even heard of Thanksgiving. Kid and I observed the fourth Thursday in November with lukewarm showers and cold Super Bock beer. There may have been some chicken and rice involved, although there is no evidence of it in the one "holiday photo" of us sitting at the Club Nautico bar.

The first 24 hours back at sea were a blur. And, apparently, rough. Perhaps Kid thought if he didn't tell me I wouldn't notice. Fair enough, since I was mostly pretending that nothing bothered me. Some tumultuous conditions I discovered were worse-than-average only after reading his notations in the log: *A wave broke over the stern in a partial broach.* Later I'll look up "broach" and learn that that was potentially catastrophic.

Carina was rolling—a lot. I wasn't sick or queasy, but I wasn't 100 percent either. For three days I tried to feel the rhythm, but never felt quite right. The good news: We were flying. 136 miles. 137 miles. 400 miles in three days.

We were, it turns out, sailing through a part of the ocean where, a decade later, the most powerful hurricane ever seen in the Atlantic would form. Tropical Storm Irma would spring to life right there, just west of Cape Verde. She would begin, according to NOAA, as "a weak wave of low pressure accompanied by disorganized showers and thunderstorms," just one of many likely insignificant weather systems flinging themselves off the coast of the African continent every few days in August and September. But a perfect storm of conditions—above-average water temperature, not enough Sahara Dust or dry desert air, the right "spin"— would fuel her. Thirty hours after forming off Cape Verde, she would grow into a major hurricane. By the time she reached St. John, she would be a Category 5 beast.

Everybody always wants to know about the storms: *How was the weather? Were you scared?* I sailed through ominous weather. Two mornings on *Yellow Bird* we were cloaked by a spooky fog so thick we couldn't see the bow of our own boat. I was so wrapped up in the opaque strangeness of it I barely processed how dangerous it was. I have photos of skies so black they're cartoonish in drama. But though storms like the one we had on *Carina* might distinguish an ocean voyage, they're not what characterizes it. It's the sameness. The lazy days of staring at the same horizon, searching for the slightest change in the waves, looking for signs of any other life out there. The long nights lying back, feeling the rocking of the boat, watching the sky change, moon and stars appearing to make more progress than we did. The hour upon hour of nothing but ocean and sky.

Back in Antigua, before my first crossing, I asked an Italian sailor what it was like sailing across the Atlantic. He was also a writer and answered in monotonous verse: *Mare, mare, mare, mare, mare, mare, mare. Terra.* Ocean, ocean, ocean, ocean, ocean, ocean, ocean. Land.

I heard that sailor's voice as, day after day, I stared out at ocean, ocean, ocean, ocean, ocean, ocean, ocean.

Loveliness unfathomable, according to Melville. I had started

Moby Dick. I read. I napped. I don't know how much Kid actually slept. He seemed to have his eyes closed more than I did, yet already had read two books and was hungrily eyeing mine.

Our meals were simple, mostly out of cans. We'd been fishing, but not catching anything. There seemed to be nothing out there, no fish to eat, no dolphins to see, no whales, no smells, no boats. Dinner was usually rice or pasta with tinned tuna or vegetables, maybe some garlic or cured meat, or canned potatoes and spinach. I thirsted for the delectable Canary Island oranges I had found in the market in Tenerife, bursting with a juicy sweetness I swear I'd never tasted, or maybe it was just our unearthly surroundings, heightening all the senses. They were long gone. Without refrigeration we only had fresh fruit and vegetables for the first part of the trip. Nearly all of the produce we replenished in Cape Verde rotted and had to be tossed overboard.

We had 75 gallons of fresh water on board, stored in two large red jugs. Plenty for drinking, plus the occasional shower. Showering cured any lethargy and rose to the level of an extreme sport up there on the foredeck—those big seas, the rolling boat—but the sun shower hanging from the mast was good and warm from the southern sun, getting hotter by the day. It felt almost decadent. After months in Europe, a couple of gelato-, cheese-, and alcohol-free weeks hadn't hurt, either. I felt hyper-alive. I confess to a little thrill being out there stark naked with the sun shining down and the hot water on my body and the most impossible view. The belief that a bare-breasted woman on a ship can calm the seas and ward off storms is a maritime superstition dating back to Pliny the Elder. Who was I to argue?

My hair was a rat's nest, unruly from the wind, and when I couldn't stand it anymore, Kid cut it. You know those pirate movies where the girl wants to run away to sea so she chops off all her hair to look like a boy and ends up looking really sexy? Yeah, it didn't look like that. I think it was Day 16 of our crossing.

Hours stretched into shifts that became a day, then a night, then another day. Yesterday fused with the day before. Days slid by without event. You would never, however, tempt fate by calling a day at sea boring, or even routine.

"'Steady' is a good word," suggested Captain Kid.

One night I scribbled notes to describe what a typical three-hour watch was like:

"Hey, Margie."

Kid's voice would usually interrupt a dream.

"Your watch."

Jump awake, rub bleary eyes, grope for glasses in the little hammock swinging over my berth. It's rolly. Sit up with legs extended across the narrow cabin, feet up against Kid's bunk. Take a minute to get it together.

Boat is going to and fro. My body, or parts of it, move side to side. I'm braced, so my butt's not moving, but limbs and head bob and wiggle like a marionette, hips and joints all working independently.

The floorboards creak.

A comforting sound. Defiant against the ocean.

Ocean makes a swishing noise. Like being underwater— bodysurfing at the Jersey Shore, water rushing past your ears —not the quiet diving in the Caribbean.

Kid's hat swings from a hook. At the foot of his bed: shelves, full of books, manuals. Advanced First Aid Afloat. *Rain-coats hang by the mast. To the right, forward, where some boats have a V-berth,* Carina *has storage: laundry baskets full of lines and supplies, two bigger hammocks, one once*

full of fresh fruit, but we ate the last apple this morning.
There's canned fruit cocktail, canned mandarin oranges,
canned strawberries—oh, for some Canary oranges!

There's a forward hatch. Barometer. Clock. Shoes. Life
preservers. My big red duffel is up there. So's our ditch bag.

To my left, aft, the galley. Two-burner propane stove.
Kitchen basics: saucepan, frying pan, plates, spatula,
wooden spoon, two forks, two mugs—just two of everything
means no dirty dishes pile up. Over the small sink is the
yellow & black EPIRB.

Emergency Position Indicating Radio Beacon. In case we
needed to be rescued.

Behind the companionway steps—the ladder up to the
cockpit—is our cooler, also emptying now, along with bleach,
laundry detergent, kerosene, flashlight, dustpan, clothes-
pins, sails, water jugs, first-aid kit. Life raft.

Across from me, on port side, is the chart table (air horn,
another flashlight, binoculars, slide ruler, GPS, VHF,
hand-bearing compass, maps, fire extinguisher). Stowed
behind a green canvas: toilet paper, paper towels, baby
wipes, Ziplocs (a staple of sailboats, to keep things dry).
Taped above the chart table is a postcard of Coral Bay.

The cabin top has a hatch and six portholes.

There it is. Our 30 feet.

If there's anything to report, Kid will fill me in. Once I'm
up, he'll fall into his bunk.

And I did mean fall. The move had the finality of a gymnast hitting the mat after a dismount.

> *Dressed in T-shirt and underwear, climb on deck, use the bucket—hanging on to the boom gallows and a lifeline for support—and look around. Then go back below, put on the teakettle. Propane stove is hard to light in the wind.*

> *Finish dressing. Rain pants to stay dry in the drizzle and a fleece if it's cold. Kid doesn't seem to get cold, but I do. If I can, try to do some upper body exercises or stretches while waiting for water to boil. Tonight it's raining so I wait below, hatch closed and drop boards in so the wind doesn't blow out the flame. Three boards seal up the companionway completely.*

> *Eat a square of dark chocolate. Usually save that for later in my shift, but early tonight. Hunt for tea bag.*

> *Flashlight's not working. Battery must be dead. There's a yellow flashlight in the galley but it doesn't fit in my pocket. Refill the pitcher that has the water purifier. (Did I remember to close the seacock after dinner?)*

An open seacock would let seawater flow into the boat. This was one of my most important jobs: Don't do anything stupid.

> *Water boils. Hug post for balance to pour hot liquid—a move I've mastered. All sorts of little tricks for leverage and balance: a hip against the chart table, foot wedged sideways against a slanted floorboard. Sometimes I pour the water over instant coffee in a mug in the sink, add evaporated milk, but tonight it's tea. My mug says Bird Watcher's General Store, Rt. 6A Orleans, "A True Cape Cod Original."*

Getting the tea on deck is a little trickier. Mug handles broken from sliding around. Baby wipes (Pampers Baby Fresh) good for cleaning coffee and tea spills on fleece.

Open hatch. Rain seems to have paused. Waning gibbous moon is hanging low, illuminating the sea. Minutes ago it looked black. Weather out here like that. Good wind and waves. Force 5, I guess, but not a squall. Perched on the middle step, I can see Sirius, the Dog Star. Only the brightest shine through tonight with the clouds and the moon this big. As my eyes adjust, I can see the big swells astern. We are surfing in the moon glow.

Take a sip of tea. Place the mug on deck.

One more step up the ladder and I can turn around and look forward, over Paisley, our rowboat, securely stowed on the cabin top. Scan the horizon for lights—signs of ships or other sailboats. Nothing.

Not surprising. We hadn't seen anything for days.

Try to step gingerly as I climb into cockpit and get settled. "One hand for the boat." Don't want a sprained ankle out here. Or any injury.

Sip tea. Look around. Sip some more. Look around some more. Go below and check clock. It's been 15 minutes. Really? 2:45 to go?

Back on deck by the tiller, but Mona does the work. My legs are a few inches shy of spanning the cockpit, but with the cushions I'm almost stabilized. Every so often Carina dips port and foam spray blasts across deck, bow to stern. Another rogue wave. In a three-hour shift, chances good I'll get doused, but OK. I like the rush up here, and the water is warm—a reminder that we're heading to the Caribbean. Hundreds of miles away, still, but the latitude is right.

Stand up to look around. Try to be quiet, but accidentally kick one of the drop boards in the companionway and flashlight falls out of my pocket. The drop to the cabin floor was bad enough, but now it's rattling loudly as it rolls vigorously from side to side. "Sorry!" I whisper hoarsely. "It's OK," says Kid. "I wasn't asleep."

I hated to disturb him. My most useful function—on this boat he could sail alone—was to let him get some sleep. My two jobs: Don't do anything stupid and let the captain sleep.

While below, check clock. Two hours and five minutes to go. Refill the teacup. Water's tepid, but it'll do.

Back on deck, sitting by the tiller.

Our compass is red, with white numbers, in a black casing. Our heading: 285. Almost dead west. Realize I haven't checked in days. Been so steady, I can tell by moon, sun, stars, we're on track. Haven't changed course since ... when? Saturday? Sunday? What's today? Wednesday? No, Thursday. I think it's Thursday. I'm sure it's December. Been December for about a week.

Sit for a while.

Sit awhile longer.

Grab cleat to hoist myself up.

Scan horizon. Is that a boat out there? No, a star. I think. Hard to tell.

Back at the tiller. Sit for a while.

Sit awhile longer.

Seems reasonable to check the time again. Shine flashlight on clock. An hour to go. Shine flashlight on toes. Nails faded and chipped. One big toenail's black from stubbing it on a rock on Cape Verde. Another one looks funky. Don't remember what happened there. Pedicure for sure.

Use the bucket again. Dump contents.

Get some water. Brush my teeth.

I could practice my knots, but I've gotten fairly proficient. There's no tidying up to do. The sheets—the ropes—are all nicely coiled, just how I left them two mornings ago.

Switch sides in the cockpit.

Stand up. Sit down. Stand. Sit.

Some watches go fast. Some seem interminable. Tonight's feels relatively fast.

Some nights I'm wide awake. Others, it's a struggle. Tonight: In between.

Think about story ideas. Things I need to do. I'm not supposed to be here. I was supposed to be home in September. I've got phone calls to make.

Run through song lyrics in my head. Madonna and Irving Berlin.

Clouds obscuring the stars now, but the moon still shines through. Watch the sea, listen, try to think of better words to describe how the wind sounds.

Give up.

Sit in silence.

Sit in silence some more.

After a while, go below. On nights I wear the harness I'm a tangle of buckles and suspenders but tonight I just have to peel off my muggy rain pants. Swipe face with a Pond's towelette.

"Hey Kid," I'd say. "Your watch."

Once the captain was on deck, I'd collapse into my bunk, sleep for three hours, then do it all over again. And at noon, another X went on the map, another circle, another hundred miles or so toward St. John.

"She's sailed all around the world!" people will say about me later, generously. But the world is big. We were sailing just one small part of one small map.

"*MAKE sure you stay until whatever is supposed to happen happens!*" that woman at Skinny's had instructed me. Was that only a year ago? So much had happened since then. Like I used to tell Tom Paine at the *Sun Times*: I can't write fast enough. A year? It must be 10.

But time was meaningless out there.

Sailing for a month, I would spend a lot of time alone. It's hard to explain how solitary it was with another person on board. Kid and I ate dinner together but since we alternated keeping watch, one of us was usually above deck, solo, while the other was below, sleeping or trying to sleep. Every time I came up for watch —every night, twice a night, for how many nights now?—we exchanged less than a minute of conversation. I tried to gauge Kid's thoughts by his face—a look of contentment, a furrowed brow. Every now and then during my watch he would come up on deck, quickly look around, check sails, scan the horizon, check the compass, make a minor sail adjustment, check the horizon again, then retreat to bed without a word.

People will be incredulous when we tell them no, we didn't sleep together. Even out there for a whole month. If there were moments when I glanced over at his bunk and wondered what it might be like to stretch out next to him, they were fleeting, displaced by the simple truth that there was something in our relationship, some instinctive balance in our friendship, that contributed as much to the harmony on board as our expertly set sails. It seemed foolish to tamper with that.

So night after night it was just me. Day after day I looked at a constant seascape, yet words eluded me. My descriptions were overwrought. Every log entry sounds like hyperbole, except that it's all true. It was just ocean, everywhere. A panorama of ocean. I took photos but all I got were poor snapshots, slender frames depicting but a few degrees of my 360-degree world. Capture the breadth of the sea? The expanse? The blue? Impossible.

More days melded together. Shake out a reef. Put it back in. Shake it out again. Put another X on the map. Then another. Another 24 hours goes by without seeing another boat, or even a fish, or changing a sail. Sleep some more. Get up. My back ached from sitting, inertia. My elbows hurt. Elbows? No clue. My skin was itchy. Was it the sheet or blanket? The salt air? Don't know. Blame the heat, maybe. My knee was sore from the same spot banging the edge of the bunk over and over and over. It rains. Then stops.

It had become a mental challenge more than a physical one. My mind on those long night watches was like the bodies of water on the moon I spent all night studying—a Sea of Tranquility, an Ocean of Storms—one minute agitated, a swirl of racing thoughts and emotions dug up from the bottom, and the next, at ease. Twelve hours of darkness down near the equator is a lot of uninterrupted time to be alone with your thoughts.

The weather got hotter. I needed sunscreen. I read more. I finished *Moby Dick*.

I passed into my longest sail ever.

Sailing for a month we would see a full cycle of the moon. If the moon was up high enough on my first watch, I knew it would set on my second. I learned the sky like this, noting the position of the stars and the moon, attending majestic sunrises, watching the world get light on the dawn patrol.

The night of the full moon, I finally got to see, at daybreak, the sun rise out of a shimmering sea in the east at the exact same time the giant moon was dropping below the horizon in the west. I took a few dozen pictures that morning. I knew they wouldn't turn out but I kept shooting anyway, hungry to preserve an ephemeral moment that I had dreamed of tasting since one of my first nights on St. John.

And at some point in there it occurred to me that all these things that kept happening, maybe I was making it all happen. This was a revelation. Maybe I was the magnet, making everything align, and that made me feel happy and strong.

Sailing for a month, from the Canaries to the Caribbean, we would sail across four time zones, but time was a fabrication. The clock signified what we told it to.

How did we know when we crossed a time zone? Our watch schedule was three hours on, three off, throughout the night. Kid took the first watch after sundown. When my second watch ended without any sign of first light, we turned the clocks back.

The sun rose and the sun set and that was how we marked our day. And I decided when the time changed.

EVEN ARISTOTLE (BORN 384 BC) knew that the world wasn't flat. The ancient Greeks had a hell of a lot figured out more than 2,000 years ago. In *The Odyssey,* Homer rattles off celestial names that connect his heavens to our current sky: Bootes the herdsman, the Great Bear, Orion. Ptolemy began mapping the stars in the second century. Today, there are 88 constellations recognized by modern astronomers; 48 of them appear in the *Almagest,* Ptolemy's astral treatise written circa AD 150. Sure, it would be another thousand years plus before Copernicus's heliocentric theories definitively put the sun at the center of the universe and a hundred years more before Galileo blew the whole thing open with his telescope, but out there, surrounded by water, witnessing the reliable and punctual rising and setting of the moon and the sun out of and into the sea, it was easy to see why those learned men thought the universe revolved around them. Out there, the geocentric world of Ptolemy and Aristotle seemed just about right.

Night after star-filled night I was gazing at the same ever-changing sky as Aristotle and out there on *Carina,* without a flicker of ambient light, my view was no different from his. Night after night the stars and planets kept me company. I consulted my little star guide and learned their names as they promenaded above me. I knew every constellation in the Northern Hemisphere. Ptolemy's Pegasus and Perseus, Cygnus and Cassiopeia, Auriga and Aquila. The winged horse and the hero, the swan and the queen, the charioteer and the eagle. Scorpio and Taurus and all the other creatures of the zodiac: The lion, the archer, the twins. If I looked hard enough, would I see my own destiny written up there among them?

Like the horizon spread before us, I still couldn't see what lay just beyond, but I was surely moving toward it, just as surely as the chain of X's on our chart continued to extend in the general direction of Antigua. Day after steady-five-knot day we sailed across the Atlantic. *Carina* was moving westward as assuredly as the sun.

Sometimes after dinner, after the oil lamps were lit, Kid and I would linger on deck and talk. Kid told me he's been obsessed with weather since he was four years old. This conjured a scene of pure Americana in my muddled brain, a sepia image of a small, dark-haired boy slamming a screen door and stepping out on his mother's back porch to survey the skies, perhaps across a dusty prairie, never mind that he hailed from coastal Massachusetts. He, on the other hand, meant that he liked to watch The Weather Channel on cable TV.

I also, finally, got a little insight into one of the questions I had been asking since our first sail together: *What made you build this boat, and then just sail away?* Kid told me about growing up, working as a teen in the boatyard on Cape Cod, listening—for years—to all the older guys talk incessantly about their dreams of sailing around the world.

"None of them ever did it," he said.

One evening in the lower latitudes, the sky a stunning canvas of glittering stars, we saw a constellation Ptolemy, on his ancient star map, called Argo Navis, the mythical ship of the Greek hero Jason. The constellation was low in the sky, with one wildly bright star shining furiously, reflecting off the ocean like the moon. It was the main navigational star in the southern hemisphere, the second brightest star in the entire night sky. It was Alpha Carinae—Carina.

Kid, his own journey now light years from those Cape Cod winters where, plank by plank, he built his boat, was seeing it for the first time.

WE WERE BECALMED.

I was alone on watch in absolute stillness. There was not even a suggestion of wind.

The last gasps of air had blown away a few stray clouds and exited behind them, vanishing. For 12 hours we had had veritable dead calm. After a full day of our boat just sitting, motionless, Kid doused every single sail. I'd never seen *Carina*'s rigging naked like that, except at anchor. With all the canvas on deck, the view of the sky was unobstructed.

When it got dark, it was divine. The stars—every star imaginable—dropped all the way to the water's edge. The glistering Milky Way stretched above. Meteors streaked across the sky.

Were you close to God out there? a friend will ask later.

I was close to something.

The world was incandescent. Stars reflected in the water, a mirror image of the heavens reaching down into the depths of the sea.

And the silence! It was a void, absent of sound. No rocking. No wood creaking. No wind vane squeaking. No sail shifting. No lapping of waves. Nothing.

Then, amid all that silence, I heard what sounded like someone taking a breath.

Poetry, I thought. It was the languishing sail, sighing, yearning to be raised again.

Then I heard the deep, heaving sound a second time and realized—it *was* a breath.

A steady inhale of air.

A burst of sigh-like exhale.

A whale.

She was so near.

Anything that close to our small vessel should have been cause for concern, if not heart-stopping dread. Something large hitting our boat, even unintentionally, could sink us.

My heart skipped a beat but did not stop. This awe-inspiring creature must have been almost close enough to touch, but I didn't feel threatened.

Illuminated as the sky was, I could see nothing below. The sea was translucent. I leaned, breathless, over portside and searched the darkness for a silhouette. I heard more breathing—forward, off the bow. Then starboard. All around the boat, stealthy, investigating. I caught one flash of movement beneath the surface of the water—lit by bioluminescence—but no distinguishing shape.

It could have been dolphins, but the cadence didn't seem right. That slow, deliberate respiration—the rhythmic inhale and exhale—must have been a whale, or two. A mother and her calf, I deduced.

Just as suddenly as they arrived, they left. I strained my ears against the returning silence, still holding my own breath. I listened as the breathing swam away, in a northerly direction, until I could hear it no more.

For a moment, I was unable to move. As I sat there, enthralled, I felt a whisper of breeze brush across my cheek. It was blowing from the northeast. The trade winds were returning.

And then I felt it. It washed over me.

The peace.

HERE IS the last email I received before setting sail:

From: A Landlocked Sailor
Subject: The Odyssey

You began this odyssey as a lowly swab and are returning as an old salt. This is the leg of the voyage that will rest most firmly in your psyche. There no longer is any question whether you have the mental and/or physical stamina for such an odyssey, but the greater challenge—indeed, the greatest challenge of all—is whether you have mastered

your demons. But I think you know the answer to that
question already—and will be able to sit at the tiller and
gaze at the stars and consider yourself the master of your
world. And the master of your own heart.

When you eventually return from the sea, you will be a
different person. You will be liberated from fear. Not physical fear—that's a little part of it—but you will no longer fear
—yourself. You will live comfortably within your own psyche
—your soul. That's the definition of peace.

That was exactly right.

I was out there with myself, and my inimitable young friend,
and his boat, and the sea. That's it. Nothing else existed. Nothing
else mattered. What did anything matter if you'd never looked up,
seen a sky like that, and felt part of something bigger. Something
transcendent. Eternal.

That night of the whale I tapped into some wellspring of
rapture and wonder. In a moment of perfect clarity, I knew
without a scintilla of doubt I was where I was supposed to be, felt,
acutely, the "rightness" of it, as one friend would say. That despite
the unknowns—decisions unmade, conundrums unresolved,
quests and questions unfinished and unanswered—despite it all,
knew, absolutely, that the universe was unfolding exactly as it
should. That it was blasphemous to believe otherwise.

This was me. This was my life. This was the epiphany.

Maybe I couldn't describe it, but I could feel it. I could feel
the freedom.

And it is that feeling I hoped with all my heart I could hold
onto when—16 days after leaving Cape Verde—we spotted land.

10

JUST GOT BACK

I t was nighttime when we spotted the lights of Antigua and Barbuda on the horizon. Safety dictated that we wait for daylight to bring *Carina* into port, so we sailed a little closer and, about five miles off the coast, set the sails so we'd be hove-to —more or less "parked" for the night. We would sail into the harbor at dawn, but we had made it. Our transatlantic voyage was over. Captain Kid honored the occasion by falling into a deep and imperturbable sleep.

It had been 28 days since we left the Canary Islands. Sixteen since Cape Verde. Sixteen days without seeing land. We had sailed around an eighth of the globe. More than two dozen little X's with circles around them illustrated our rhumb line across a great swath of blue. We had sailed across the Atlantic.

Our first stop after dropping anchor in Antigua was the Mad Mongoose, decorated for Christmas. December. I had lost track of time. We left Europe as the sailing season there was waning, and the cycle was beginning all over again in this part of the world. The winter solstice was nigh, auguring the mythical halcyon days when Aeolus, god of the winds, calms the seas.

Like the gods, we feasted on ambrosia—cheeseburgers and fries, ice-cold Caribs—and chatted up the other sailors having lunch. I felt like the fucking queen of the world. *We just sailed across the Atlantic Ocean!* I told everyone we saw. Sixteen days without seeing land! Nearly 3,000 nautical miles! I had logged 11,125 miles, spending 176 days at sea since my very first sail on Thanksgiving two years earlier! I needed all those exclamation points because it was a tough crowd. Almost everybody at the bar had just crossed the Atlantic. But *Carina* was no ordinary boat. Thirty feet! No engine! If that didn't make an impact, I informed any blasé listener that we had a bucket for a bathroom for a month. That usually did the trick.

After lunch we went back to *Carina* to pick up our stuff for showering. A real shower on land, a shower with water pressure, was going to feel so good. I went below to grab my towel and shampoo and never made it back on deck. Kid found me passed out in my bunk. I slept for 14 hours.

Three days later we set our course for Coral Bay. We retraced, in reverse, the 200-mile journey we had made the previous spring. On our very last night, I kept watch as the lights of the Virgin Islands came into view. Virgin Gorda. Tortola. A few cruise ships lit up brighter than any island. Then, that glow in the distance: St. John. There's always something magical about seeing St. John from the water.

Just before dawn, Kid set the sails. Then he gave me the helm.

The morning was, seriously, I am just running out of adjectives, but let's go with stupendous. Cerulean sky over lush green hills topped by wispy clouds and surrounded by the bluest blue water. We sailed past Ram Head, where I heard the supernatural voices calling me out to sea, and John's Folly, where, during one of my first weeks on island, I listened to the voices of real-life sailors regale each other with stories of being "out there." We sailed past Johnson Bay, where I rigged up a Sunfish and had my first solo sail. Then we sailed into Coral Harbor. Where the saints from KATS taught me what to do with the tiller that was in my hand. Where I found my confidence with a crew of women on a boat painted Fighting Lady Yellow.

For a little objectivity, here's the final entry in *Carina*'s log:

Anchored in Coral Bay towards outside in 20' of water
at 0800.
18°16' N
64°13' W
Conditions: good
Sky: clear
Temp: 73

But here's what it doesn't say:
We dropped anchor right in front of the Cliffhanger.
And I thought "coming full circle" was just a cliché.

I had always thought it was an accident, landing in Coral Bay. Some of my neighbors thought otherwise. "It means you're supposed to be here," Mean Jean would say. But did I belong? Had I lived on St. John long enough for this to qualify as a homecoming?

My question was answered immediately. A friend on another boat dinghied over to welcome Kid and me with coffee. Roughly five minutes after that, another friend buzzed over to update us on all the news. *They took down the old surfboard menu at Skinny's and now they have menus on the tables! Shipwreck has new tiles on the bathroom floor!* A boat full of kids on their way to the Saturday morning KATS class sped by. Everyone waved. We went ashore and had breakfast at the Donkey Diner, where I got my name put on the Wall of Shame for not having enough money to pay my bill.

"My God, you're an official pirating scallywagging sea wench!" said Erin. "I'm so proud of you!"

When I first moved to St. John, I was introduced to a lot of people like this:

"This is Joe. He just got back."

"That's Annie. She used to work here, but then she left. But now she's back."

I thought it was odd that so many people had that "just got back" thing tacked on to the end of their names. Now I was one of them.

"You remember Margie," Cruz Bay Julia must have said a few dozen times at the Mongoose Junction Christmas party later that night. "She just got back."

Just got back? I felt like I had never left. In just a few hours, at one party, I saw about half of the people I knew on St. John.

"What did you think about all those nights out there on watch?" asked one erudite old salt.

I launched into a rambling mishmash of metaphysics, navel-gazing, overblown literary metaphors, new age mumbo-jumbo, and spiritual epiphanies, concluding with, "And what about you? What do you think about when you're out there, alone?" Someone must have an articulate answer to this question.

"I count the women," he replied. "I think about all the women I've slept with."

Yup. I was definitely back.

The quintessential *Welcome home!* moment came the next day at Skinny's. I was eating a blue cheese burger, medium rare, and telling a story about a classic boat I raced on in Saint-Tropez. I had an attentive audience, hanging on every word. When I finished, my friend Badlands Frances smiled and said she had a good story, too.

"I was at Mosquitoes," she said, turning to me and explaining, "That's the new breakfast place near Aqua Bistro. And I saw this gecko climb on top of a grasshopper."

She paused, for dramatic effect.

"Then the grasshopper jumped!" Frances exclaimed, gesturing in the air. "And the gecko held on! The grasshopper and gecko went LEAPING across the floor TOGETHER."

The three locals sitting across from us, wide-eyed and rapt, nodded with the same enthusiasm with which they had just listened to my story about sailing in one of the most prestigious regattas in Europe.

"Wow," said one.

"That is amazing," said another.

"When did they open a new breakfast place?" I inquired, thinking of that Skinny's waitress who once asked *What is it about this place?* Because there it was, right there. The locals had a refined appreciation for the little things in life. *Las cosas pequeñas.* Once they decided you were pretty OK, they'd share their passions, and support you in yours.

And you could always come back.

A WEEK LATER, I was celebrating the New Year with Jazz and Ellen in Philly. We inadvertently crashed a private party at a hotel. Jazz scored some champagne and sent me in search of food. I walked up to a group chatting around a table of hors d'oeuvres.

"Hi," I announced. "I just got back to Philadelphia after spending a month sailing across the Atlantic Ocean in a 30-foot boat. I am really hungry."

The lone woman in the crowd arched an eyebrow. "That's the most amazing story I ever heard," she said, "to get cheese."

The guy sitting next to her handed me the entire tray.

I didn't know when—or if—I'd be going back to Coral Bay. I had said my goodbyes and flown home to Philadelphia to see my family for Christmas. I needed to regroup. But I was determined to hold on to my sailing high and minimalist lifestyle. US Air did its part by losing my luggage. St. John transplants often talked about "going shopping" in the basements and attics of relatives' homes, or wherever else they stashed their worldly goods before moving to the island with a backpack. I got a taste of that, foraging in my storage locker for winter boots and sweaters. I had everything I needed. This was good because somehow, on January 2, I got a job.

I set up temporary camp in the spare bedroom at my brother's house. He was sorry, he said, that the mattress was on the floor and there were no drawers for my clothes.

"That's OK," I reassured him. "Since I don't really know what I'm doing next, I don't want to get too comfortable."

"You're pretty lucky," he observed. "You just got home and you got a job right away, and a place to live."

Yeah, that falling into place thing? Happened a lot.

I started my new gig, writing at a university, and had my desk and computer moved three times in two days. The tech guys kept apologizing for disturbing me, which only made me laugh.

"No worries," I said. "I'm just part-time. I don't want to get too comfortable."

Then it turned out the job had full-time potential. Would I be interested?

If I was ambivalent, a lot of people around me were not. They threw around phrases like "401(k)" and "dental insurance" and "you're crazy." The job had appeal. Money, for example. It would have been so easy to rent another apartment, move all my stuff out of storage, and essentially resume my old life. If I said yes, I'd still have plenty of time left over to think about what I *really* wanted to do next, right?

Wrong, cautioned another friend. "Don't take that job. Because if you do, every day your odyssey will slip away a little more and a little more ..."

It was already slipping away, and I was panicked by how swiftly. The ocean felt far away. I couldn't taste it or smell it or feel it. Was I really on that little boat in the middle of the Atlantic *four weeks ago*? I was beginning to feel like it had never happened.

"Restless Sea Legs Syndrome," pronounced one clever friend.

I was in a quandary. But I did have plenty of time to mull it over because I had an hour-long commute. It was dark when I got home, although there was too much ambient light to see stars. I knew the sun was rising late and setting early, but I no longer knew at what time. I had set my clock by the sun for two years, but I was no longer living that life. I wasn't even talking about it.

After those first few weeks, I was old news. My ecstasy, feeling like the queen of the world, had been reduced to two simple sentences: "It was amazing. Thanks for asking."

"It's the same everywhere," wrote a sailing friend from the U.K. "One time I walked into my 'local' after an absence of a couple of years traveling to exotic countries and friends just looked up at me and remarked, 'Haven't seen you for a while, been away? Want a pint?' And local gossip was resumed!"

It was OK, normal. Some days I craved normalcy. It's awful to have longtime friends clam up when you ask them what's new because they insist their lives are boring by comparison. But I didn't want to be too normal.

When I needed an ego boost, I talked to the friend who called me "a seeker" and raved about my "hero's journey," the one who wanted to know if I was "close to God out there" in the middle of the ocean.

Did it change your DNA? she asked me.

Great question, unexplored, because I was busy fielding another, more common, question, the one almost everyone was asking:

So, you're back?

I hadn't even been on St. John a year when the question most often asked by friends back home was not *How are you liking it down there?* or even *How's the weather?* It was: *What are your plans now?* I didn't often have a plan beyond—lunch, maybe, or a waitressing shift the next day. Why did people keep asking me this? Did I need a plan?

Was I back?

This question left me flummoxed. Or maybe it wasn't the question that was baffling, it was the premise. Somewhere along the way, I don't know exactly when, residency in the Virgin Islands, working on sailboats, living abroad, all of it had ceased to be a sabbatical or a vacation or time off and had become, simply, life. Couldn't I be "here" without being "back"? There was no "back." It was all forward. Blissful, liberating, sometimes terrifying, not always smooth, but always forward motion. Which reminded me how much I missed being on the boat.

One cold, snowy night I went to a yoga class taught by my friend Theresa, a former crime reporter who quit the newspaper business to teach yoga full time. She told me I was her inspiration. I reminded her that I had Mickey Mouse health insurance. She told another woman in the class that I was her hero anyway.

On that evening, she inspired me. We breathed. In. Out. Stress melted away. When we went into tree pose, standing on one leg, arms raised high overhead, I was on the bow of the boat, surrounded by big, blue swells, nothing but expansive sky in front of me. I was balanced; equally grounded and buoyant.

I was back. Back on the water.

I left feeling happy and energized. I went home to my brother's with a clear head. Then I shoveled snow.

I didn't want to get too comfortable.

"HEY MARGIE! When did you get back?" For the next 10 years the question persisted.

Four months after sailing across the Atlantic I was back on *Carina*. I was still sleeping on my brother's floor when Captain Kid called saying he needed crew for Antigua again. I had just finished my taxes. There it was in black and white (and red) proof: "Odyssey" was not a Real Job. But how much did I need? I lined up a couple of freelance writing gigs and hopped aboard. Crippling doubt, I had learned, would blow away with a few glorious days of sailing. It is impossible to worry when you feel so free.

I spent another season boat hopping and then, right around the time I found enough work to keep me in the Virgin Islands, I also found a lump in my neck. Cancer. Not a death sentence for me but it would kill my plans to continue living in the Caribbean, premium health care not being one of paradise's stronger selling points. I went back to Philadelphia, where I'd be landlocked for a year. My oncologist said if I didn't get seasick, I'd probably do well with the chemo. He was right. I got better. And when my treatment was over, the first thing I did was fly back to St. John. Julia put me up. Belle took me sailing. I went hiking with Erin. I swam in the Elixir. Chemo and radiation cured me, but St. John healed me.

I went back and forth for a while, not sure where I belonged. Then, during one stay up north, I met Steve. Mutual friends—Philly sailors who had been following my journey—thought we might hit it off. We did. Our first date lasted three days, after which I was back on St. John for six weeks. Had I been with one of my more uncompromising girlfriends—Belle, for example—I might have ignored the daily text messages that followed. But on that visit, I was staying with New Age Billie, who didn't believe in playing hard to get. She believed in *LOVE*. That not responding meant *FEAR*. Steve lived in New York City. If I was scared I'd have to give up St. John to be with him, I should remember I could always come back. I answered the texts.

Steve wore a Skinny Legs T-shirt the day I met some of his friends in New York. "Skinny Legs! I've got a great Skinny Legs story," one of them said. "So does she," Steve said, pointing to me, but before I even had a chance to say, politely, "You first!" the friend was happily jawing away, reminiscing about the day trip out to Coral Bay that he and his wife took while vacationing on St. John back before they had kids.

Steve and I fell in love. Got engaged in Paris. Had a wedding at the Jersey Shore. At 46, I was too old for kids, but finally got my wish to be a bride. And after I was married, the first thing I did was take my new husband back to St. John.

In hindsight, honeymooning in Coral Bay wasn't the best idea, not, at least, if your definition of a honeymoon includes a healthy dose of privacy. Island friends who couldn't reach me on the phone —whether due to still-sporadic cell service or because I was otherwise engaged and didn't pick up—would routinely pop by the villa where Steve and I were staying without warning and unannounced until they appeared on the deck outside our bedroom. The home, Caribbean Bliss, had been under construction when I worked at Skinny's; the owners, regulars, who'd come in for burgers after a long day on the job site. Our stay there was a wedding gift (now *that* was a good tip)—a beautiful basecamp from which I could introduce Steve to my tropical Elysium and the mortals, my friends, who resided there. An undertaking that, thanks to the surprise visits, proceeded at an accelerated rate. I had a tolerant groom.

After that, life resumed in New York. I tried going back to broadcast journalism, but the business wanted younger people. I started freelance writing for non-profits, "meaningful work" that didn't pay a lot but let me make my own schedule. I could set my clock by the sun again, and did, although I sometimes needed an alarm to remind me to go outside and look at the sky. I sailed a bit up north, too, but I was spoiled. I had already sailed with the best. But life was good. Living in the city was stimulating and I loved being married to Steve. We were close to old friends and family. I was happy.

Steve and I made it back to St. John almost every year, often to house-sit in late summer when New Age Billie took her vacation. We'd sail with friends, float in the Elixir, and batten down the hatches when anything menacing loomed, but the hurricane warnings on our watch never amounted to much. Forbidding skies, some vainglorious wind, maybe, but in the end, another false alarm. For 10 more years, small storms came and went. Big ones hit elsewhere. St. John stayed off the radar.

Things changed. Fun Christina went off to Spain to "use her brain" and become a teacher. Captain Kid sailed through the Panama Canal and on to the Pacific with my uncracked copy of *Anna Karenina* on board. Miss Lucy met her good Lord at the age of 91. Pirate Bill died, and so did Irie, the Rastafarian who picked out my hurricane flashlights at Kmart, too young, when his truck overturned at a switchback and toppled down a cliff. His photo continued to keep watch at Skinny's from over the bar stool where he used to sit.

The *St. John Sun Times* changed hands and then folded. Skinny's changed, too. Doug died and when Moe retired, he sold to a long-time employee. KATS kids grew up and went off to college. Some of my carefree, 20-nothing friends became mothers and business owners, settling into their weathered skin, aged by sun and hard living. More mature Coral Bay folks were getting hips and knees replaced, anti-government hippies who had been muddling through the past decades without health insurance suddenly extolling the virtues of Medicare.

Skinny's made *Esquire*'s list of the Best Bars in America: *Skinny Legs is one of those rare points on the face of this dirty globe from which all good feelings emanate. Travelers wash up at Skinny's for the harmonic convergence and stay for the rum punch and a cheeseburger grilled behind the bar in the open for all the world to smell.* And Coral Bay made a *New York Times* list of top places in the world to travel—ranking just after Mexico City; Bordeaux, France; and Malta (*Malta!*)—with an exhortation to go soon. The village/hamlet/burg was in danger of being despoiled by development.

The island was getting more built-up. More exclusive. More than once I'd gotten into a taxi at the airport to discover everyone crammed into the cab was headed for Coral Bay. "The country" had gotten trendy. But its heart stayed the same. You could still find a beach all to yourself, if you knew where to look, and then stop at Skinny's for lunch being pretty sure you'd run into someone you knew. "Did you just get back?" they would ask.

I could always go back.

Until 2017.

CATEGORY 5

HURRICANE IRMA

Colin was tracking the hurricane, plotting its course himself. He didn't trust the weather guys. He didn't need to. He's a good sailor. A good navigator. And he trusted his own instincts. He would take the facts and do his own calculations. He laid out a nautical chart—a paper map—in front of him, penciled in the coordinates, and drew a line.

To properly prep a boat for a storm takes time. To do it right takes at least two days and he had several boats to prep—including his home. So he had been preparing for a week. He doesn't freak out anymore. He's been through so many scares, he doesn't panic, unless it's coming close. But he gets ready, regardless.

Colin was on his 80-year-old classic sailboat, *Buxom,* already secured in Hurricane Hole, staring at his map. Irma had been gaining strength for four days. Even without a direct hit, she'd be fierce. Two days out he knew it was going to be bad. Every single update confirmed the worst. Thirty hours out, he started to worry. Before that, predictions estimated the eye would be 30 miles north of Anegada in the BVI. That was all right for St. John. Plenty north. But the next update said the eye would be 15 miles north. Then five miles north. All he had to do was connect the dots. If Irma kept jogging down in that pattern, she would go right over St. John.

The day before the hurricane Colin and his fiancée, Leah, worked feverishly, doing all the last-minute prep, laboring until dark. *Buxom* had 13 anchors out plus line to the chains and doubled chafe gear. There was nothing more they could have done, to any of their boats or the boats they took care of for others. They were in the safest creek in Hurricane Hole, and Hurricane Hole was one of the safest places in the Caribbean. They did it right. Everyone did it right. Everyone boarded their houses up right. Everyone took it seriously. Before most storms, people will say they're not worried. All the time, during storm prep, people will say they know what's going to happen, it's not going to hit, the storm's not going to do this or that. Drives him nuts. But not this time. No one said that before this hurricane.

Colin and Leah and the dog headed to a villa high on Bordeaux Mountain where they would ride out the storm. That's when he started getting the phone calls. An old friend from St. John, now living off island, that he hadn't talked to in years. People from high school he hadn't heard from in forever. They were all calling to see if he was OK, if he was ready.

That hit him in the gut.

———

Anna had been through hurricanes on the boat before. In a Cat 1, down below? It was fine. Even with the kids. But this storm? No way were she and Steve going to stay on the boat with two kids. What they really should have done was gotten on a plane and gotten the hell out of Dodge, but it was too late for that. At least they had a secure place on land to take shelter.

Steve handed each of the kids a trash bag. "Pack everything that you can't live without," is what he told them. Anna thought that was pretty heavy-handed. They were only 8 and 5. But he'd been through typhoons in the Philippines. Maybe he knew something she didn't.

———

Bryan knew a hurricane was coming, but you couldn't tell from the weather. The sun was out. There was no rain. Of course, you knew from the satellites, it was heading right at you.

Even before the wind blows, there's the anticipation. You've prepped. Tied down everything you can. Boarded. Shuttered, stowed, stocked. Water, food, medical supplies. Found a safe house. Found the people who don't get on your nerves too much, who you don't think you'll feel like killing if you're stuck with them, holed up for a few days, or weeks. For Bryan, that was Erin and Lindsay. They'd all stay at Erin's down in the valley.

After you scramble around, you wait. You sit on the porch, outside, as long as you possibly can because you don't know how long you'll be locked in the house in the dark. Bryan called his parents in Kansas. He had cell service for longer than expected. "I'll talk to you on the other side," he told them. "Don't assume anything. Don't worry."

Four hours later, he called them again. "We're still here!"

It still hadn't started.

———

Belle had planned to stay with Captain Elliot on *Silver Cloud*. She thought his padded steel ship would be safer than a house, even if it flew onto the road, like it did in Hurricane Marilyn. It's a steel box, Belle thought. Unless it sinks, it's probably a pretty safe—albeit, rough—ride.

Friends told them to get the hell off the boat. They took their dog and went to the villa with Colin, Leah, and another friend. The mansion had a bona fide bunker on the bottom level, with bunk beds, a bathroom and kitchenette, and a DVD player with a cache of disaster movies. When Irma started blowing, they ran the generator and watched *The Perfect Storm*.

They were keeping themselves busy, keeping their cool. The two dogs kept them entertained. The wind was blowing hard. All of a sudden, they heard loud, weird, popping. Was that the roof getting yanked off? Or something else?

The house was ripping apart above them. With each new pop, creak, or crunch, they imagined what part of the house was being demolished.

At least the bunker was solid. You had to walk through the pump room to get there. The bunker had a solid door, but the pump room door had a glass jalousie. If you stood in the right spot, you could peer through the slats and try to piece together what was happening. They took turns looking out. Irma had snapped the welds on the hand railings outside, rolling up the metal like pretzels. That was the popping sound. The shutters had blown away. Colin saw a full-size turpentine tree fly past the door. A 30-foot-tall tree just flew by.

Their ears were popping, too. It was painful. They were high on top of the mountain, but Colin felt like he was 90 feet under water, like he was scuba diving. The pressure kept dropping. Every gust of wind felt like it was screeching through his ears, making his head swell. Then his ears would pop, and it would feel OK until it happened again.

The floor beneath them started to split. Next thing they knew, they had a 15-foot crack in the solid masonry floor. Water was shooting up. They were starting to flood.

Prudence was with her husband in their wood-frame house. The wind was shrieking. Her husband was pushing on the door, attempting to keep it from smashing into the house, when Prudence noticed the wall was moving.

As if the hurricane was breathing.

Out, in …
Out, in …
She stared in disbelief.

"Is that supposed to do that?" she yelled over the noise.

Her husband looked over his shoulder at the undulating side of his house and yelled back: "Do you want to hold the door, or do you want to hold the wall?"

It was dark. With everything closed tight, with the storm shutters, you couldn't tell night from day. Like a Vegas casino or something. Bryan was with Erin in their safe room. A tiny closet bordered by concrete, more concrete, and a stairwell. It was the lowest place they could shelter without risk of drowning. The space was as big as the two of them with Gus, Erin's dog, in between, and they needed to wedge in Lindsay. She was frantic and kept darting in and out. They couldn't keep her in. They sat, cross-legged, water up to their knees, petting Gus so furiously it's a wonder he had any fur left. Water was coming through the wall. They were ass-deep in water.

They were startled by a bang. Then it was pandemonium. The ceiling must have given way because suddenly things were crashing down on them. There was a waterfall coming down the stairs. A two-story waterfall, like a muddy river flowing through the house. Water gushed straight down. Brown mud squirted out sideways.

Their eyes started burning. They smelled gasoline. There were four containers of gasoline stashed in a high place in the laundry room. One of them must have tipped over. There was gasoline in the water flooding their cramped closet.

There was one door in the house not barricaded in case they needed to make a run for it. They would have to get the door open so Bryan could run out and do something about the gas can. They waited for a break in the wind and counted: *One, two, three!*

The door busted open. "Bryan, run!" Erin yelled. Bryan ran into the storm, found the five-gallon jugs of gasoline, and hurled them into the air. *Whooooosh.* They took off. He never saw them again. At least they were no longer spilling into their so-called safe room. He ran back inside. They shoved the door shut and bolted it back up.

———

Sylvia was in someone's multi-million-dollar villa. She should have been well protected in her downstairs room, all cement. She was lucky to be there. She had put her little clock on the bedside table, treating the place like a hotel. And that was her mistake. When one of the narrow double doors blew open, instead of running away and saving herself, she ran toward the door to close it. She didn't want the bed to get wet. It was borrowed finery. She reached out to grab the door and felt herself getting sucked out. She flew onto the patio outside and that's where she stayed for the next two hours.

She tried to crawl back inside. It wasn't that far—not even eight feet. But every time she got close, she slipped back, like she was on an incline. Like something out of the Three Stooges. On the third try, her dog came out and she was afraid he'd get blown to Kansas. She grabbed his collar and lay down on top of him. She rammed her elbow into a crack in the patio and hung on to an extension ladder that was on the ground. It wasn't secure, but maybe the extra weight would keep her from being blown away.

Lying down there she saw all her stuff get sucked out of the house. Her poncho. Her glasses. Her clock. The shirt she was wearing turned to spaghetti, shredded by the winds.

The other half of the mahogany door blew off and hit her, hard. She wondered if her foot was still attached because she couldn't feel it. She couldn't see anything because now it was a whiteout. Did she need a tourniquet? Would she be Peg-Leg Sylvia from now on?

She must have been in shock because she wasn't scared. She'd been more terrified on the open ocean, sailing in the North Atlantic. For a lapsed Catholic, though, the Act of Contrition came back pretty fast. She was ready. She was 67. She'd had a great life. Now it was over. People would say, *Remember Sylvia? She went out in Irma.*

She passed out.

Anna and Steve, their two kids, two adult friends, and three cats. They were all in a container house. When the windows started bowing in and out, they all squeezed into the bathroom. It felt safe, but there was a vent with a fan that whirred the entire time. *Wheeeeeeeeee!* It sounded like tornadoes. Their ears were popping. Flying debris pinged when it hit the container. Ping after ping after ping. They were sweating. Anna had insisted that they all wear long sleeves. It seemed prudent at the time. Protection. Warmth in case they were wet and cold. But crammed in that hot, small space with no air for four hours, they were baking. Zach was scared. He was old enough to know what was going on. Lilith was just bored. Steve was the rock. He was the epitome of calm, even when the container started rocking. Not Anna. All she could think was: *My God, did we make the right decision? This is stupid.* She had her baby girl in her arms. *What did we do?* Zach wasn't the only one who was scared.

Matt's plan was to ride out the storm downstairs. His family home up on the mountain had survived plenty of hurricanes. Worst-case scenario, he'd barricade himself in the closet. So he was surprised when pretty early on—hard to say exactly when because the timeline is so weird—a big window in the main part of the house got sucked right out. He wasn't even sure he saw it happen.

He definitely saw other windows get sucked out. This was a problem. The storm had just started, and he had a gaping, four-by-eleven-foot rectangle of a hole in his house. It was like watching a hurricane on a wide-screen TV.

He knew what was going to happen next. Every other window in the house was going to blow out. It took a moment to understand he was no longer safe. He would die if he stayed there. It was a lethal environment.

He retreated to another part of the house, closing a door behind him—as if that would shield him from the gaping hole.

There was glass everywhere. His brain wasn't processing. *Just don't do anything stupid,* he told himself. The door was bulging. The slats in the door started vibrating. And then it was like a movie. The slats blew out one at a time: *Ff-ff-ff-ff-ff-ff-ff-ff-ff!*

He took cover in the closet. His last-resort safe spot. It was only about two-and-a-half feet wide, two feet deep. There were a couple of inches of seawater on the floor. He folded his body into the tiny space, crammed beneath and between the clothes hanging above. Every now and then he peeked out from his foxhole. He saw an eerie glow in the milky water flooding into the room. What the heck was that?

He realized it was his flashlight, dumped to the floor when a dresser toppled over. He ventured out to retrieve it. He would need it when it got dark.

He kept thinking he should take photos, shoot some video. But there wasn't much to see. Just white. It was a sea of white, from all the moisture in the air. He would have needed an underwater camera. Visibility was no more than 12 feet. It was like being in a fog. Not very dramatic. Would have been a boring video. White visuals and white noise.

It was loud. His ears kept popping from the pressure. He heard grinding and breaking. The volume was up so loud.

BEEP! BEEP! BEEP!

The smoke detector was going off. On top of everything else —soaking in gas, wading through a river of mud flowing through the house, risking his life outside in a goddamn Cat 5—now Bryan had that noise grating on his brain.

BEEP! BEEP! BEEP! Note to self: Next hurricane, disconnect the fucking fire alarm. He couldn't take it anymore. Adrenaline was coursing through his veins so hard. He grabbed a baseball bat and tore outside again, clutching the railing as he climbed to the second floor. Shit was flying everywhere. It was like a tornado inside the house. He jumped up on the futon, took a flying leap, and smashed the smoke detector to bits.

Erin had followed him. She looked up and saw—a skylight? She tried to make sense of the barrage of crap she saw whizzing through the air. All she could think of was *The Wizard of Oz.* There were bowling ball-sized holes in her roof and pieces of her neighbor's house were flying through them. The neighbor's roof, ripped from its rafters, was coming through her roof, punching holes—*DITT-DITT-DITT!*—like a daggerboard.

DITT-DITT-DITT! That was the non-stop sound now.

———

Sweet Sarah and her boyfriend, Thomas, were cowering in the bathroom when the house started coming apart.

They could feel it. The house had lifted. Twice. The windows were blowing in. They had watched the roof peel off. The house on the hill above them must have come apart, too, because pieces of it were flying over them.

They had to get out.

They grabbed a couple of buckets and put them over their heads. If part of a neighbor's house, or a branch, or anything else, came hurtling at them, at least it would hit the bucket or their shoulders instead of their skulls.

Thomas said if they didn't get out soon, they'd be buried

under a pile of rubble. *Oh my God, we could die,* Sarah thought. She was inside her home and she could die.

They were going to have to make a run for it. The landlady's house was 35 feet away. They couldn't see it, but they knew where it was. Sarah could see the tree, about halfway there. They couldn't get the door open because of all the debris piled on the stairs. They would have to jump out the window. Thomas told Sarah to go first, he'd follow behind her. But she was too scared. She knew she couldn't do it unless she was chasing after him. So he went first.

It was a five-foot drop. Sarah jumped, fell down, got back up, and ran in the direction Thomas had disappeared, trying not to think about all the things that could hit her in the head. They were being bombarded. She had to dodge God knows what. Thank God it was daytime because at least she could see in front of her eyes. At night it would have been 10 times more terrifying. She slipped and fell in the mud. She was wearing nothing but a nightgown. She just kept telling herself to keep going. She might die on the way, but at least she would have tried.

Sarah couldn't see Thomas but she could, just barely, hear his voice. It sounded like a whisper. It was crazy. He must have been yelling, screaming her name, but it came out like a muffled cry, miles away.

She was hyperventilating when she got to the landlady's garage. Thomas went upstairs to pound on the door. What if no one heard the knock over the noise of the storm?

Luckily, someone let them in. Sara couldn't stop thinking that she could have been killed in her own home. And it was only her feet carrying her away.

———

Ira and his family had been planning to make chicken and Johnnycake, but the drumsticks never got cooked. At twelve o'clock, all hell broke loose.

A waterspout came off the sea. It was like somebody turned on a fan and it skipped one and went to three, then from three to about FIVE. And that was really scary, Ira thought, because a fan doesn't have a five. The wind was pushing the wall in, and the air started to pop, and there was the freight train sound. *Vv-vv-vv-vv-vv-vv-vv-vv-VVH!* The roof began to move.

Ira and his girlfriend and daughter ran from the kitchen to the main bedroom and bathroom. Ira tried to shut the door behind them, but he was fighting the wind. He couldn't get the door closed. Then, as he was pushing, Irma started pulling. She pulled the door—and Ira—out. It was terrifying.

But—somebody up there said: *Let me help you.* Irma swallowed the door, but she spit Ira back out. Like she didn't like his taste. She tossed him back inside, knocked him to the floor.

Thank God he was wearing his motorcycle helmet. His daughter always teased him for wearing it during storms. Called it his hurricane helmet. He landed below the bed where the two women lay, protected by part of a wall. He doesn't scare easy, but he felt himself trembling. If he had gotten sucked out, he'd have been out to sea.

He couldn't get up because pieces of the island were flying over his head. *Whoosh! Whoosh!* For hours he was down on the floor, delirious. Water blasted from a fire hose while wind lashed at him from a giant hair dryer. He was getting pressure-washed and blow-dried.

They were taking a beating. It was constant. There was no calm. The storm was a monster.

But—he was alive.

Ira's grandfather had been blown off that same hill in 1924. He was near a window in another massive storm and got sucked out. He did not survive. When they found him, he was like a pin cushion. He had lost so much blood. He died that day. In those days they had no morgue, so they buried him the same afternoon.

That story kept flashing back into his mind, freaking him out.

Because he was on the same hill as his grandfather. But God was in the middle. God must have decided it wasn't his time.

The sound changed. Colin could tell the wind was different. There had never been a break—no calm, no eye—but he was almost certain they were on the back side of the storm. That meant Coral Bay got the eye wall.

They had to see for themselves. The first person to reach the door outside the bunker peered out through the slats and turned around with an ashen face.

Is it that bad? asked the next person in line, before having a look and turning around with the same reaction.

Colin looked outside.

Everything was brown. Everything was gone. There were no trees. No houses. Nothing. It would have taken an army months to do what that storm did in hours.

They had friends who stayed on their boats in Hurricane Hole. He wondered if they were alive.

The closet door was gone. Matt didn't know when that happened. It was hard to know how long it all lasted. There had never been a period of calm. He must have been in the south side of the eye wall the entire time. He had watched the main door get sucked out. He'd heard stories of people trying to hold a door, but he would have just been sucked out. The closet held, though. It was a wood closet, reinforced by the stacks of magazines he never throws away. But it was like a pressure washer had been unleashed inside the house. That is, if a pressure washer had a setting powerful enough to throw a refrigerator.

Everything outside was annihilated. There wasn't a leaf left on a tree anywhere. The trees were broken and jagged, not like a horror movie, just surreal. There were shards of glass everywhere. Shards of glass were under rocks, they had flown with so much force. He saw a huge piece of lumber, L-shaped, hanging from a tree branch. The lumber was pastel green. That was the color of the interior paint upstairs.

That's how he knew there was no more upstairs.

Erin walked outside, took one look around, and thought: *Everyone I know is dead.*

She had been through hurricanes before but had never seen anything like this. Tumbled cars across the road. Boats on shore. Houses completely gone. Her whole fucking neighborhood. Massive destruction. She saw a pink teddy bear impaled on a spike of a tree, 40 feet up. A tricycle protruding from some wreckage. The trees were just sticks. Like that song their friend Mark S. always sang: *All the trees are brown.* The ground looked like it was covered in green confetti. Like if you dumped out that bag on your lawn mower, grass confetti everywhere. Like some ultimate, insane rave party. Put on by Satan. It looked like a nuclear bomb had hit.

When Sylvia came to, she crawled back inside her borrowed villa. She knew she needed medical attention. There was blood everywhere, and she was worried about ruining the beautiful baby-blue towels. The owners would be pissed at her for not being more careful. Then she went upstairs and saw that the entire upstairs had imploded. Exploded? The roof, and everything under it, was gone. The custom-made wooden hurricane shutters with the steel bars had been pulled right out of the bluestone walls. There was nothing she could have done about that.

Somehow she made it to a neighbor's house and banged on

the window. She was bloody from head to toe. They cleaned and bandaged her, fed her. Then she went to sleep.

Sarah was flabbergasted. *So this is what it's like right after.* There was nothing left. Not one building that wasn't touched. Everything was ruined. Walking around Coral Bay, everyone was a zombie. She was stepping over trees and looking at dead donkeys and wondering if people had died. It was terrifying, not knowing if other people were killed. There was no communication. They were completely cut off.

The wind was still blowing, but Anna needed air. They had been taking turns, trying to ascertain the damage from a peep hole in the bathroom, but now they were anxious to get out. They prepared themselves. If it was dark when they opened the door, that was good. It meant the roof held. If they saw daylight, they were screwed. They opened the door. Dark. Everything had held. The house was OK. Then they went outside.

It was eerie as hell. All the leaves were gone. The lush brush, all gone. The trees were gone. Like a 15-foot chainsaw just took everything down. There was a house right next door that Anna had never seen before. Their container was one of the few dwellings that survived. Jeep Rental Joseph's house? Gone. Wakeboard Wendy's house? Gone. It was mind-blowing.

It took a day just to get out of the driveway, to bushwhack through the detritus. When they finally got to a better vantage point, they grabbed the binoculars to look out toward Hurricane Hole, see if they could see their boat. Did they make it? Then they saw the pile of boats. Did ANYBODY make it?

Up until that moment, Anna thought they'd be going home. Even when they were in the bathroom with the container-rocking and the ear-popping and the debris-pinging, she never thought they weren't going home. Not until she got outside and saw what happened did she realize there was no way the boat made it.

And yet. They lived through it! She felt a weird sense of euphoria. They had just cheated death. It was kind of an ecstatic feeling. They made it.

Rooney had been outside during the storm. If Irma was going to kill him, he was going to watch her do it.

When the winds died down, he went to check on his neighbors. Their house had collapsed. He swore they were dead.

Rooney didn't know Ira was under the rubble, watching him. Ira would have given a million dollars for a picture of his friend's face. Rooney's skin is dark, but he looked white, like he had seen a ghost. He couldn't believe it when he saw them crawl out from under that house.

Ira lost a tamarind tree that had been in the family since before his grandmother. It was from Danish times. They had a tree house in it when he was small. A big, wide tree, just pulled out of the ground, roots and all, by tornados. Gone. Ira thought he was going to die. That Irma would kill him—like that other hurricane had taken his grandfather—and leave the tree. If anyone had told him he would live to see that tree go? He'd say, no man. That tree is going to be here. My grandkids will see that tree. So sad to see a tree like that go.

The women left. Ira's girlfriend got into the jeep and plowed her way out of the remains, determined to get to the road. But Ira couldn't leave the house. He needed to collect himself. He stayed, alone with the dog, in what was left of his home. For three or four days, he just sat there.

PARADISE
(PART TWO)

II

CATACLYSM

When Hurricane Irma hit St. John on September 6, 2017, she was the most powerful hurricane ever to come barreling across the Atlantic. She was four hundred miles wide. Her eye was 30 miles wide, bigger than St. John. She thrashed Antigua and Barbuda, St. Bart's, St. Martin, and Anguilla, and then unleashed on the Virgin Islands with winds over 200 miles per hour. A Category 5 demon, she attacked with a force never before seen in the Caribbean.

I was in New Jersey, watching it all on TV.

If it had been September 6, 2016, Steve and I would have been on St. John, house-sitting for New Age Billie. But she had moved away, and we were at the Jersey Shore, where outside the late-summer weather was beautiful and inside I was glued to the screen. The Weather Channel had been yammering at me for days, tracking the hurricane, updating its position, predicting its path, comparing the models, speculating about where and when the storm might hit—Florida. The meteorologists never mentioned the islands. You couldn't even see the Virgin Islands on the map. The satellite images showed a mammoth storm obscuring half the Caribbean, but I knew the center of it—a sickening swirl of angry red—was sitting right on top of St. John. Hurricane Irma was devouring my island.

As a journalist I had covered hurricanes and as a resident of Coral Bay I had prepared for them. But I never had to huddle in a bathroom praying for my life while one tore my house apart around me. I never had to cower in water up to my waist, thinking *My God. This might really be it.* I don't know what it looks like the instant your roof detaches and blows away. I don't know what it feels like when the pressure drops so low, you think your head's going to explode. But I do know what it sounds like when you're a thousand miles away, waiting to hear what happened.

Silence.

There had been a few dispatches from Coral Bay earlier in the day—Facebook posts about final storm preps, a video when the wind and rain started—but sometime mid-afternoon, probably when the power went out, the posting stopped. It all went silent.

And stayed silent.

For two whole days after Hurricane Irma passed directly over St. John, there was silence. An image from space showed a rock in the ocean, a sterile brown splotch that used to be all green, but there was no information, no news about deaths or destruction, no communication with anyone who knew anything about what happened. Nothing. Anyone not there could only guess.

When the first photos from the scene finally surfaced, they told a grim brown and gray story of annihilation. There were no green hillsides or palm trees. No red flowers. No yellow birds. No pink houses or white sailboats.

But the first thing I noticed was the color of the water.

There it was, still. That water. That blue. Encircling the post-apocalyptic landscape in a tight embrace, with all the promise implicit in those 42 shades of crystalline perfection.

Exactly how much promise anyone else saw in this surreal scene would depend on where they were standing.

Survivors started checking in—from Cruz Bay. All the early news was from Cruz Bay, as if Coral Bay no longer existed.

Gradually, a fact or two broke the silence. Someone from Coral Bay walked nine miles across the island to find power and a cell signal. Someone waited in line for six hours to make a one-minute call on a satellite phone. Someone managed to transmit a photo of what appeared to be a giant piece of cardboard on which survivors scrawled their names. If you saw a person's scrawled name, you could assume they were alive. But there were no answers to any other questions. How was everybody? Did the boats make it? Was Skinny Legs standing?

Then, as more victims found ways to report in—several days after Irma hit—there was a faint cry for help. A sort of bewildered Dr. Seussian plea, like all those *Whos* living on the dust mite in *Horton Hears a Who!* raising their voices together to shout *We are here! We are here! We are here! WE ARE HERE!* Residents were shell-shocked. In need of everything. Afraid of being forgotten.

Help arrived first in an army of small boats. A fleet of private vessels from St. Croix and Puerto Rico ferried in supplies and evacuated the most vulnerable. A Caribbean Dunkirk. Then the Navy and Coast Guard. The military had seen the images, too— the hurricane maps all red and yellow, those NASA images showing all brown where there should have been green—and sent, it was reported, ships stocked with body bags. Helicopters airdropped food and water. The Red Cross set up shop. Law enforcement tried to restore some semblance of order. Reporters found St. John on the map just in time to relay more horrifying news: Hurricane Maria was headed for the island. A second Category 5 storm. A one-two punch.

Recovery operations shut down. News crews pulled out. Residents who could, evacuated. Even the military was forced to retreat. Anyone left behind hunkered down in anything that was still standing and braced for another onslaught. Hurricane Maria blasted through the Virgin Islands, then devastated Puerto Rico, next door. Emergency relief efforts had to focus on an even more desperate populace there. St. John disappeared from the news.

The governor of the U.S. Virgin Islands called his territory's residents "the forgotten Americans."

A month after Hurricane Irma, there was still only a trickle of information. There was no phone service in Coral Bay. No power.

Two months after Irma and Maria—or Irmaria, as the back-to-back hurricanes came to be called—I still had not spoken to anyone who lived through the storms. Not Erin, not Belle, not anyone at Skinny's, not anyone in Coral Bay. All those people who befriended me, helped me, taught me, inspired me, pushed me into going so far—I had no idea what happened to them.

I wanted to go down and find out—and help—but I didn't want to be a burden. I didn't want to consume precious resources or be in the way. But I couldn't sit and do nothing. I didn't know what to do.

And then I got a message from Erin:

Come.

I got back the week before Thanksgiving. Ten weeks after Hurricane Irma. Regular flights to St. Thomas had only just resumed. I was all nerves on the plane. I couldn't wait for my first glimpse, to see something with my own eyes, but when I finally did, it still didn't tell me much. The sun was shining. I saw green and blue. Normal.

I disembarked from the back of the plane into that first blast of tropical heat. There were construction workers all over the airport, but the tourist greeters were there, too, offering up the free rum punch to the sounds of steel drums. My bags came, taxis were waiting, and before I knew it, I was on my way to the ferry dock and, again, it was almost normal. Looking around I could see storm damage, but there was traffic, and people, and business being conducted, or so it seemed, or maybe I was just distracted by the young woman sitting next to me in the cab who was also returning for the first time (I heard her tell the driver) but spent the entire trip staring at her phone, apparently shopping for a leather jacket. Didn't she want to look around?

I made the four o'clock ferry and, on the boat, saw the first people I knew: Chef Harry and his wife, Kelly, whose wedding I had attended at Hawksnest back when we worked together at Shipwreck. The couple had been through both hurricanes and were just getting back from what should have been a respite up north, but the time away was too short and they were returning to chaos. They couldn't get the things they needed to rebuild their Coral Bay home. Harry had no job because Shipwreck was flattened beyond resurrection. Kelly, the National Park ranger, got lost driving around the island, so unrecognizable was the terrain where she worked for years, so foreign the beach where they got married. They looked wrecked. Slightly wild-eyed. Beyond exhausted. Later, I will hear this described as "the look."

Twenty minutes later we docked in St. John. Harry and Kelly disappeared into the crowd. Bustling, in-charge relief workers swarmed into view. Men and women in clean shirts labeled Bloomberg or Johns Hopkins greeted the ferry, off-loading boxes and bags, crucial supplies of something-or-other, tangible evidence that things were happening. This brave front was the island's narrative. The rallying cry was *St. John Strong!*

Waiting for me at the end of the dock was Cruz Bay Julia. She was one of the "do-ers." My friend who liked to joke that she did "as little as possible" was head of the Love City Fund, her job to help St. Johnians in need even before the worst storm in the island's history. Now she had a lot of company in her tiny office. FEMA and the Coast Guard and the National Park Service and the Army Corps of Engineers. Kenny Chesney's Love for Love City Foundation and Bloomberg Philanthropies and Love City Strong. She rattled off acronyms that I assumed spelled disaster relief and recovery: VITEMA, VOAD, DIRT, something called the BBC that apparently had nothing to do with British broadcasting but before I could get an explanation, she was off on another topic. She told me about the successes and setbacks of her day—the hurricane rumba, someone called it. One step forward, six steps back. Julia was relentlessly positive.

We had dinner at Mongoose Junction where the lights were

on and the place was buzzing. It was a good night, everyone said, because Sun Dog Phillip cooked on Tuesdays. Phillip was one of the best chefs on island, I was told. The dry-rub mahi was delicious.

Friends of Julia's waltzed by the table, over the moon: Their power had just come back on! After 10 weeks, a cause for celebration. Everyone seemed upbeat. But something about the whole scene felt off. I asked about Coral Bay, got head shakes in response. They heard it was bad. Even on the island, firsthand information about Coral Bay—eight miles away from where I was sitting—was out of reach.

Julia wouldn't answer my questions about her own little apartment, which she called Fort Julia. She had been off island during the hurricanes, and I suspected her home was ruined, but she wouldn't let me see it. Instead, we stayed at Coqui Cove, a villa she managed that fared well in the storms. The house was clean and comfortable. There was no power, but Julia had portable solar lights, plus a generator. She turned the generator on long enough for us to settle in, take brief hot showers, and flush the toilets before retiring for the night. The stars were out. The tree frogs were singing. Normal.

Not normal were the torrential downpours that kept me from getting to Coral Bay for two more days. The weather was malevolent. Nearly seven inches of rain fell during Irma, five more during Maria. It didn't stop there. After the hurricanes more rain followed. Biblical rain. An average year sees 48 inches. 2017 would end with a record-breaking 76 inches of rain, 42 of them in September, October, and November.

"The rain made everything green," said the man handing me keys to a rental Jeep. "Maybe God knows what he is doing. Maybe the island needed a cleansing."

A lot of the green was weeds but it was a welcome sight as I finally got on the road to Coral Bay. So were the bursts of red and orange from the flamboyant trees. The purple bougainvillea. And, always, the blue of the water. Those colors made for a stunning—

and incongruous—frame for the scenes of obliteration I was looking at. Nothing but rubble where the Chateau Bordeaux lookout used to be. Headless palms sticking out of Maho beach. An historic building at Cinnamon Bay, clawed open and exposed to the sea. Mounds of wood and metal that used to be somebody's home, clinging to the hillsides. The destruction was random: a house intact next door to a house collapsed, a "blue roof" tarp from the Federal Emergency Management Agency covering what was left. Blue used to be just the color of the water, but it had become a primary color of the land.

Downed and dead power and telephone lines still snaked across North Shore and Centerline roads, which were cratered with fetid potholes and littered with rocks from mudslides. Towering scoops of detritus occupied what was left of any shoulder or turnout, often turning the road to single track. There were more animals than cars. I saw donkeys. Mongooses. Goats. Deer. A lone bananaquit. It was hard to take it all in, harder still while trying to keep my eye on those treacherous-on-a-good-day roads. So many trees had been denuded or ripped from the roadside altogether, I could now see just how close I was to the cliff's edge.

I slogged across the island. Eventually I was inching down the other side of the mountain and Coral Bay came into view. I must have gasped. The pictures I'd seen did not prepare me.

"Coral Bay is lagging behind in infrastructure repairs," I had heard someone in a recovery office in Cruz Bay say. *Recovery slow going in Coral Bay* was the front-page headline on a recent edition of the *Virgin Islands Daily News*. Lagging? Slow going? Those statements were laughable. *Coral Bay a Combat Zone* would have been more appropriate. It looked like the hurricanes had just hit.

There was still just one road into Coral Bay so I knew I was in the right place, but I felt lost. Nothing looked right. All the landmarks were gone. The red roof of the Moravian Church, gone. The *Welcome to Coral Bay* sign at the Triangle, gone. Cars and roofs and homes and businesses, gone. People, too. Gone.

I turned at the Triangle, toward Shipwreck, and drove right past the place I used to work. How had I missed it? I doubled back. The restaurant wasn't demolished, it had vanished. Three barstools had been propped upright in front of the non-existent bar as if to summon the tourists, there just weeks before in search of conch fritters and mango coladas, now just ghosts.

I drove around in a stupor. The losses were catastrophic. The place looked beyond help. Beyond hope, even. And then I saw Erin. When I saw my friend in the flesh, breathing, in front of me, I felt a heartbeat. I knew I was back in Coral Bay.

Erin did not fare nearly as well as Cruz Bay friends but she was also—on this day, at least—relentlessly positive, her boisterous laugh buoying the people around her, her hugs consoling a young woman who started sobbing when we saw her in the Dolphin Market and asked how she was.

Erin needed to stop at Connections to see what that day's deliveries brought in. Jenn, the KATS instructor who taught me to sail, owned it now. She cried when she saw me but was too busy to stop working. Erin couldn't get the screws she needed to put a new roof on her house, but Jenn had to make a trash run every day to get rid of all the catalogs taking up precious space in her cramped office. Even in a hurricane, the junk mail gets delivered.

Erin opened a care package from Boston. Plumber Kathy sent a pair of work boots and clean socks—a big hit. A bag of trail mix was roundly rejected. Nobody wanted to see another bag of trail mix. I spoke up on behalf of the spurned gift. (I'd sent a few boxes of it myself.) People want to help and don't know how, I offered. Some well-meaning church sent blankets and sweaters. Not much use in a place where it's 80 degrees—at night. Medical supplies not from an official source had to be thrown away. Getting unwanted stuff off the island was as challenging as getting the needed stuff on. There's a reason relief organizations ask for cash.

I wanted to bring as much as possible with me when I flew down, but every single person I was able to communicate with ahead of time said they didn't need anything. "You know how it is down here," Julia always said. "When you don't see it, you don't know you need it." The truth was that many needed almost everything. This one needed a roof. That one needed water. Let's not even talk about the jobs just yet.

The final item in the care package was a Kenny Chesney Christmas CD with a $5 bargain bin sticker on the front. Erin gave it a big thumbs-down. Jenn snatched it up. Nobody was allowed to say anything bad about Kenny. Chesney was one of those people who had fallen truly, madly, deeply in love with St. John, and he'd funneled millions to the island since the hurricanes. It's because of him that Connections had a generator, meaning Jenn no longer had to conduct business in the dark, with a flashlight, in a hot and buggy office. It's because of him that Skinny Legs was getting a spanking new roof, and a real one at that, not just a piece of old sail cloth. To hear the locals talk, you'd think the country music star himself was hammering in the nails.

The new owners of Skinny's had been off island during the storms and in the information vacuum that followed, the rumors flew: Skinny's made it. Skinny's is totally gone. Skinny's is not only fine, but open! Serving up breakfasts, feeding storm survivors like it did after Hurricane Marilyn! It wasn't true. Just another piece of disaster misinformation, tinged with hopefulness and wishful thinking. Skinny's was destroyed, but not Shipwreck-destroyed. They could rebuild. James, the only cook left from my time there, the one I played darts with, was there every day to help, never mind that his own home was not OK. I thought of the island elder who once told me that after a hurricane, what you most need is "a purpose." *You need something to do. You have to stay active, so you don't get depressed.*

We needed the four-wheel drive to get through the muck that counted as a road to Erin's house. As we pulled up to her property, her façade faltered. Everything was trashed. The house, the car, the yard. Standing on her deck, she enumerated the losses. The roof was gone. The interior was dank and moldy. Her possessions were ruined. The food truck business she'd just opened was a total loss. Yet Erin believed every one of her neighbors was worse off than she was. The family next door was living under a tarp. The concrete apartment building beyond, where Arlene gave massages, was destroyed. Arlene had fled mid-storm when the roof went. We could see her car, upside down. Across the main road, by the water's edge, the pink building where Heidi drafted blueprints for sustainable housing and Elliot silkscreened T-shirts looked like a wrecking ball had smashed through it, more than once, exposing everything inside to the elements, and the looters. To the right, up the mountain, we could see where Pat and Dennis, the owners of Shipwreck, used to live. Dennis had a stroke.

The neighborhood's thick, lush terrain had mutated into something barren and bleak. Without trees, Erin's home had a water view, and we could see Coral Harbor. Normally there would be dozens of sailboats bobbing in the fresh breeze. Instead, boats were piled in heaps on the shoreline or sunk. Many of those boats were someone's home. Anna's home. Colin and Leah's home. Belle's home.

Erin pointed to a house across the valley with its second floor shorn off. The home belonged to a family with two daughters, she told me. After the storms, after their bedrooms were blown away and their life's belongings scattered in the wind, she watched the girls run down the hill, over and over, shrieking with joy every time they found something salvageable, or maybe just recognizable, to pluck from the rubble. *Daddy! I found a shoe! Look Daddy, my award certificate from fifth grade! Daddy! Daddy! The sewing machine!*

Erin showed me the musty closet where she and Bryan and Lindsay huddled, cross-legged, during Irma, water rising up to their waists. I had brought her new sheets and pillows, and I'm still embarrassed that she put them on the bed where I would be sleeping. She showed me how to pull buckets of water up from the cistern to flush the toilet. Pointed out all the hazards while it was still light: the yawning hole in the floor where they accessed the cistern; the stair railing on the left that was about to give way; the network of extension cords zigzagging across the floors to position as many fans as possible toward the beds, the only relief from the bugs. The generator would drone all night to keep the fans turned on.

The stove was out on the deck. A hose was strung to wash dishes. Erin, who I knew was one of the best chefs on the island, cooked dinner for half a dozen people—pasta with fresh vegetables, which had only recently begun appearing in the grocery store. Her kitchen was a shambles. She tried to shrug it off with a joke. She'd been thinking of downsizing anyway. Bryan suggested she put together a Cat 5 cookbook. Recipes featuring post-hurricane staples: Vienna sausages, SpaghettiOs, that off-brand spam that tastes like pancetta if you use your imagination. The meal was delicious. Halfway through, Erin mentioned she'd had to pick weevils out of the pasta. There was a brief pause in conversation, but nobody stopped eating.

AT 7:30 in the morning there was a traffic jam in front of the Disaster Recovery Center, across from Coral Bay's destroyed firehouse. I heard construction sounds. Chainsaws. A fleet of BBC trucks hit the road. BBC Electrical Services was the Joplin, MO-based utility contractor hired to repair the power lines. The linemen were working 12-hour days, seven days a week, the new heroes of St. John. The cavalry, someone called them. Eye candy, too. Amidst the obvious progress were other signs of hope. Three National Park beaches were officially open. One of Miss Lucy's sea grapes was flourishing on the beach in front of the closed restaurant and otherwise razed property. Delicate pink flowers bloomed across the top of the fence around the Coral Bay ball field, which was being used as a trash transfer station. Fat tufts of leaves emerged from the top branches of spindly trees, another image straight out of Dr. Seuss. An enormous tamarind, keeled over and uprooted, sprouted dainty shoots of green. While it's hard to see new growth as anything but positive, Erin confessed to wanting to send a big "Fuck You!" to Mother Nature for flaunting her fertility, for bouncing back when she, like so many others, could not.

We drove out to East End. It was one of those clear days that give a spectacular view of the BVIs. The British Virgin Islands had been devastated by Irma, too, but from a distance exuded normalcy. They were velvet green, verdant, and the sky and water were Caribbean blue, and then someone pointed out that Thanksgiving was just days away and there was not a single boat in Sir Francis Drake Channel. Not one. Not normal.

Erin checked on other friends whose property she had not seen. One home was covered with a blue tarp. Another was open to the sky. Someone was living in a tent. A big stone house looked untouched, a fortress. Everyone was in survival mode. I saw more people with "the look."

"I can tell you weren't here for it," one bedraggled woman said, inspecting me. "You're too clean."

"That hurricane was luck and chance and good and bad," said an islander who counted himself among the blessed, even though he lost his roof and his car, and both he and his wife, he said, were suffering from "hurricane brain."

I watched people greet each other, their faces inscrutable: "How are you?" "I'm good. How about you?" "Good. We're good." In some cases, I knew what "good" meant for one person who was speaking, and I can tell you it wasn't good. I could only imagine how the other person in this conversation was defining "good."

Sometimes I asked the question. "How are you?" I would say, more anodyne greeting than query, because it was impossible to tell who wanted to talk and who didn't. "Good," some would say, and I wouldn't have to ask any more questions because an hour and a half later, they would still be talking. About the 200-plus mile-per-hour wind. About the bathroom where they hid during

Irma's screaming eye wall. About the aftermath. The pulverized landscape. The people who came to help. The flotillas from St. Croix and Puerto Rico. The helicopters dropping food. The first responders. The rescuers who went door to door. The Red Cross working with any semi-functional restaurant to serve hot meals every day. And then the second storm. Maria. How the helpers all evacuated, and they still had no communications. They couldn't get the hurricane's coordinates. The second time they didn't know what was coming, or when. It was the island's own can-do spirit that saved them. People got out there as soon as it was over, said one survivor. "People were out there in flip-flops and chainsaws."

Every day was Groundhog Day, someone said. You started with the Shop-Vac, sucking up the previous night's rain or dirty water that seeped in from the ground. You worked all morning, cleaning up the mess. Call it whatever—debris, detritus, junk, waste, dross, crap, shit—it was everywhere. Mountains of it. You had to climb over it. Throw it away. Pry open a door and like a cartoon, another mountain of crap spilled out, muddy and moldy. A team of people worked day after day in a tiny place just getting rid of crap and weeks later it looked like they hadn't made a dent. You stopped around noon for the free meal and water at the fire station. Sometimes you got the good lunch—a piece of fresh fruit, or the turkey and cheese. The sandwich with the white cheese was OK. The yellow cheese was gross. If you had any energy left, you tried to go back to work, but the heat in September and October was intolerable. Without trees, without shade, people had to wear long sleeves and hats to protect themselves from the sun, UV rays one more hazard to worry about. You couldn't get a cold drink. You could wait half a day for a block or bag of ice and still not get it. If you wanted dinner, you had to boil water. If you wanted to shower, you had to haul water up from the cistern. You'd sweat while taking the shower. If you slept, it was only because you were exhausted. Try sleeping in the buggy heat with no fans or mosquito nets. But you were so tired. You fell in bed, passed out cold. They didn't need a 7 p.m. curfew. There was nothing to do at night and nowhere to go. And it was so dark. With every light on the island off? Black. At sunrise, you got up and did it again.

Residents who were off island during the storms had to wait weeks to get back. It took three weeks for commercial flights to resume after Maria. By that time, someone in the emergency management office had decided what hurricane victims needed most was a break. In another twist of apocalypse surrealism, some returning residents stepped off the ferry in Cruz Bay to find a party in the wrecked streets. The Cool Session Brass band was jamming in the park. St. John Brewers was handing out cold beer and ginger beer. "Welcome home!" one survivor greeted new arrivals, thrusting Painkillers in their faces.

The stories came out in pieces, as broken as the surroundings. The things they lost. The things they salvaged. The things giving them nightmares. For every victim reluctant to talk, another considered me the chronicler.

"Make sure you write about the bugs," someone said. They came in waves. The Jack Spaniard wasps, the mosquitoes, the no-see-ums, some big green things.

"Write about the hurricane diet." Everyone's lost at least 10 pounds; some of the men, 30.

"How are the taxi drivers faring?" They had no work.

"What about the kids?" A dance instructor said her dream was to organize a free trip to Disneyworld for her young students. She asked them to write down why they needed a break: "I'm tired of doing my homework by flashlight." "I'm being skinned by mosquitos." "I'm afraid of the dark." Anna Banana, the bartender from Skinny's—now a mother of two—told me how, when the family evacuated from the boat where they lived, her daughter had wanted desperately to take a favorite doughnut pillow with her but there was no room in the dinghy. The little girl soldiered through the storm, a five-year-old trooper, who didn't cry until a few days later when, asking when they'd go back to the boat to get her pillow, finally understood they were never going back.

"Write about PTSD." Three different friends, in separate conversations, mentioned wanting to learn more about PTSD. Not that they were worried about themselves, mind you, but they thought "some people" might be suffering from it. Any heavy rain or violent gust of wind was capable of triggering flashbacks. Almost every female friend—except for Belle—cried when I saw them, and I saw more than one grown man on the verge of very public tears. People were smiling, and they were determined, and they insisted they were optimistic, and it was just not possible that they were not very, very tired. The DIRT (Disaster Immediate Response Team) volunteers checking up on their neighbors carried clipboards with a list of assessment questions. One of them was: Do you feel you need emotional support? No, came the replies. I need a roof. I need a job. It was suggested that maybe the wording of the questionnaire should be changed: Do you feel like punching someone in the nose? That was a hard yes.

Some survivors had no break—no brief respite someplace safe and whole, away from the unimaginable loss—and none was in sight. Some were counting the days to a break coming up. One man told me he had been lucky to get up north to "decompose" for a couple of weeks. I wrote "decompress" in my notes but thought later that maybe he had it right.

ON THE SUNDAY before Thanksgiving there was more torrential rain. Businesses closed, plans had to be cancelled, roads were flooded and blocked by rockslides. Everybody holed up somewhere. It was damp and depressing. Forty inches of rain is unbearable.

They say fire is cleansing, but when water enters your house, it doesn't purge. It leaves behind a toxic mess. To clean it up you have to haul out mud and debris, dispose of shattered glass, throw away soggy furniture and textiles, get rid of the garbage. Disaster recovery experts call this "muck and gut," but some of St. John's local relief workers—victims themselves—didn't like the sound of that. These were their neighbors' lives they were talking about. Instead, whenever they accompanied distraught residents to what was left of their homes, they said they were going "treasure hunting." Together they would sift through the remains for anything worth saving—a piece of jewelry, a dish, a photo, a book—any buried keepsake, some sign that life "before" had not been eradicated.

They were a hopeful bunch, these island relief workers. Whether born of denial or natural optimism, their capacity to look at something so desolate and see mostly blue would prove to be a force in the aftermath as powerful as the hurricane winds. But their treasure hunting had an urgency, for anything not rescued soon, any memory of "what was" not foraged from the remnants and preserved with great care, was in danger of disappearing—scavenged by opportunists, lost in the rebuild, reclaimed by the land, or blown out to sea—in any case, gone forever.

12

THE NOTALOTTAYACHTA REGATTA
(THANKSGIVING, 2017)

On Thanksgiving Day the sun was shining and the climate was bittersweet. Families were separated, one parent on St. John, trying to rebuild; the other somewhere else, having evacuated with the children. Island kids were being enrolled in new schools, living with aunts or grandparents in New York or Oklahoma, North Carolina or Florida. Residents and relief workers mingled at the free turkey dinner hosted by the Rotary Club in Cruz Bay Park. And in Coral Bay, Long-Haired Ken was spearheading Thankspigging.

Of course he was going to have it, he told me. Why was I even asking? It was more needed than ever, with so many people without kitchens. Or homes. So his sponsor pool was "a little depleted." He'd make it work. The only question was where, as Skinny Legs had been ravaged, but by Thanksgiving, Skinny's was starting to resemble her old self again. The bar was newly varnished. Hot-pink paper pigs with white tulle wings and green pipe-cleaner tails hung from the rafters of the new roof.

The first person to greet me was Puerto Rican Pete who, I imagine, would survive actual Armageddon. His presence on Thanksgiving in Coral Bay was comforting, a vague sign of business as usual. Pete had recently acquired a bit of fame. His latest venture—a swim-up, floating bar called *Angel's Rest*—had been written up in the *New York Times* the previous spring, just a few months before Irma ripped the canary-yellow pontoon boat to pieces. *All that I owned swoooosh gone!* Pete wrote on Facebook. *Time to turn the page and start another chapter.* But after an outpouring of virtual support, Pete had a change of heart. In a burst of post-traumatic entrepreneurial spirit, he returned to Facebook 10 days after the hurricane, pledging to rebuild and promising a day of fun and free drinks later to anyone who sent him $100 now.

Pete had been at every Thankspigging since it started 17 years earlier and he wasn't missing this one. "I lost everything so it's nice to be here with people that probably lost everything too," he said. Chef Benji, who roasted the pig, said he was thankful to be helping out his friend Kenny, and his community. Jeff from Drunk Bay Brewing, another regular, fried three turkeys and brought beer. He wasn't happy with the brew, done "under extreme circumstances," but it was free, so he was not expecting any complaints.

I snapped a photo and, just like at my first Thankspigging, was reproached for pulling out the camera, first by Ken, then by Pete. "Don't take a picture of that!" Ken pleaded. He was embarrassed by the "little, skinny pig," a fraction of the size he wanted but all he could get. Pete was doing the carving. The aging pirate didn't want his picture taken until he took off his glasses.

Football? Please. There wasn't even any power. But those who could brought homemade side dishes and desserts, and before long the bar was crammed with food. "We need some normalcy and a sense of camaraderie," said one survivor as she arranged platters on the buffet. Life was hard without power. Without telephone, television, or internet. "You hear stories that the military can go into the middle of the deep dark jungle and set a system up in 24 hours and here we are, almost three months later."

And yet, she thought she was lucky. Everyone thought they were lucky. Everyone thought they did better than their neighbors. This was a community that prided itself on taking care of its own. No man was an island. If someone needed help, you put out a jar. But this time? There weren't enough jars.

The line for dinner snaked all through Skinny's and out into the parking lot. The roast pig was mouthwatering. Long-Haired Ken made a speech. They weren't just *St. John Strong!* "We're Coral Bay Fucking Tough!" he toasted. The crowd cheered as Ken showed off the Thankspigging commemorative T-shirts. The theme was Irma La Douche.

One thing Coral Bay did not lose was its sense of humor.

Two days later, as was tradition, sailors from the Coral Bay Yacht Club convened for a regatta. The NotALottaYachta Regatta.

At first glance, it looked just like my first Thanksgiving regatta, like all those other regattas. Another picture-perfect Caribbean day on the water. Same bright sunshine. Same puffy white clouds. That impossibly blue sea. But everything was wrong. Once-proud sailboats lay in splinters up on the rocks and all around the shoreline. Most of the boats that were floating had no rigging. No masts. *Calabreeze*, the last of the Coral Bay Cowhorns still sailing on St. John, was among the mountain of wrecked vessels. Birdie couldn't even find his boat, *Dolphin*. Belle refused to talk about *O'dege*, but I could see her Fighting Lady Yellow hull across the harbor. She was mastless. The racing boat looked sad and lifeless, like all the fight had gone out of her.

Not so for her captain who, as commodore of the yacht club, was hell-bent on making this day happen.

Belle and I were standing on the deck of the haunted tall ship *Silver Cloud*. A black-hulled, 110-foot fortress of iron, *Silver Cloud* looked like a pirate ship and, like many of her Coral Bay neighbors, had a checkered past. A Great Lakes pilot schooner, she was built in 1899 in Thunder Bay, Ontario. Her history included action in both world wars, rum-running during Prohibition, missionary work, drug smuggling, and sitting on the bottom of Lake Ontario for 20 years after sinking in a storm. Captain and crew sometimes heard the faint sounds of a radio, somewhere below decks, still tuned to a 1930s Cleveland Indians baseball game.

Captain Elliot Cook Hooper—a descendent of that Captain Cook—took possession of *Silver Cloud* in Key West in 1987, spent the better part of three years restoring her in Trinidad, sailed her to St. John, and arrived in Coral Bay on September 17, 1989 —a day ahead of Hurricane Hugo. In the aftermath of that disaster, *Silver Cloud* rescued 10 boats, and Elliot's new business, Coral Bay Salvage, was born. Eight years later, *Silver Cloud* was the victim. In 1995 Hurricane Marilyn batted her right out of the water. She would spend nine months on the side of Coral Bay's only road, shutting down traffic with every attempt to get her floating again.

I have a photo of *Silver Cloud* from a flotilla a decade earlier that shows what she's supposed to look like. Bright white sails and trim. Fresh paint on deck and topsides. A line of colorful maritime signal flags flying high. The passengers that day were children from Guy Benjamin Elementary School, Coral Bay's only school, which was now permanently closed. The flotilla was raising money for the school's playground. I remember how joyful those kids were on that hot spring day, jumping over and over from the bowsprit into the cool Caribbean Sea.

Silver Cloud was serving as committee boat for the NotALot-taYachta Regatta. She couldn't sail. The three-masted schooner had no masts at all. Irma had snapped them like a trio of twigs. Her flags were strung across the deck, faded and in tatters. Despite the captain's best efforts, *Silver Cloud* looked tired, like everyone aboard her. One of the few ships still floating after Irma, she had been hard at work since, leading the salvage efforts in Coral Bay. Captain Elliot pulled sunken boats out of the drink, testing to see if they were worth saving. Thirty-seven boats so far. Zero worth saving. "It's a horror show," he said.

Belle appraised the handful of jury-rigged boats tacking around *Silver Cloud*, waiting for the race to start. She was irked.

She expected better turnout. She had a few choice words for some yacht club members who stayed home. Where was the couple whose boat survived?

Survivor's guilt, someone said. They didn't want to put their good fortune on display.

What about the guy who said he'd crew but didn't show?

"He's being a pussy," Belle said.

"Some people aren't ready, Belle," said Erin.

The commodore was unconvinced.

"They should grow a pair."

AMONG THE SAILORS not at the regatta was Eddie Z. Eddie grew up landlocked in Ohio, and first set eyes on the Virgin Islands in 1995, two days after Hurricane Marilyn. He came down for a two-week job putting tarps on damaged roofs and ended up staying 22 years. After a few years of island life, Eddie bought a boat and then taught himself to sail, and anyone who thinks that sounds ass-backwards hasn't spent enough time in Coral Bay, where your lifelong-sailor neighbors will be more than happy to help you master your new hobby while simultaneously taking delight in watching you plow your boat up onto a reef every now and then.

Eddie learned enough to start doing charters on his 36-foot ketch, *Roadrunner*. When the conch shell blew, it meant Captain Eddie was taking a boatload of tourists out for a sunset sail or whooping it up with a free ride for the locals on a slow day. On August 28, 2017, he advertised a last-minute special for the next day. It was not promoted as a valedictory sail. The captain had no reason to think it would be his last time at *Roadrunner's* helm.

After that sail, as Tropical Storm Irma formed off the coast of Africa, Eddie flew to Colorado for a Labor Day weekend wedding, which is where he was when Irma strengthened to a Category 5 hurricane. Flights were cancelled. The ports closed.

Eddie couldn't get home. But *Roadrunner* was secure in Water Creek in Hurricane Hole, the protected harbor in National Park territory. Eddie had done all the prep work—scoped out his spot, set all his anchors—and friends helped him finish the job. His boat got slapped with an orange sticker, a warning for putting out too much line. Eddie ignored it. A Coral Bay sailor who had died —tragically, and somewhat mysteriously—before the storms had taught him how to prepare. Eddie trusted Vince. He'd take the fine.

While Eddie waited out Irma stateside, he set up a Facebook page where people could share information about St. John. A few days after the hurricane, he shared news of his own: *Roadrunner* was floating! A small miracle, given that most of the boats in Hurricane Hole sank, or were tossed on land. Maybe it was that extra 20 feet of line. Eddie was vindicated. He was fine. His boat survived. He was one of the lucky ones, or so it seemed, until 10 days later, when he posted that *Roadrunner* was for sale. A good price for the right person. Her captain would not be returning to St. John because he no longer had a job there and wouldn't for the foreseeable future. "I'm starting a new life out west somewhere," he wrote. He would spend Thanksgiving in northern California, 3,750 miles from Coral Bay.

FOURTEEN "BOATS" raced in the Coral Bay Yacht Club's 36th annual Thanksgiving Regatta and, commodore's displeasure notwithstanding, many of the stalwarts were present and accounted for, helming anything that would float. Colin and Leah on *Buxom's Revenge,* pieced together from scraps of their sailboat, sunk and in two pieces. Surfer Lori on *Wizard,* "Frankensteined" with this and that with help from a friend, plus a mainsail plundered from a neighbor. Michael on *Indigo,* a glorified raft named for the restaurant that fed the residents of Coral Bay in the days after Irma. *Indigo* was a parody of a square-rigged catamaran, crafted from a couple of patched-up inflatable dinghies, a wheelchair, and an old ceiling fan "to make it look like propulsion." Every bit of her was salvaged, including the crew. The boat had to be towed out into the harbor for the start of the race because she could only sail downwind. The unproven seaworthiness of the vessels prompted a special rule: Life jackets were mandatory.

Rounding out the ragtag fleet was a sprinkling of Sunfish and Lasers from KATS—the small boats I learned to sail on. Anna Banana and her family lost their boat, which was their home, all their possessions, and their business, but she was out there sailing. Donkey Diner Doug, who looked like he was trying to remember how to sail a little dinghy, had written an obit for his big boat, *Runaway: RIP ... With the exception of my late mother,* Runaway *has been with me longer than any woman ... Davy Jones rest your soul.* English Clare sailed with her seven-year-old son in his child-sized Opti (short for—fittingly, I realize later—Optimist). When the roof came off their house, everything inside was ruined by flood or blown away, except that little sailboat. "We haven't got a house, but we've got a boat!" she said.

The countdown began. Someone picked up *Silver Cloud*'s VHF to relay the start sequence. Someone else pointed out that no one racing had a working radio. There was a frantic search for a whistle, but between KATS/Connections Jenn's formidable lungs and Erin's natural bullhorn cheerleading, the ladies had it covered. The two-minute warning was called out over the stern of the boat. Now what about a timepiece? Did anyone have a decent watch? Are we doing that? someone asked. A decision was made to just note winners, not times. "Remember when we used to have regattas with official time?" Erin said. Belle hopped into a Laser, ready to start.

"Racing!" Jenn yelled.

"Look at us!" shouted Erin. "We're having a regatta!"

While the larger boats headed out to sea, the rest of the sailors singlehanded Sunfish and Lasers on a course set up around *Silver*

Cloud. Some of the racers had not sailed small boats in a decade or more.

"You're on the start line!" Belle hollered at one struggler.

"You want a Heineken?" Erin encouraged.

On the first of the round-robin races, Vicki got a sheet wrapped around a cleat, lost steering, and capsized. Sailor Shirley flipped over, too, but quickly uprighted her boat, scrambled back on board, and was off again. To where was a bit confusing; the markers kept drifting because the small anchors securing them were dragging. Big Steve motored around, trying to reposition them. "They're not gonna stay," he shouted. "You got anything heavier?"

"Oh my God, PURE EXCITEMENT!" said a straight-faced spectator.

"It's like a big-screen TV!" gushed Erin, someone who hadn't had television—or any power—in three months. It was the best thing she'd done since the storms.

Every so often a dinghy buzzed the committee boat. One had a messed-up tiller. Another lost a clew tie-down. This one needed a Heineken. Uh-oh, Shirley tipped over again. Anna Banana had a disabled rig. Her hands hurt but she was laughing. She didn't tip over. That was her goal. "So I'm a winner!" she said. The small boat racing turned out to be so much fun, someone suggested it become a regular part of future regattas. "Screw the big boats," said Elliot, adding, "Because there aren't any."

The NotALottaYachta post-regatta party was held aboard *Silver Cloud.* Erin grilled hot dogs and burgers. The captain, who had to move his silkscreen business back on board after his studio space was leveled, printed souvenir T-shirts down below. People were happy. Many of them were on the water for the first time since their lives were torn apart.

"Being on the water is healing," said Vicki, the KATS instructor who hooked me up for my first long-distance sail. She and her husband, Lord Thatcher, should have been racing their boat, but *Trinka* sank in the storms.

"Life goes on. And that's just stuff ashore," said Shirley, drenched from capsizing. "I survived! I'm a survivor. I'm still surviving. That's what I do. I survive."

———

THE FIRST WEEK OF DECEMBER, Eddie Z. announced that *Roadrunner* had been sold. By the New Year, he would be in Denver, where he had a job lined up for a month. Beyond that? Who knew. But, once again, landlocked.

13

HURRICANE RUMBA

By December I was landlocked, too.

After Thanksgiving, I returned to New York, to work and family obligations. Like all those other times after leaving St. John, I felt like I'd left a piece of myself behind.

I still didn't really know what happened. Nobody did. And what about the long-term impact of two major hurricanes? After that initial disaster voyeurism, when the storyline fizzles, and the cameras move on, and the news fades from the headlines—assuming it was ever in the headlines—what happens next? What happens to the people who survive but lose everything except their lives? What happens to a place? Is paradise lost?

It was a mentor from my old TV days who suggested maybe I was the one who should go back and try to find out. Never mind that I hadn't been employed as a journalist in over a decade.

"I don't have a platform," I whined.

He thought that was beside the point. He was no longer in the news business, either. But we both knew a story when we saw one.

Once again, I didn't really have a plan. But I thought maybe if I could go back several times over the course of a year—in between paid assignments at home, whenever someone could offer me a place to stay—I might be able to answer some of those questions.

I returned in January and one Sunday morning was walking the path along Leinster Bay. It was so different. There were rocks and coral where there used to be dirt. The mangroves looked dead. Didn't there used to be a "fairy forest" approach of overhanging trees? I struggled to bring memories into focus. It was hard to remember what it used to look like.

A beached boat blocked the path, a cartoon snorkeler painted on the side looking surprised to be hovering over land. A little farther along, another sailboat, named *New Horizons,* was hard aground. New horizons indeed. Irma had altered the topography of St. John.

The National Park beaches were all open—although you had to bring your own shade since the trees were gone—greeting the smattering of tourists who arrived on the cruise ships that had begun returning to St. Thomas or stayed in villas with minimal damage. The two big resorts were still closed, one indefinitely. The hiking trails were open, too. The one I was on with friends that morning, the Johnny Horn, was familiar. The views were not. But they were gorgeous, and it was a glorious day. It was high season, after all, that time of year when the grandeur of the island's natural beauty is enhanced by textbook Caribbean Vacation Weather.

I took photos. Vibrant pink flowers carpeting the landscape. Butterflies leading our way. A sailboat or two on the water in the distance. It had been nearly five months since the hurricanes and pretty pictures like this had been popping up in Facebook posts and on island blogs. I was back up north when I first saw them, bundled against 20-degree cold in New York, fighting off the doldrums that come when it's dark at 4:30 in the afternoon.

Social media has filled the vacuum left by the demise of old-fashioned news coverage, with mixed results. Never was I so happy to be on Facebook as in the week after Irma, when people could share information about who was safe. Throughout the fall, social media was an outstanding tool for those in a position to help to organize relief efforts. Come winter, though, plundered islands, desperate for tourists to return, started going online to put their best face forward—often with little context. Posts with nary a mention of any hurricane were wildly skewed. *Look!* they seemed to say. See the crystalline water beckoning. Hear the siren's call of that tropical beach you fantasize about on a frigid winter's day. After those post-storm satellite photos showing all that brown where there should have been green, these colorful images were a hopeful sight. They were also unfiltered. I knew this because I was looking at the real thing with my own eyes. But were they the truth? They deceived. They didn't show the scenes of devastation, just out of frame. They only told part of the story.

Was the island even ready for tourists? Opinions were fierce and disparate. Those who fell on the good side of luck and chance were naturally eager for business to get going again, as were those less fortunate who depended on tourism for their livelihoods and, moreover, their futures on St. John. Others saw the weakened infrastructure and strained ability to serve the local people and said the island was not close to ready. One person squarely in the not-ready camp reminded me that the clinic had been condemned and there was scant access to health services. There was little room for error.

We climbed higher. A brief rain shower cooled us off just as it was getting a little too hot. All the trails were hotter than normal. As on the beaches, there was no shade. But there was bright green grass beneath our feet, and that was something new, also welcome.

We were walking over land that used to be covered with sugar cane. We stopped at the ruins of the Murphy Great House, once home to St. John's biggest sugar producer and a slave trader. There was a sweeping view of Waterlemon Cay and the Annaberg Plantation, where hundreds of slaves once sweat, bled, toiled, suffered, and died in a place we now call paradise. A young woman in our group—a first-time visitor—had taken the

Annaberg tour and recounted grisly details, giving our hike a sobering narration.

Coming down the other side of the summit, the slope was muddy and slick from so much rain the previous few days. I pussyfooted through the slippery muck, claiming the view of Coral Bay as an excuse for my feeble pace. From up there I could look down on Emmaus Moravian Church, where on a normal Sunday morning you might hear the choir singing. But not this day. The historic church—more than 200 years old—was silent and vacant, appearing untouched since Irma ripped off its red roof.

The pastor and his wife had been inside the manse when it began to fly apart. They were in the kitchen putting Johnnycake in the oven when they heard the wind shift. Then it started whistling. Tornadoes. Outside on the hillsides there was nothing but white. They moved toward the bathroom, the most protected part of the house, but the pastor detoured to his office, hoping to save important documents. As the storm intensified, his wife screamed for him to COME, to abandon his search, but he couldn't hear because of the noise. She was frantic. When she went looking for him, he shouted to her that the roof was gone. They retreated to the bedroom, where they huddled until the storm ceased.

They survived. Providence had been at work. The church's flooded fellowship hall was supposed to be a shelter but, at the last minute, the fire marshal had denied permission. Who knows how many people might have been in there?

Across the street from the church, in the ball-field-turned-trash-transfer-station, piles of metal, wood, and other debris grew. Remnants of lives towered neatly in sorted heaps, waiting to be carted away. A travesty to use a recreation space, some said. A sign of progress, said others.

Around the corner, a life-size doll sat on the porch of Pickles in Paradise, hoisting a martini glass. The restaurant was open for brunch and a saxophonist played as diners—tourists, locals, and recovery teams full of get up and go—ate omelettes and stuffed French toast. As the island rejuvenated, residents were also putting forth a brilliant display of resilience, belying the recent trauma. A Coral Bay friend told me, giddily, that her check was coming on Wednesday. It's what she told me on my first trip down two months earlier: *My check is coming on Wednesday!* It's what the insurance company had been telling her for weeks, and now months.

This was the context. That indefatigable woman helping other victims? She was homeless. That persevering man rebuilding his neighbor's roof? He was separated from his kids, who were staying with relatives in the States. That bubbly lady serving up the free meal hadn't had power—or water—for five months. That smiling little boy had been doing his homework by flashlight. Oh, also homeless? The photographer taking all the pretty pictures.

Nature, in such a fertile place, was recovering much more quickly than the people who lived beneath her blossoming trees or beside her immaculate waters. People, it turned out, were not as ripe for transformation as the plants. Sometimes a picture needs those thousand words.

WHEN I RETURNED for that second trip, I got an airport pickup from Cruz Bay Julia who was on St. Thomas shopping. She had managed to squeeze onto an overcrowded car barge from St. John that morning, her vehicle wedged between the dump trucks and garbage trucks hauling waste off the island. On many days only one barge was running, a single lifeline to the outside world. There should have been at least four boats, but only two survived the storms and it was a rare day that both were making the trip across the Sound. One more anomaly conspiring to interrupt the supply chain, to halt the recovery. Everything that comes onto the island—food and water, mail, medicine, fuel, building materials, relief workers—as well as the refuse going off, has to go by boat. Everything. As the President of the United States said about Puerto Rico, "This is an island surrounded by water. Big water. Ocean water." He got that right.

Julia needed to buy new furniture for Coqui Cove, the villa she managed. The first real renters—not the National Park workers who had been staying in the house since the lights came back on—were coming at the end of the week. A brand-new $5,000 generator sat on the property, uninstalled. The perimeter of the house was a construction zone, with laborers putting in 12-hour days. The deck around the pool needed to be replaced but the tiles hadn't arrived. *Soon come,* the suppliers said. The pressure was on.

It was KATS Jenn who, in an early dispatch from the front lines, described life in the aftermath as a rumba: *Steps to the left side, steps to the right, and repeat again ... but how many steps forward and how many steps back keeps changing.*

Those with money to pay for supplies and the means to procure them were rebuilding. Those who knew how to build or fix or clean were working. On a hill approaching the traffic circle in town, there was a yellow road sign reading "AHEAD" in black lettering. Above it someone had nailed a piece of wood, painted a tropical aqua, with the words "Better Days" written in a cheerful purple. *Better Days Ahead.* A rosy sentiment. Those without money had miles to go.

St. John was not hurting on the scale of Puerto Rico, but many people were suffering. Pre-hurricanes the poverty rate, territory-wide, was over 20 percent. Disasters do discriminate. Against poor families. Against the seniors.

Life was in flux, and a study in contrasts: An amalgam of superhuman progress and stifling inertia. Functioning-pretty-well juxtaposed with broken-beyond-repair. Cruz Bay versus Coral Bay. There'd always been a disconnect between the two sides of the island, but the chasm seemed wider than ever; the sense of being relegated to second-class status, deeper. I was shocked by how few people from town still hadn't driven the eight miles to see what was happening on the other side.

Some people had only just gotten the power back on, and there was no guarantee it would stay on. Think about that: Five months with no power. Every aspect of a daily routine has to be improvised. The new normal meant turning the generator on once a day to goose the fridge, take a shower, flush a toilet. No power means no water. You could run the generator all night, but then you're annoying your neighbors, not to mention running through fuel. Then it's the rigmarole of buying more, another hour and a half in line, another full day gone.

Soon come. Progress was slow. Painfully slow. Islanders were used to slowdowns and shutdowns, but not like this. Internet and cell service were temperamental in town and practically non-existent in Coral Bay. A new era in island communications had dawned since Moe had to drive around looking for a waitress to cover a shift at Skinny's. Residents had grown accustomed to having phones that actually worked. Think waiting on hold for your insurance company or bank is a drag? Try doing it with service that cuts off after you've been on hold for an hour. Have the money to hire a plumber or electrician? Lucky you. Except you can't make a call. Now you're back to hoping you'll run into a contractor while you're out doing your errands.

By some estimates, the island population was about half of what it was pre-storms, but people were returning every day. There were fewer people with that wild-eyed "look." Fresh blood was welcome. It was overwhelming, how much there was to do. Preposterous amounts of paperwork. Small tasks took on Sisyphean proportions. Whole days were wasted trying to get one thing done. One woman said she put "accomplish nothing" on her to-do list every morning, just so she could cross it off at the end of the day.

Everyone was waiting for checks—from FEMA, from other government agencies, from their insurance companies. Like my friend in Coral Bay, the one whose check was promised on

Wednesday, they needed cash to start rebuilding. But another Wednesday comes and goes. Maybe next week.

ON A WEEKDAY MORNING, I made the rounds in Coral Bay. I drove past Coral Bay Organic Gardens, from which Josephine supplied her famous greens to grocery stores and the best restaurants on island. Thirty years of work gone in a few hours. Her son was struggling to save the family farm. Crabby's snorkel shack, under new management, was wrecked. OK, so it was, in fact, a shack, but it was a viable business, somebody's livelihood. Some business owners confessed to a crisis of faith. The island had betrayed them. Why risk rebuilding? Why all the work and the heartache and the hardship when it could all be gone again? It was daunting. Futile. Better to just walk away.

I noticed Oasis had set up a makeshift drive-through. The restaurant was another open-air shack, but it was taking advantage of the razed periphery, letting cars drive around the back and order food from a window behind the bar. A Coral Bay chuckle.

I stopped at the Cliffhanger and tried to peek inside. It had been remodeled, pre-hurricanes, and now hid behind a locked gate, but it appeared to have withstood Irmaria. There was a slick new parking platform that let you pull in, easy, right off the road. Whoever lived in it now wouldn't have to do that crazy Jedi move to back down a steep driveway. Testing out the parking platform, I turned around and headed back toward the Triangle.

Now, even long-time residents found driving terrifying. "I never knew there was an 800-foot drop-off," said one woman of a road near her house. "I was driving it like I was on the Indy 500 in the old days. I couldn't drive it for the first two months. It scared the bejesus out of me." With trash piled everywhere, there was even less room to maneuver, and you had to worry about flat tires. One man told me he didn't leave home without an air compressor and a couple two-packs of tire patches. If you only needed, say, three patches a day, that was a good day. But the breakdowns you really had to watch out for were the mental ones.

When I popped into Connections, I heard the same story from Jenn. Driving up to Bordeaux, she told me, people would shout *Stop the car! Stop the car!* and get out and walk the rest of the way. The same thing was happening to her, my strong, self-sufficient friend admitted. "Something that you had BALLS about before. I'd drive anywhere!" She didn't realize how much the foliage camouflaged. Now it was all revealed: The eroding road under that hairpin turn. The cliff's edge. The perilous drop-off. Now she started hyperventilating. She got light-headed. Nauseous. Vertigo.

"Now I have fear," she said, voice breaking.

We were interrupted when someone walked into the office. "How are you?" "Good! You?" "Good. I'm good." This was the only answer. *Good.* Where do I get one of those free generators, a man wanted to know. Across the street at the DRC, the Disaster Recovery Center. The door opened again. "How you doing?" "Good. You?" "We're good." Is the mail in yet, a sailor asked. He was thrilled to open a package of the Great Courses DVDS. His disintegrated in Irma and the company replaced them. For free! He was ecstatic, holding them up for me to see: Bach and the High Baroque. I wondered if he even had a DVD player. Or a boat.

How do you deal with it, I asked, when Connections quieted down. The fear? How do you handle that?

Jenn answered in a whisper. "I cry."

I SPENT a week talking to survivors. The mechanic who was sucked out of his house, clutching a door handle, on the same piece of land where his grandfather was blown to his death in a hurricane in the 1920s. The boat builder who was knocked unconscious and lay outside, bruised and bleeding, as the eye wall passed over, slashing her shirt to shreds. The waitress who jumped from a second story window as her home collapsed around her. The sailor who thought he could ride it out on his boat and, when the boat started sinking, swam for his life and clung to a rock. A caretaker showed me a tree impaled by flying debris from Irma. A piece of wood cut deep into the heart of the trunk, lodged there with the force of a giant swinging a sledgehammer. What if that tree had been a person? Wood puncturing not bark but flesh? I thought of Sweet Sarah, running for her life with a bucket over her head. I heard secondhand a story about a family huddled together on a sofa bed that, after their house blew apart, slid down a hillside with everyone on it, safe. It sounded apocryphal; exaggerated, at least. But maybe not.

The stories trickled out as slowly as those first bits of information post-storm. Not everybody was ready to talk. Not Belle. Not Julia.

Miraculously, no one from St. John died in Irma or Maria, or so it was reported—erroneously. No one died on land. But Richard Benson, a charter captain and father, died on the water, and land and water are hard to separate on an island. There had been a few write-ups about Benson. He died trying to outrun Hurricane Irma on his 84-foot wooden boat, *Goddess Athena*. His body washed up in the BVI. His boat was still missing. I was confused when, later, I heard conflicting details. The boat was a metal trimaran not a wooden monohull. His boat washed ashore in the Dominican Republic; his body was never found. Wait, wasn't it the other way around? I finally realized, talking to Captain Colin in Coral Bay, that we were talking about two different people. There was a second death.

"We keep hearing nobody died on St. John," I said.

"Nobody died," Colin said. "Just two boaters."

THINGS GOT DONE. By the end of my stay, the new furniture had been delivered to Coqui Cove. The last tile got laid before the first guest arrived. My friend in Coral Bay got her insurance check. It didn't come on Wednesday, but it did come on Friday. Private money was flowing in, too. Bill Clinton—who, during his presidency, designated the water around Coral Bay a national monument—paid a visit, with a promise of cash from his foundation. It couldn't come too soon. Hurricane season was just four months away.

14

MAROONED

Later that winter, when I was back in New York, I was scheduled to go visit Pat, the owner of Shipwreck. She was living across the river in New Jersey, staying with family and nursing her sick husband, debilitated by the stroke he suffered after Irma. My plans to see my former island boss were scuttled by, of all things, a blizzard, and I'll confess to being a little relieved I didn't have to look her in the eyes. What could I possibly say to someone who lost everything, including her foothold in paradise? She must have stared out at the icy landscape and concluded that her Caribbean life had all been a dream.

So many hurricane survivors were far from home. Jungle George evacuated after Irma and wouldn't return. There were no jobs. No places to live. Sweet Sarah was preparing to leave Coral Bay. Another casualty of a spectacularly demolished economy. She knew her boss was being fair, dividing the work evenly among the staff, but a shift or two a week wasn't paying the bills. Plus, it was exhausting listening to the second-home owners complain about minor damage or the vagaries of island building. Didn't they realize they might be talking to someone who was homeless? Who escaped with only the clothes on her back?

It took me months to track down Captain Marty but one

spring afternoon we were hunched over the bar at a place called Peg Legs in Tortola with another old sea dog, Captain Robin. Marty had been mostly MIA since his beloved boat, *Ruffian*—his home—sank in Irma. Some say it was one towering wave that took out a cove packed with sailboats, an entire fleet submerged or dashed on the rocks in one fell swoop. But we were avoiding that subject, talking instead about old times.

I had met Captain Marty a decade earlier at a regatta called the Dark and Stormy when, in a typical Coral Bay misadventure, the boat I started out on ran aground. Captain Marty dinghied out to help get us off the reef, and I recognized him as the man Team Skinny Legs referred to as the Turkey Sandwich Guy. When *O'dege*'s jib ripped at the Sweethearts Regatta, he lent Belle one of his sails. When it didn't fit properly, he came back with sandwiches. I remember thinking: What's this guy's deal? He just dinghies around rescuing sailors in distress? Like some knight errant of the high seas?

After we were towed safely to port, Marty invited me to join the crew of *Ruffian,* a fast boat named for a champion thoroughbred who broke a string of horseracing records. I was wary. I had never sailed with someone I didn't know, but it was either that or stay behind on land. I hopped aboard. It was kismet. Marty turned out to be from the same New Jersey town as me. We were born in the same hospital. We had a sublime sail from Tortola to the fabled Tierra Anegada—drowned, or flooded, land, the Spanish had christened it—and when we arrived, our captain saluted his crew and the marvelous day with his trademark toast: *Some people will never get a day like this in their whole lives.*

After the celebration, I faced a dilemma: Where would I sleep? Bunking on *Ruffian* would be awkward. And there was the stigma. Have a sleepover on a man's boat and, even if you kept your clothes on, conventional wisdom says you didn't.

In the end I was too tired to give a damn about my reputation. I needn't have worried. Captain Marty was the consummate gentleman, giving me the best berth and sleeping, well, I'm not even sure where—or if—he slept. He may have been up all night because when I awoke and stumbled up to the cockpit, there was the chivalrous captain sipping coffee and listening to NPR. I'd been radio and television news-free for over a year in Coral Bay. How he tuned in to public radio in that remote spot, I still don't know. We sat on deck and talked. Marty told me about his late friend Bernie, a World War II veteran who used to sail with him on *Ruffian* and whose flag Marty flew in his honor during regattas. It was a most civilized morning, one that reminded me to trust my instincts. Captain Marty's kindness was a gateway to jumping on all those strangers' boats that got me across the ocean and back.

After coffee we dinghied over to *Kuralu* where the engaging Captain Robin, a Brit, was mixing up Bloody Marys while his crew shucked oysters for breakfast. Robin gave me a tour of his catamaran, pointing out the plaque he won at the inaugural Dark and Stormy. "I came in first that year, they immediately changed my rating, and I haven't won since," he sighed. Two years later, a friend of Robin's would let Fun Christina and me stay on her little sailboat in Valencia, Spain, when New Zealand challenged Switzerland for yachting's biggest prize. That's the thing about Coral Bay. One minute you're on a boat, running aground before your race even starts. Next thing you know, you've got a front-row seat at the America's Cup.

I thought these captains were old salts back then. Now both men were just shy of 80, and one of them was foundering like the boat that precipitated our friendship. I looked at the two of them sitting side by side, both wearing their Mount Gay racing caps. Robin's was bright red, new and unweathered, from the BVI Spring Regatta held just a couple weeks prior. Marty's cap was faded, sun- and salt water-bleached to an acid-washed pink. His was from the Sweethearts of the Caribbean race in 2016, not too far in the past unless you were a marooned seafarer, in which case it was forever ago.

It was hard not to compare the fortunes of these two friends.

Robin was, that very day, overseeing a frenzied push to get his new boat, a 31-foot sloop, ready to launch. He had a time slot to "splash"—put the boat back in the water—that afternoon, but the bottom was still being painted, and the pulpit had to be installed, and a few other odds and ends needed tweaking, and you were unlikely to get anyone's undivided attention at the marina for more than a few minutes. The boatyard was packed, injured vessels all around, the pungent smell of fiberglass heavy in the air. Nautical triage.

Captain Marty, meanwhile, had just flown in from somewhere to look at a potential new boat, but his lead didn't pan out. Eight months now he'd been looking for a ship, and not one of his leads had panned out, disappointment after disappointment piling up on top of the destruction, the weight of it all obvious in the slump of his shoulders. He was cagey when I asked where he had been living, admitting only to visiting friends around the U.S. He'd put some 16,000 miles on his car in the previous months, he told me, visiting and boat shopping. I pictured him driving aimlessly, lost, in the bigger sense. A castaway. I wondered how many nights he had slept in his car.

For every person doing all right, there was someone sitting next to them who had lost everything. Their story was being played out everywhere, winners and losers, side by side.

The last time the three of us were together my father had just died. We had been in a similar position, slouched over a table of drinks, and talking about death.

I had been at sea on a boat delivery when Dad passed away, meaning I didn't get the urgent voicemails saying he was dying until we got to port and by then he was gone. We had been mostly estranged, our relationship rocky, but I was still consumed with guilt. I was sad that we'd never fully reconciled, I told the two surrogates sitting across from me.

One old salt nodded. He had been having troubles with his son. The other old salt said he regretted not having a chance to tell his father certain things before he died. There was a brooding moment of silence.

Captain Robin sighed. "Let's talk about sailing."

Somehow the conversation that long-ago day had been more upbeat than the one we were trying to have at Peg Legs.

I suggested a drive over to Soper's Hole, where both men used to keep their boats. "You don't want to go there, sweetheart," said one. The harbor that served as the finish line for all those bygone regattas was on the West End of Tortola, just across the water from the East End of St. John and Coral Bay. Like Coral Bay, West End was wiped out. If you look at a map, you can visualize Hurricane Irma barreling straight down the Sir Francis Drake Channel, her eye walls squeezing through the cut, crushing the two defenseless pieces of land on either side. "Soper's Hole is a ghost town," sighed the other.

One of them asked for the news from Coral Bay. My turn to sigh.

Skinny Legs had reopened. That was the good news. But despite the gumption of the NotALottaYachta Regatta, the yacht club was floundering. Belle, fed up that there hadn't been a meeting, gave notice on Facebook, above a photo of an ancient sailing ship:

> There should be a Coral Bay Yacht Club meeting today at Skinny's at 4:30. Your former commodore is willing to continue in some capacity, but not as a one-woman show. If you would like to see CBYC continue and not go down like the Phoenician ship below, please express your interest in writing or show up!

It was hard to have a yacht club with no yachts. For many sailors, the only outing on the water had been a memorial service for Mark S., a popular local who was always out and about in Coral Bay. He died in his sleep, one of several deaths since the storms. A man repairing his deck fell and it was fatal. Another regular at Skinny's, who lived in a neighborhood called Hard Labor, told me his friend had just died. He blamed the stress. Isn't that a hurricane casualty? he wanted to know.

How is Belle? the old salts asked.

Last time I saw Belle, she told me she was doing fine. She hadn't cried since the storms. Not even at Mark S.'s memorial.

"Maybe I should work on that," she said.

The yacht club did manage to give away $5,000 in a scholarship contest. Kids were asked to write about the hurricanes. There were 10 winners and a pile of rejected essays referred to as "the losers." No political correctness in this crowd. "That's the way I was brought up," said one judge, with no apologies, after seeing me wince. "This kid wins, that kid loses." Look around and it was impossible to argue. Winners and losers, side by side.

After lunch, Robin went back to his boat, and I went with Marty to Road Town where I would catch the ferry back to St. John. We stopped at another marina for more drinks. We didn't need more drinks but I was not ready to end our visit and I knew my friend was getting antsy so I kept inventing more activities so he'd stay. Drinking was an activity we could agree on.

We sat overlooking the harbor. Lots of yachties walked through, including boaters who knew Marty, people who hadn't seen him ... since. Our friend was grieving, and others stopped, briefly, to mourn with him, not just for the loss of a home but possibly the loss of a way of life. People reacted like anyone offering condolences, with a weird variety of responses from sadness and sincere concern to nervous laughter. It was all getting to be too much for Marty, I could tell, this funereal air. Our time was waning.

Robin launched his boat as planned that afternoon and, two days later, got his first sail on her with his family. The boat was named *Jera*, a Celtic word meaning "harvest" or "a good year."

Marty, when we parted, was headed to Virgin Gorda to look at a boat called *Godspeed*. When we finally said goodbye, he was still holding it together, and I was the one weeping.

15

STILL WALKING TALL

J uly third is a holiday in the U.S. Virgin Islands. Emancipation Day.

On July 3, 1848, thousands of enslaved Africans in what was then the Danish West Indies converged on Fort Frederik in St. Croix to demand freedom. News of their victory arrived by boat a day later in St. Thomas and St. John.

Emancipation came more than a century after the St. John slave revolt of 1733, which started in Coral Bay. On what came to be known as the night of the silent drums, slaves stormed the fort protecting the harbor, then swept across the island, taking and retaining control of the plantations for six triumphant months. Not until French troops sailed in to help were the Danes able to quell the rebellion. Rather than be recaptured, many of the enslaved jumped to their deaths, leaping from cliffs into the blue water below.

I listened as this history was recounted at the emancipation pageant, a solemn event held just before St. John bursts into the final celebrations of Carnival.

Emancipate us now! Emancipate us now! Men and women chanted, their insistent refrain accompanied by the steady beat of a drum. There was a haunting blow of the *tutu,* or conch shell, and I envisioned the Freedom statue across the street from the ferry dock—the exultant man blowing a conch shell of his own—coming to life to join in. The primeval moan conjured the ghosts of thousands of enslaved men, women, and children, their souls permeating the oppressive air, mingling with the spectators paying respect to their ancestors.

The pageant was attended primarily by the eldest third of St. John's West Indian population and, for inexplicable reasons, held at midday, under a punishing sun. The seniors came early to get a seat under the tent and, by the time the exuberant bamboula dancers took the stage, were withering in the small bits of shade. The dancers—clad in madras skirts and headscarves of red, orange, green, and yellow plaid with white ruffled tops and petticoats—were completely covered but oozed sensuality. They whirled around multi-colored woven baskets, hips gyrating to the pulsing rhythm of the drums. Every now and then a small puff of breeze cut through the heat, and it was heavenly.

The audience was almost entirely Black, and I was reminded of a magazine article from a few years earlier that described St. John as segregated. An affront, I thought, when I first read it. Was the author talking about the place I loved? Yes, there were stratifications—deep ones—economic and racial. *Segregated,* though, felt too harsh. *Segregated* didn't go with all those other descriptions of St. John: *Idyllic. Love City. Paradise.* And yet. With everything laid bare post-storms, there was plenty of room for reckoning.

Scanning the crowd, I saw, under their ever-present hats and inclined toward each other, the heads of two sisters, ancestral St. Johnians, whom I had interviewed on a previous trip: Miss Claudine, 81, lived in Brooklyn, but her 87-year-old sister, Miss Esther, still called St. John home. She had been in a shelter at Bethany Moravian Church when Irma struck.

"The storm was coming madly," she told me, describing how the fellowship hall had started shaking. Irma rattled the windows, then pried off the kitchen door. It was mayhem. They needed to barricade the hole in the wall. They were fortunate because there was a construction man big enough to move the heavy fridge and freezer. "He supervised and we all pitched in," Miss Esther said. I pictured a team of octogenarians, adrenaline fueling their frail bodies.

When it was over, she ignored the curfew and snuck out. She needed to get to her house, check on her books. When she saw that her roof was gone, she knew instantly how much was lost. Her piano. Photos. The pictures that had been hanging on the walls—it had never occurred to her to take them down and put them someplace safe. And all the books.

Miss Esther's roof was either the wrong type of construction or too far gone to qualify for FEMA's Blue Roof program, so she didn't get the blue plastic sheeting that covered many of her neighbors' houses. And then her niece—Claudine's daughter—came from New York in a "mad rush," insisting that her aunt join the family up north where she'd be out of the path of Hurricane Maria, which was rapidly approaching. She left her home with the roof gaping open and the windows blown out, nothing secured because there was no time.

"My niece took charge of that whole scene," Esther said. "I really didn't want to leave the island."

"What a trip!" Claudine interjected. "She didn't tell you!"

The New Yorkers had been worried sick about their 87-year-old matriarch. First Esther had refused to go to the shelter. The night before Irma, they had been up until midnight, pleading with their stubborn sister/aunt to go someplace safe. Because Esther did not want to leave her home. She held her ground as long as she could, but in the end gave in and went to the shelter. And then, no news. After Irma, the family had no way of knowing if Esther was alive.

"That was a scary situation," Claudine said. "Couldn't find out anything."

Claudine's daughter flew to St. Croix where, for the first time in her life, she played the doctor card. *I'm a physician and I must get to St. John.* She hitched a ride on a private yacht ferrying security workers across the sea, then tracked down her aunt.

Esther was "looking very much an immigrant" when they evacuated, she said. "I had a bundle or something. I couldn't even find a suitcase." They lined up at the National Park dock with the rest of the Irma survivors desperate to get off island ahead of Hurricane Maria, eventually getting on a boat to Puerto Rico.

"What the devil happened after that?" Esther asked. Was it a flight straight to New York? A hotel at the airport? She couldn't remember. "Well anyway, it was a roundabout trip. I spent, what, two weeks in New York?"

Claudine harrumphed.

"Three?" asked Esther.

"Five days!" said Claudine.

"It was only five days in New York?"

"Only five days."

"Oh," said Esther. "I thought I had spent two weeks."

"Five days," Claudine said again. "She wanted to come back. We were upset."

Esther didn't see what all the fuss was about. She no more wanted to leave her home and go to New York than she wanted to leave her home and go to that shelter.

"But don't forget," Esther protested, "I left everything wide open! I had to come back." She had jewelry from their mother. Family heirlooms. Souvenirs from her travels. And she had those books. "I really had some books I did not want to lose."

I had met the two ladies at church one Sunday at Bethany Moravian, where Esther sheltered. With Emmaus Moravian in Coral Bay destroyed, both congregations were meeting at Bethany, near town, even though Bethany was also heavily damaged. The altar, organ, and piano were ruined. White folding chairs sat on plywood where there should have been pews. The roof was a blue tarp. When the sun shone down, merciless, the blue lit up like stained glass.

Both churches date to the 18th century when Moravian

missionaries ministered to slaves. The book of Caribbean Mora-vian Praise includes prayers for Emancipation: *Liberator God, we lift up before you, blacks in the Caribbean who have suffered a painful history of slavery. Remove, O God, the scars and mentality of colonialism and imperialism ...*

Current church leaders had been having a heck of a time getting the Coral Bay congregants to come "all the way" to Cruz Bay for services, although, noted one of the elders, no one seemed to have trouble coming all the way into town to, say, go to the hardware store or a restaurant. Even in the house of God, there was a Coral Bay/Cruz Bay divide.

We need to stay strong, said one church leader. Prepare ourselves better. For next time. With climate change and global warming, hurricanes yet to come would be worse. And where was anybody going? There are disasters everywhere. Maybe not hurri-canes, but something else. Earthquakes. Tsunamis.

"Where am I going?" asked a mother of six. "We have roots here. I will tell you the same thing my grandmother will tell you: My umbilical cord is buried here ... This is my island. This is my home ... Yes, my home is gone, but this is still my home. This is where I'm born."

Miss Claudine and Miss Esther were born and raised on St. John. Claudine remembers when the first Jeep drove through. There was no road when they were growing up, only a trail. If you wanted to get to Cruz Bay from their home in Coral Bay, you rode a horse. Both little girls became schoolteachers. Her parents valued education above all, Claudine said. Their mother was a teacher, their father a mason who helped build the Coral Bay school.

When I told Claudine I used to waitress at Skinny Legs, her eyes widened.

"You worked at Skinny Legs?"

I braced myself for what she'd say next. I certainly didn't remember ever seeing anyone like Miss Claudine—a proper lady, dressed in her Sunday best—popping into Skinny's for a cheeseburger after church. Did her whole opinion of me hang in the balance?

"I love Skinny Legs's hot dogs!" she declared.

Her friends couldn't believe she ate there, she laughed. *You go to Skinny Legs?* they scoffed. They didn't think it was classy enough.

After that, I seemed to run into Claudine and Esther everywhere. Lunching at Mongoose. Waiting at the ferry dock to shake the big, meaty hand of Bill Clinton the day he came to town. At a meeting in the Julius E. Sprauve School (JESS) where seniors—many of whom had sheltered at the public school during Irma, waist-high in water—confronted their elected officials, demanding they do better. Now, here it was, July, and Esther's home of 50 years was still not habitable.

"I really was so stupid," she said, after the pageant. "After the hurricane, I had visions of Christmas meal in a refurbished house."

Many of her friends and neighbors were in similar predicaments. They were not in good shape to withstand more storms. "It's frightening," she said. But Esther, at 88, was taking matters into her own hands.

"Next hurricane, my plan is to go to Aruba and wait out the news."

CARNIVAL ON ST. John starts in late June and climaxes on Independence Day, beginning with J'Ouvert—literally a "dawn" or "daybreak" celebration, but in practice the culmination of an all-night bacchanal. The island desperately needed a party. A big one—the Transfer Centennial, marking the 100th anniversary of the Danes selling the Virgin Islands to the Americans, making them a U.S. territory—should have been celebrated in 2017, but America's Paradise got hurricanes Irma and Maria instead.

On July 4, I met up with Cruz Bay Julia for the parade. Her

home, Fort Julia, was about the size of a she-shed and Irma destroyed the roof, but she was still insisting she didn't need anything. She whipped a plastic baggie out of her purse to pay Slim Man for parking. "You like my wallet?" she asked with a twang, pulling bills out of the Ziploc. "I'll get you one for Christmas!"

I don't know where she hoarded the various costumes she was always able to pull from thin air but she was dressed entirely in red, white, and blue. Crisp white shirt. Blue shorts and hat. Red scarf knotted around her waist. Red high-top Converse sneakers. Even her water bottle was red. Where do these women with the tiny shacks and boats and tinier closets and cubbies get their accessories? At a performance by the newly formed St. John Recovery Choir, hurricane survivors gave a Motown concert decked out in sequined dresses and sparkly shoes. Singers who did not have these items at their disposal improvised with flashy table runners, courtesy of an island wedding planner, worn as sashes. They belted out a jubilant rendition of Stevie Wonder's "Higher Ground."

The Middle Age Majorettes had disbanded but that didn't stop Julia from sharing a few dance steps with any of the dozens of other troupes that paraded by. My friend was the mayor of Carnival and I was her sidekick, trailing behind as she made loop after loop around the route, greeting and hugging, well, everyone, it seemed. Even before the hurricanes, Julia worked tirelessly, spearheading the Love City Fund's various projects: Securing funding for the senior center so she'll have a place to go when she's old, she joked. Working with the homeless—so she wouldn't be one. There's money in her family but she didn't expect to see it. Her mother was saving the furniture for when her daughter got serious about her life. The daughter was 55.

The day was another scorcher, but no one was missing this. Parade-goers did what they could for protection, slathering sunscreen and donning wide-brimmed hats and baseball caps. Someone was wearing red, white, and blue flag sunglasses.

Someone else had heart-shaped shades. Oh wait, that was Julia. Another person was wearing rose-colored glasses. Actually, a lot of people crowded onto the small streets were wearing rose-colored glasses. You just couldn't see them.

The parade was a celebration of prelapsarian mirth. There was a whole brigade of little Carnival princesses riding in shiny cars, flaunting rhinestone tiaras, itchy lace and ruffles, and 1,000-watt smiles. One was in a magenta dress with white polka dots; another sported stars and stripes, with red crinolines under her red-and-white striped skirt and, dangling from her ears, American flags. The Carnival queen, dressed in a regal white gown, waved a scepter. The first responders—St. John Rescue, the police and fire departments—also had a place of honor. The citizenry proclaimed allegiance with cries of *St. John Strong! Love City Strong!*

There were squadrons of women and men in classic Carnival finery. Bejeweled cuffs and winged backpieces flashed. Elaborate headdresses bounced to the throbbing beat. Feathers shimmied in fuchsia, sky blue, and electric orange. Fringed and beaded bikini bottoms swished. One woman had purple lips. Another, feathered feet. Someone was blowing bubbles. There was bedazzled skin everywhere. All kinds of skin. Black. White. Brown. Bare, sweaty, exposed, all-hanging-out skin, and a lot of it, normal in this conservative culture only on this day. Sweat poured through melting makeup, through the smiles.

There were two "indigenous peoples" groups, scantily clad but overheated in loincloths and animal skins. A battalion of kids from St. John School of the Arts showed the "face of recovery." They wore handcrafted masks—the fruits of an art project—adorned with bits of coral and driftwood, reclaimed trash, glitter, shells, IRMARIA spelled out in Scrabble tiles.

It was sweltering. Flatbeds rolled by with passengers tossing out bottles of water, more in demand than the free Carib beer. On one of the floats were the Love City Pan Dragons—the youth steel pan band—their happy calypso melodies resonating through the muggy air. Most of the players were students. Irma took their homes and the parade route took the public school kids right past their demolished school, but Irmaria left the pan yard alone. The young musicians got their instruments out of storage three days after Hurricane Maria and started playing again.

The parade marched from Mongoose Junction to the post office, down to the ferry dock, then up toward the Quiet Mon pub. As it passed the judging booth outside Cruz Bay's Connections, a few women under a tent held up placards rating the groups. Julia jumped in to join them. All 10s for the Love City Pan Dragons! All 10s for the recovery masks! Closer inspection revealed that all the placards have 10s on them. Everybody gets a 10.

We parked ourselves upstairs at Quiet Mon to watch the end of the parade. On one of the final floats, a woman in gold boots and drooping orange feathers was hunched over, getting high. She looked deflated, like a Macy's balloon at the end of the parade, the heat of the day and the weight of the year forcing the breath right out of her body. Behind her, watching over her, a lone moko jumbie clopped by, perched high on his stilts, doing one-legged stunts. Did he see any evil spirits approaching? Legend says his height gives him that power—to see harm coming and ward it off.

"The Moko Jumbie, if you asked him," wrote Trinidadian historic preservationist John Cupid, "he would say from under his masked face that he has been walking all the way across the Atlantic Ocean from the West Coast of Africa, laden with many, many centuries of experiences and, in spite of all the inhuman attacks and encounters, yet still walking tall, tall, tall."

Carnival ended with fireworks exploding over the water in Cruz Bay. The soulful sounds of soca and reggae played into the night. A few more hours of fun. Of freedom from the year.

The next day, Tropical Storm Beryl formed. By the end of the week, it would become the season's first hurricane.

16

PRESSURE

(HURRICANE SEASON, 2018)

Most people don't remember Hurricane Beryl. It wasn't much of a threat when it passed by St. John. "A big nothing-burger," one islander called it. But for Chef Harry, hunkering down in his home on a windy ridge, listening to the howls and rattles, it was excruciating. The last straw. He put his home, Chez Breeze, on the market. Harry built the house himself. It had a custom kitchen and handmade hurricane shutters and nurtured gardens. He and his wife had lived there since they got married on the beach at Hawksnest. *Enjoy the fruits of our labor of love,* the listing read.

He was the second friend in a week to announce he wanted out, one saying he could no longer stomach it, the other saying she could no longer afford it. Irma destroyed her business. Did I want to buy her house? She'd throw in the car.

"Until you have PTSD, no one can describe it to you," Harry said. He knew he was suffering from it. The anger. The irrational behavior. He tried not to dwell on it. They paid somebody to help with that. Beryl was a nothing storm. Completely nothing. He knew, logically, that it was nothing. They'd had stronger winds when the Christmas Winds blew. But after Irma? He felt vulnerable. Pissed off that he had to start thinking about it again.

The wind was also blowing hard on the day I interviewed him. My Jeep rocked as I climbed the cliff road to his house. It was unsettling. I tried to imagine what that wind would be like times 10, or 15, and couldn't.

Harry's cottage looked lovely, but it had taken months to get it to that condition, everything back in place. Not like after the hurricanes, when he'd find an ink cartridge in a sauté pan. When things that weren't supposed to go together were thrown together. When the house looked like someone threw all the potted plants inside, added water, and shook. A putrid milkshake.

Harry's Shipwreck job was gone, and so was his side gig mixing spices. He had run the business out of a shipping container on his property. He showed me the spot where the container used to sit and, way down below, where it landed—unscathed. It clearly didn't roll. Irma must have just lifted it up, *Wizard of Oz*-style. Harry thought he'd see the Wicked Witch's striped stockings and ruby slippers sticking out from under it. "I looked," he said.

It was easy to see where the container touched down because there were construction workers there, pouring concrete for a new house. It was being built by a friendly young guy, Harry told me, a newcomer. He had been walking up and down the road introducing himself, very sure of himself. "And I'm so not sure of myself," Harry said. "At all. About anything."

Something about this description sounded familiar. "I met that guy!" I said. Of course I did, because you met everyone down there. He'd been prattling on about the house he was building in Coral Bay. An outlier, I thought at the time. Not so much oblivious to the destruction as impervious. Some nut all excited about his new life while other people were reeling.

It was OK, Harry said. It was time for new people. It was paradise for new people. It was paradise for him, too, for a while. Not anymore. He couldn't even get in the water, and he loved the water. He didn't know why. He just could not get in the water.

He didn't want to complain. They were lucky. But he was not

going through it again. It was exhausting getting the house ready. Isolating, too. All the drudgery, most of it alone, while Kelly was at work. He pointed at a dead tree that needed to come down. It would be a torpedo in another storm. Hopefully the house would sell soon so it would be somebody else's problem, but they needed to find a buyer, not to mention new jobs. Kelly could apply for a hardship transfer from the National Park Service. He had fantasies of showing up at her office and doing something crazy to move the process along. He was kidding, he said. Sort of.

IT WAS around the time the Sahara Dust arrived that the cracks started to show.

Sahara Dust can suppress hurricanes, all that dust and dry air anathema to tropical storms. But, as it travels the same path as most major hurricanes, it also serves as a reminder of the formidable forces lurking, the deadly threats that can originate an ocean away. When the summer skies grew hazy and the dust descended, it was like a little bit of fingerprint powder revealing a clue—right there on the façade—that, before, you couldn't quite see.

I had sensed it for months, the tension building with each subsequent visit, but nobody would talk about it.

On the surface, everything was fine. Throughout the winter and spring, that was the mantra—*Everything's fine!*—any inner turmoil safeguarded from scrutiny by a now pervasive, banal exchange of pleasantries: *"How are you?" "I'm good. How about you?" "Good. We're good."* People might have been a little touchy or irritable. But overall? Everyone was fine. Really. Just ask them. One of the bartenders at Skinny's refused to go to the beach he used to love, but he was fine. Belle was fine. Tough as nails. She hadn't shed a tear since the storms, but she was fine. The elderly woman without a stove or refrigerator, who hadn't been able to cook a meal in 10 months was fine. The young man who lost his house and his car and his boat was fine. The indomitable spirit of Coral Bay was just fine, thank you very much.

Then a longtime resident posted on Facebook that he felt he didn't belong anymore. He was angry, depressed, and over-whelmed. And worse, a "friend" told him he had no right to feel that way since he was off island during the hurricanes and did not lose his home. Was there something wrong with him? Everyone else had such a brave face.

A floodgate opened. Catharsis in the form of comments spilled onto his page, offering support, confessing to a litany of tribulations and runaway emotions: sadness, fear, despair, general pissed-off-ness. Someone revealed the existence of an informal therapy group, an AA-type gathering where people could lean on each other, talk about how they were feeling in a private place.

Latent anxieties, simmering for months, were boiling over in public, too. People who had been living too long with their neigh-bors under such awful conditions were starting to get on each other's nerves, foibles morphing into major character flaws. Be kind, someone would urge. Forgive. Be patient. Everyone's so testy. Be careful what you ask, you might get an inventory of woes. Watch out for so-and-so's mercurial moods. He's full of recriminations. This one has these loops of stories that he'll tell over and over. Mention any part of the story, he'll jump right in and go again. That one's a ghoul. She got off island to visit family, but it didn't seem to help. "The devastation is home now," she'd say, with "the look" in her eyes.

"I have to admit, it's pretty rough," said one Coral Bay tough guy.

One morning I saw Erin and Bryan at the Aqua Bistro bar, downing shots of Fireball. I'd last seen Erin all gung-ho, passing out bear hugs along with the prize-winning chili she cooked up for a fundraiser. Next I heard, she'd quit her latest chef job. Some-thing about running out of buns. "On a personal note," she'd written in response to her friend's Facebook lament, "I feel like fucking crap most of the time & pretend like everything is hunky fucking dory. It's not."

Erin was sleep-deprived and losing her mind. Her neighbor— she loved him, she swore—had one piece of galvanized aluminum on his roof that banged all night long. *Bang bang bang.* She was about to go off on him. His whole house practically flew through her roof during Irma. It wasn't his fault. That's what happens in a hurricane. But could he please do something about this noise? She'd been listening to the *bang bang bang* for 10 fucking months.

"I don't like wind anymore," Bryan said. "It's windy as fuck where I'm staying."

"It's drip, drip, drip," Erin said. It was the rain that woke her up, freaked her out.

"Do you still get hurricane dreams?" Bryan asked. He hadn't had one in a while but the other night he dreamed he was on a trimaran, spinning through the air.

Erin started humming *Wizard of Oz* music as Bryan trailed off, as if in a trance. "Hadn't had one for months but had one the other night. It was windy that night."

We were sitting not far from where Arlene, the masseuse, used to live. The concrete apartment building should have been a bunker, but Irma demolished it like a house of straw. It had been Erin and Bryan's safe house, the place they would go if they had to make a run for it. Arlene did have to make a run for it, at the height of the storm, when the roof went. She described it as Godzilla popping the top off her home with one swipe of a mighty arm. Before that, a window had blown in and she remembers getting a broom and sweeping up the glass—in retrospect, a ridiculous act. She saw her cat, Lanky, fly out the window. She was with her grandnephew, and they needed to escape, but they couldn't budge the door. They had to wait for the pressure to change so they could get out. She must have hugged the side of the wall going down the stairs outside. She saw a car roll by—her car, Lulu—and dodged it. Everything was brown. The trees were sticks. Toothpicks. There was a beam spiked in the ground. When she got to her neighbor's, he gave her a pillow. All she wanted to do was lie down. She lay down with the pillow in two inches of water.

Now Arlene was healing high up on a bluff. After months of camping out in what she called "the bomb shelter," she got a reprieve, caretaking a villa while the owners were away. It was peaceful. A sweet spot, with no jumbies—no ghosts or spirits of dead people—she had told me while giving me a massage, her stream-of-consciousness toggling between woo-woo hippie stuff and jogged traumatic memories, some hurricane-related, some not. She dug into a knot between my shoulder blades and recalled protesting the war in Vietnam. She was at Kent State. Saw the students get shot right in front of her.

She was doing OK after the storms. She had another apartment in town that she rented out to some "volunteers" who wanted to come down and help with recovery. The renters complained about the condition of her apartment. She thought maybe if they wanted to help, they could start by scrubbing the apartment, but whatever. Ninety-three days later, Lanky came back. Unbelievable. That cat showed up 93 days after Irma. She didn't really have a meltdown until she got back up to the States. She had a PTSD attack at the mall. No idea what triggered it. She was at one of those vision stores, just trying to get her glasses fixed.

You never know what's going to trigger it, Jenn said, through tears. It comes and goes. Every time I walked into Connections she started crying. On one visit, another woman came in and, seeing Jenn blowing her nose, laughed. I was waiting for the punch line. "This hurricane shit!" she said. She had just had her own good cry. "The triggers are so funny."

"I'm not really sure why I'm crying because things are getting better," Jenn sniffled. She had just shown me photos of the progress on her home. The new kitchen. New windows.

I diagnosed Jenn with compassion fatigue. She had her own problems but had to absorb the hardships and neuroses of every single person who walked into her office needing something, and everyone needed something. I told her even Mother Teresa made her nuns take time off to avoid burnout. Cruz Bay Julia had just told me that. Julia, I determined, had compassion fatigue exacerbated by survivor's guilt. I knew she had been guilt-shamed for not being on island during the hurricanes. My friend was a paragon of persistence and positivity, but it didn't matter how much she did in the aftermath. She couldn't change that one simple fact: She wasn't there. She dealt with it by working harder and not talking about it. She was fine, though. Just ask her.

I WAS STAYING at Caribbean Bliss on that trip. The house where I honeymooned sustained relatively minimal damage, got quick repairs, and, with the vegetation thinned out, now had an even wider-angle view. Every night at sunset the sky was a kaleidoscope of color, streaks of deep purple and fire orange fading as the lights of St. Thomas twinkled on. And in between that lovely panorama of twilight on a glittering harbor and my enviable perch on the deck of a luxury villa was a house with no roof. Luck and chance and good and bad.

Looking at pictures from my honeymoon, I could just make out the no-longer-extant red roof poking out of now-gone foliage. With no trees, there was nothing to hide what looked like a dollhouse—sliced open, wholly exposed—in the hands of a tantrum-prone child. It must have once felt invincible with its sturdy concrete walls and stone masonry. On the right, splintered rafters reached across the top of the house to nothing, a skeleton with half its ribs. Verdant land was visible through blown-out windows. I could see straight down into the bedrooms. Nobody was home.

I wondered how strong a wind it would take to pry one of those two-by-fours loose and send it airborne. Just up the road was St. John's dump, full to capacity, sheets of corrugated roofing stacked next to heaps of trash and hurricane debris, potential projectiles all. It had been breezy the past few nights, great sleeping weather I would normally call it, although not for people who have been traumatized by wind.

There had been a rainstorm before dawn. Just before it started, something woke me up—some early bird or a tree frog off his cue. The creature song stopped for a split second of silence and then the rain bucketed down, a tinny, popping sound as it pinged and ricocheted off the galvanized metal of the roof, a muted thud when it hit the awnings. In an instant the air had changed, becoming cooler. Heavier. And then that distinctive smell of a tropical shower. It was blissful to be lying in bed, half awake, dry and safe, and hear that surround-sound downpour, know that it was nurturing the land and filling the cisterns. In a few minutes, it was over.

"It used to be my favorite thing," Sweet Sarah had told me. She was still living with a tarp for a roof. When the wind came— "starting to build and starting to build and starting to build"— the tarp moved, making strange noises. She hated it. She used to love the rain and wind but now it scared her.

When the sun came up, I went out on the patio. A mourning dove cooed. *Whoo-WHOO-whoo-whooooooo.* An elegy. I should have been writing. My laptop was open on the glass table in front of me, but my fingers were wrapped around a warm coffee mug. My bare feet rested on cool, damp red brick. A gecko—or was it an anole?—nipped at my ankle, snacking on mosquitoes. Bougainvillea petals, still wet from the rain, popped with color, magenta and pastel pink. The hillsides, lush and hydrated, released intoxicating whiffs of jasmine and frangipani. The only thing missing was the rainbow, which was bound to appear any moment.

A hummingbird gathered nectar from one of those red, spindly plants. The breeze flapped the broad leaves on the—what kind of tree was that? Maybe one day I'll learn the names. This place I claim to love and I can't identify the trees or tell the lizards apart. I used to know all the stars, every single constellation, but that knowledge has faded after too many years living where there's too much light at night. Truth is, a lot about my time on St. John has faded. You think you won't forget (*Do not forget this!*) but you do. After the hurricanes, everything was different. But maybe I didn't even get it right the first time around. There is an unreliable narrator, and it is me.

I stared at my notes and wondered, not for the first time, what the hell I was thinking. This island, these people, had given me so much, I was desperate to give back but I couldn't build, I couldn't write big checks, I couldn't even muster enough self-sufficiency to get out of a literal rut when my perfect-condition rental Jeep with the four-wheel drive got stuck in the mud. I was a burden after all.

People were sitting down in the midst of their tragedies and telling me their stories—why? Because I was the one always with the pen and the notebook? Because they trusted me? They shouldn't. I was an interloper, letting them down. The *Sun Times* was defunct, most of my reporting contacts gone. Hurricane Irma was old news. The media had moved on to the next calamity. I told myself I could at least bear witness, but if I wrote stories that nobody read, well, tree, forest, etc. My pitches had failed to move anyone in a position to publish. No one is interested in another hurricane victim story, I was told, as I was on my way to interview another hurricane victim, still in shock, wondering where his dreams went. Nobody cares about place, I was told, as I tried to describe a place, before and after, forever changed.

Maybe they were right. I went back and looked at the little square of land where Shipwreck used to be. It had loomed so large! Given me friends, and work, a community, laughter, memories. Yet the physical footprint was so small. Maybe I remembered it wrong.

"Stop showing your work to numbnuts," Tom Paine counseled over lunch at Skinny's.

I hadn't seen or heard from my old *Sun Times* editor since I worked for him more than a decade earlier. In the intervening

years he had, as far as I could tell, been off the grid. But lo and behold, he emerged on island post-storms like one of the bush cats keeping him company in the remote little shack he was fixing up in between spurts of writing poetry. He told me Thoreau had to self-publish his book about the Merrimack River and suggested that, when I finish my blue cheese burger, I get back to work.

As if the sight of the stripped mangroves wasn't bad enough, the dumpsters across from the Love City Mini Mart were over-flowing. Piles of trash lined the coastline, rejectamenta from the hurricanes mingling with refuse from the sea. The stench was stomach-churning and attributed to the sargassum that had been occupying Virgin Island shores, but it was difficult to sepa-rate the seaweed smell from the festering garbage. Ten months after Irma, poignant reminders of the injuries she inflicted lay in wait like muggers, ready to pounce when her victims least expected it. Vestiges of someone's life confronted you when all you wanted was a bag of ice. Decide to take the scenic drive home from town and you might accidentally end up on the sad beaches tour.

The long-term impact of Irmaria on the island's ecosystem— the reefs and marine life, the forests, the animals and plants—was hard to measure. One native species expert said the effects would be visible for another 50 to 60 years. And that's without another storm. At Maho, someone planted a few baby palm trees where the lofty coconut palms once stood. The sprouts looked hopeful, protected by borders of smooth stones. Trouble is, you can't just plant things in a National Park. Coconut palms are not indige-nous. The Park Service pulled them up. Two camps formed, pro- and anti-palm planting. Even the palm trees could provoke a fight.

Look for the new growth, I heard a local schoolteacher implore, like Mr. Rogers telling kids to look for the helpers when they see something scary on the news. She might have been talking to her fourth graders, but she was addressing a group of sunburned tourists on the beach, bemoaning the state of the island.

I ran into this teacher later, at the Smoothie Stand, where she had a second job. While whipping up a Funky Monkey (pineapple, banana, coconut) and a Tart and Tasty (soursop, lime, passionfruit), she gave me an update on JESS, the public school in Cruz Bay. The student population, normally about 450, stood around 150. Some parents had taken advantage of the private Gifft Hill School's offer of free tuition after Irmaria. Many children had evacuated post-storms and not returned. More would be back in September, but they'd still be down a full third. Families remained separated, kids living with relatives somewhere else, mom or dad on island trying to rebuild.

The children didn't have books. Or a school. The plan for the next year was to build something temporary in the playground, taking away the only recreation space. And by the way, the kids didn't think Hurricane Beryl was a big nothing-burger. They cried. They were so stressed out. Even the do-gooders stressed them out. Some charity donated pencils and then expected the kids to write thank-you notes. And they were so done with the photo ops. Posing with another politician? The 11-year-olds weren't dumb. They knew they were being used.

She handed me my Tart and Tasty and apologized for her jeremiad. She wasn't usually this negative. Just having a bad day, she guessed.

After 2 Hurricanes, A 'Floodgate' Of Mental Health Issues In U.S. Virgin Islands NPR would report the following spring. Children in need of counseling they would never get were exhibiting behavioral problems. Research showed "startling" levels of depression and post-traumatic stress. A high percentage of high-school-age students surveyed said they had thought about suicide.

The English word "hurricane" is rooted in the Taíno *hurakan,* which means, depending on your source, "center of the wind" or "god of the storm." The ancient people of the Caribbean saw in the heart of the spiraling storms that ravaged their islands a swirling, furious goddess spewing chaos. Centuries of science since have not improved on that description.

NOAA defines a tropical cyclone as "a rotating, organized system of clouds and thunderstorms that originates over tropical or subtropical waters and has a closed low-level circulation." These storms and depressions become hurricanes when they hit maximum sustained winds of 74 mph. When the wind hits 111 mph, the hurricane is classified as major: Category 3 with winds up to 129 mph, Category 4 if winds are 130 to 156 mph. A hurricane with sustained winds of 157 mph or more is a Category 5. The numbers don't go any higher.

The wind on St. John during Hurricane Irma was believed to be somewhere in the range of 180 to 220 mph. One Coral Bay resident said his anemometer blew out at 285 mph. Gusts were estimated up to 300 mph. Some survivors say there was never a break. No eye.

It's unclear whether any wind gauge survived to provide an accurate reading. But if you extrapolate from the Saffir-Simpson Hurricane Wind Scale—each additional 20 mph or so of wind speed marking a new level of intensity—even the official, conservative reading of 185-mph sustained winds would seem to bump Irma into a higher category. No one who lived through it believes what roared through the island that September day was a Category 5 storm, but there is no Category 6, as many Virgin Islanders believe Irma was; or even 5.5, as Long-Haired Ken dubbed it at Thankspigging. Irma was unprecedented.

Photographer Matt suggested Category 7. He had been alone in his family home when it blew apart around him.

My old *Sun Times* colleague had invited me up to watch the sunset from what he referred to as The Slab. Driving up the scary-ass road to his property atop one of St. John's highest peaks, almost every house I passed had a blue roof or was roof-less. Irma had spun off countless tornadoes and a string of them had made the trek up the mountain before I did. After I parked, we continued ascending. Matt, juggling a couple of chairs and a cooler, occasionally looked over his shoulder to warn me about stinging nettles or a rusty nail as I followed him up to a block of concrete that used to be the second floor of his home. The Slab.

Venus was shining brightly, an almost-full moon was rising, and there were wisps of rose and coral in our wraparound view of the sky. All this muted celestial light cast shadows over my friend as he talked about all the things he did wrong. He had worked nonstop preparing for the storm, but in hindsight he realized maybe he could have done this. Maybe he should have done that. If only this, that, or the other, maybe he could have saved the house.

"The hurricane's the easy part. It's the aftermath that's hard," Matt said, over a symphony of coquis, determined to drown him out.

Living amidst the rubble, in conditions most people would consider uninhabitable, had been brutal. As a journalist, he'd seen plenty of disasters. He saw the carnage in Haiti after the earthquake that killed a quarter million people. He just never thought he'd be the one needing help. It was humbling.

He thought he'd be fine. He'd been through every hurricane since Marilyn. The house had survived all that and more. His Mom prayed the rosary! He was ready. Everything was wrapped, stacked, stowed, packed away. He had his six-pack of Corona and, his words, enough canned ravioli to both keep him alive and kill him. He knew, logically, that a Category 5 hurricane could destroy the house. "But back then," he said, *back then* referring to the pre-Irma era, a mere 10 months earlier, "I literally felt like there was something magical about this house."

There wasn't. He had drunk only half a beer, was only halfway through his can of ravioli, when a large window blew out, rendering him vulnerable to every danger outside and forcing him to take cover in his closet. Then the closet door came off. He was fully exposed, feeling not scared but guilty. That's when the shouldas started. He should have done this to prepare better. He should have done that with his life.

Afterward, his neighbor, Arthur, came up to check on him. He could hear the worry in Arthur's voice, calling Matt's name. The house didn't look like anyone could have survived. "Hey, Arthur. How's it going?" he remembered saying. He must have looked deranged, surrounded by wreckage, soaking wet, covered in paint that had blasted off the walls. He accepted his neighbor's invitation to spend the night. It seemed the smart thing to do. Everything was gone. He just wanted to grab his six-pack first. He still had that beer. It didn't seem right to go empty-handed.

Weeks after, months maybe, it hit him that he could have been killed.

"I was full-blown PTSD three months later," he said. It wasn't just the storm. He and his girlfriend, Melanie, broke up, their relationship more of Irmaria's collateral damage. He couldn't get into photojournalist mode. It was too close to home, like being a surgeon and having to operate on your own child. Plus St. John, post-Irma, was not photogenic. There was nothing to shoot. No iconic disaster photos that captured the magnitude of it all. It was just ugly. Funny, though, the things that did catch his eye: A roll of toilet paper, still on the spindle that had been yanked from the wall. Melanie's sandal. A DVD of the movie *Twister.*

The hardest part had been the loss of people after the storms, Matt said. You lost people to stress. Or because they left. Some people evacuated and never came back. Some came back months later, gathered what was left of their stuff, and left for good. Climate migrants.

AFTER BERYL CAME HURRICANE CHRIS. He went up to Charleston. Debby arrived the beginning of August, Ernesto a week later. Both formed in the North Atlantic. Debby stayed at sea. Ernesto went to Ireland. And on St. John, the recovery dragged on at a glacial pace. The island was not ready if there was another storm. There was not a single shelter.

"Everybody thinks another one is coming," said a resident, laboring on a house that was not his own. "Everybody wants everything finished by September." He didn't know why everyone thought another one was coming. Somebody must be looking out for them.

Science says he is wrong. Global warming is causing rising sea levels and temperatures. Hurricanes get energy from warm water and that big ocean they travel over is getting hot. Baleful warnings from climatologists predict, if not necessarily more storms, bigger ones. Slower and more intense. More cataclysmic, with more consequences.

2017 was one of the most destructive hurricane seasons in U.S. history. Category 5 hurricanes are rare, and here were two, Irma and Maria, on the heels of Harvey, an equally disastrous Category 4. FEMA was overwhelmed and, by its own admission, not prepared to help the five million Americans who needed it. And Hurricane Irma wasn't just a rare Category 5 storm. She maintained that Category 5 strength for a rare three days.

ANNA BANANA HAD HOPED to be far away from St. John for the height of hurricane season. She and her family had planned to sail in their new boat—their new home—to one of the Caribbean islands outside the hurricane belt, but there were too many things wrong with the boat that they didn't have time or money to fix. They would have to stay put and hope for the best. She didn't want to complain. They were doing OK. They'd lost everything twice now, started with nothing before. They had steady work and a bigger boat with three cabins, enough for everyone. She was afraid to nest. But the kids were resilient.

They hadn't been off island at all since Irmaria. Beryl totally freaked her out. When that wind picked up and started blowing through the halyards? Her PTSD kicked in. She was shaking and pacing. She was used to being on the water when storms came through. Normally she'd sleep through it, but this hit her differently. She could use a break. But leave for good? She had tried to do that once but couldn't. This was home. She couldn't imagine being anywhere else. But she didn't fault anyone who left. If they needed to leave, they needed to leave. No judgment. But Coral Bay was still going to be here. They could always come back.

17

TREASURE HUNTING IN
CORAL BAY

What is paradise, anyway?

Is it a place? An X on the map? Latitude and longitude? Or is it internal? A state of mind. Something that lives in your head, or your heart. Is it a moment in time? Does it follow you, travel with you? Can it be recreated? If it's a place, and it changes, is it still paradise?

Can you go back?

For outsiders, what are we searching for in a theoretical paradise like a Caribbean island? Is Coral Bay full of seekers, contemplating the meaning of life? Pursuing some primal need to get back to the Garden? Or is something more prosaic at work? *Some are looking for their destiny, some are looking for their truth,* the website of the Wayward Sailor, a St. John charter boat captain, philosophized. *And some are just looking for a parking space.*

"It's the peace," Mean Jean said.

Mean Jean and I were on the hunt for flamingos. It was either that or the flamboyant tour, and who knew how long the flamingos would be around. The birds had been spotted a few days earlier by an island photographer who posted exquisite images online. He lost everything in Irma, but he was still out there showcasing the glory of the place he called home.

Flamingos are not foreign to the Caribbean but they're rarely seen on St. John. Perhaps the small flock blew in from the BVIs—from Anegada where there's a colony, or the private island where an eccentric billionaire breeds them. Maybe it was another one of those mystical St. John happenings. Either way, the birds were exotic enough and, as the latest island intrigue, we wanted to see them.

We were in Mean Jean's car, heading out toward Lameshur Bay. We turned off onto an unpaved road, bumping over rocks near the salt pond where the flock was sighted, and almost immediately we got lucky. Of course we got lucky because that was, still, what happened. We spotted the birds. They were far away but unmistakable, bright pink spots set off by the murky brown of the slack salt pond, a line of green trees behind them and, in the distance, the dazzling blue of the sea.

Seven flamingos stood in position, legs crossed, like ballerinas. I snapped a few pictures. In the professional's photos, you see the curve of each graceful, S-shaped neck, the wispy details of every feather, the nuances of pinks and corals. The blurry shots on my phone were less *Rara Avis,* more *Blotches in Muddy Swamp.*

We drove around to Grootpan Bay to see if we could get a better look from the other side. Grootpan is a little hard to get to and usually deserted. We parked in some brush and hopped out, hearing the surf before we saw it. The beach there is rocky. Waves washed across wide stones, pebbles, and nuggets of coral, which clattered together when the water rolled back out. I liked to think they were gurgling bits of gossip as the sea ebbed and flowed. Giving up the island's secrets to anyone "totally open" to hearing them, as the old *Sun Times* adage promised.

We walked gingerly, careful not to disturb the cairns that dotted the beach, sanctifying the shoreline. We were alone but the little rock piles, like the Petroglyphs on the Reef Bay trail, were reminders of those who had been there before us, whether centuries ago or just that morning. We passed a tree with conch shells hanging from it. Wind chimes with no sound.

I was wobbling in Jean's path, trying to step where she stepped so I wouldn't twist an ankle on an unstable rock, and I had to keep stopping short, lest I bump into her when she stopped to take a photo. She stopped every few feet to take a photo. Mean Jean had lived there 40 years but still took pictures everywhere she went. Fish and turtles, sweeping water views from her deck, violet orchids and flaming bird of paradise. She stopped again and pointed the camera down, toward our feet. Nestled within the flat gray stones of the beach, someone had crafted dozens of tiny white mollusk shells and bits of bleached coral into the shape of a heart.

After navigating over the rocks, we had to wade through the thorny scrub, spiny catch-and-keep, and Christmas Bush—more like poison ivy than the holly it resembles—that separated the beach from the salt pond on the other side. I gave up, but Jean forged ahead—and would pay for it with an itchy rash for weeks after. But she wanted her own proof she saw the elusive birds, and she got it, plus a shot of a delicate and dew-covered periwinkle blossom clinging to a vine.

Mission accomplished, it was into the water for a snorkel. It was murder getting over those rocks in bare feet, and there was a surge, so graceful we were not, but getting wet felt so good on such a hot day. Jean had her underwater camera and took off in pursuit of a school of sergeant majors. I explored the reef. It wasn't exactly brimming with life, but I saw some tiny fish that looked like babies and took that as a good sign. When I started to get cold, I swam to shore and got out of the water the way I got in: on my ass, scraping my swimsuit bottom, and dragging my fins. I burned my feet as I ooh-aahed my way up to my towel and shoes.

"I think it's the peace," Mean Jean said again as we dried off.

Paradise isn't easy, she said. Or cheap. Daily life can be hard. Sometimes there's no work. You could lose your house—or your life—in a hurricane. She knew she got lucky this time. Irmaria spared her. When she went home to Mean's Dream—her wooden house up in the cliffs—it would be peaceful. From her aerie she'd hear the sea hitting the rocks, the mourning doves, the coquis. She rarely listened to music anymore. She wanted to hear the frogs.

"IT'S NOT THE PLACE. It's the people," said Coral Bay Carl from the deck of *Silver Cloud*.

It was supposed to be a day out on the water, and, well, technically, it was, but we were still sitting at anchor. We had a boatful of people, snorkel gear, food and drink, but the ship was not cooperating. Captain Elliot was sweating it, trying not to get his feet tangled in a hundred feet of two-inch-thick anchor chain as a jammed windlass fought him. He was losing the battle.

"I have a boat that can't go anywhere," he sighed.

"Join the club," said Anna Banana.

Everyone had been trying so hard to get back in—or out on—the water. I had had better luck another day with Colin, who had one of his Flyaway Charters powerboats up and running. I spent a carefree day island-hopping with girlfriends, benevolent wind blowing troubles temporarily away. Late in the afternoon it started to rain but we stayed in the bow, out in the open, taking in our surroundings as fresh water from the sky rinsed off the day's salt.

The Antilles. The name traces to a pre-Columbian Iberian legend. An island called Antillia—believed to lie somewhere in the middle of the Atlantic—was listed on nautical charts through most of the 15th century until regular ocean voyaging disproved its existence. But the mythical place still gives its name to the islands we were boating around, islands where the authentic splendor surely must rise to the level of any imagined Shangri-La. The beauty was extreme. It was easy to see why people professed to find a profound spirituality in its presence.

As we made our way back to Coral Bay, the mountains of Tortola and St. John took on an enchanted quality in the fog, appearing and disappearing in the mist.

"You mean like *Camelot*?" said the smart-ass in the group when I waxed lyrical aloud.

Well, more like *Brigadoon*. But yes, sort of, I said, bracing for more mockery.

"It's like that Kenny Chesney song," said one of the other girls, a romantic like me. "'Song for the Saints.' Have you heard it?"

Hard not to. Chesney's new album was dedicated to hurricane victims; the song was an instant island anthem.

The smart-ass made a face. "I hate Kenny Chesney," she groaned. "I mean, I'm grateful for all he's done for the island, but I can't stand his country pop music. I'm into gangsta rap."

"People accept you for who you are," someone said, back on *Silver Cloud* now. "You don't have to pretend to be something you're not."

"It's the people," Coral Bay Carl said again. "It's all the fucking weirdos."

I might have gone with "free spirits." But OK.

"It's *indescriptionable*," one of the Skinny's waitresses said, before correcting herself: "I meant *indescriptable*."

Is she right? Can a writer just say it's indescribable—ineffable, even—and call it a day? If not, at least I've now got "indescriptable" in my arsenal of inadequate words.

There would be no cruise, not that day, on *Silver Cloud*. Elliot did his damnedest but to no avail. His ship would remain anchored. A gang of water-loving friends spent a dry day on a sailboat that could not sail. And because that's not enough irony, one of the passengers, I noticed, was wearing a tank top with a pair of hurricane warning flags X'd out and the words "Blessing of the Fleet" underneath. As far as I knew, there'd never been a blessing of the fleet in Coral Bay, but the boat on the front of the yellow shirt was clearly *Silver Cloud*.

"You had a blessing of the fleet last year?" I asked.

"Yup," someone shrugged. They thought they'd try something new. They had had it in June. Ten weeks before Irma.

Maybe next time they'd follow Captain Eddie's lead. He had poured rum all over his boat—to appease the hurricane gods—and that boat made it. Had I heard? Eddie Z. just got back. He still didn't have much work, but he said he'd rather be broke in Coral Bay with all his friends than somewhere else with money and no friends. No real friends. Eddie had a new boat, *Here Comes the Sun*.

As I headed to my Jeep at the end of the day, a peal resonated from the belfry of Emmaus Moravian. The church was still in ruins and there were no services, even though it was Sunday. No one had heard that bell ring all year. Later, the pastor's wife would tell me her husband rang it in honor of some visitors. But standing there by the Dinghy Dock, after the day we had just had —a day marked by perseverance, resilience, and gratitude—it sounded like a benediction.

Peaceful. Beautiful. Resilient. Treasured. These were some of the words on the vision boards that had begun popping up all over the island, asking passers-by to describe, in one word, their ideal St. John. For at least one contributor, St. John was summed up in that one word: *Paradise.* But there were as many words as people: *Harmonious. Blessed. Awesome. Utopia. Home. Accepting. Family. Magical. Safe. Happy. Loved. Blissful. Maho.*

I saw a painting recently that perfectly captured Maho Bay: the geometry of her beach, the placement of her palms and sea grapes, the colors of the water lapping at her shore. Except for the period dress of the two fishermen on the sand, it could have been 2004, when St. John was my home, or summer 2017, just before Irma. The painting was from 1903. For 114 years, and more, that haven had stood, unchanged. In one day she was scarred beyond recognition. *Sic transit Gloria mundi.* Thus passes the glory of the world.

One late summer morning I was at Maho with Steve. We

could almost forget the mutilated trees behind us—palms hacked off on top, raggedy edges clawing at the sky—if we looked out to sea. On that day, morning showers had left behind rainbows, plural. God's promise to Noah. *Never again shall there be a flood to destroy the earth.* A covenant. The island was healing. Isn't that what people were saying?

"Rainbows are boring," Jazz and I used to joke, we saw them so often. And not just rainbow fragments, complete arches that began and ended in the water, the kind kids draw with their crayons. I wondered if I had grown up to live in a place I saw in my head when I was a little girl, coloring.

One rainbow was especially vivid, reaching right down from the sky and cocooning a sailboat, a multicolored spotlight transforming the white hull. The water was ... Sigh. *Indescriptable.* Columbus sailed the ocean blue. Homer had his wine-dark sea. What the hell color is that water?

I'm grappling. This is a word I associate with an exhibition I saw at the Metropolitan Museum of Art, probably on some dreary winter afternoon, of the paintings of Post-Impressionist Pierre Bonnard. According to the exhibit notes, the artist "spent his entire life grappling with white." I feel his pain. My journals and sailing logbooks and notes and drafts brim with years of efforts, most overwritten, some merely lackluster, a few bordering on good, all falling short. If only I could describe the color of the water, maybe I could—like those relief workers hunting for treasure in the wreckage—preserve a piece of paradise that exists for only a fleeting moment of time.

Maybe I should forget colors and just go with "sparkly." My then-seven-year-old niece, who lived in coastal New England, attended an elementary school with a view of the ocean. Part of her day, every day, she told me, was Sparkle Time. Her teacher stopped whatever they were doing for a few minutes so the children could look at sparkles on the water.

And here's another kid story: A Philly friend told me about a family trip to Mexico with her husband and two little boys. Just like in the islands, she remarked, they heard the phrase "no worries"—those hallmark words of paradise—everywhere:

"We missed our bus. Can you help us?"

"Of course. No worries, señora."

"I'm so sorry, my son spilled his juice."

"No worries! I'll clean it up. Here's another glass."

When the vacation was over, eight-year-old Leo confided to his mother: "What I liked best about Mexico, Mom ... is that there are No Worries there."

Maybe that's paradise. A place where second graders get Sparkle Time instead of Worries.

Steve went for a swim while I pulled out my camera to take pictures. Another addition to my collection of crappy rainbow shots. Like my words, not a single photo does justice to the scene before me, ever. There's a lesson in there, I suppose, something about appreciating the moment or the inherent perfection in things impermanent. Whatever. Is it really too much to ask, to have one small piece of ethereal beauty that I can keep?

A pelican plopped down, diving for a fish.

I watched my devoted husband, who indulges my fascination —and my history—with this island, wade out of the sea and, I swear to God, seeing him there, in that setting, at that moment, I think I must have conjured him all those years ago, right in that spot. Floating in that same salty water where I released tears and trepidations, jettisoned all the old what-ifs, opened up to possibilities.

We were alone on the beach except for two tourists, way down the other end, one on the sand, one in the water. A turtle popped his head above the surface, taking a gulp of air, and the woman in the water shouted, shattering my reverie. *A turtle! Oh my god! Holy shit! A turtle!* An exasperated eye roll would have been my normal response to such a shrill disturbance of the peace, but she was so overjoyed. She saw a turtle! It's magic when you see your first turtle.

Looking out at the road I saw Julia, fresh from her morning

hike at Francis, driving to Cruz Bay to start her day. Seconds later, speeding in the other direction, was a *Great Island Car!* with a fluorescent orange noodle floatie for an armrest and a Save Coral Bay bumper sticker. It was Sistah Blistah, the bartender from Shipwreck who taught Jazz and me how to make drinks.

There are a dozen countries in the world with at least one place called Paradise. The U.S. alone has 27. (Although one of them, in California, would burn to the ground in the state's deadliest wildfire a year after Hurricane Irma.) For Sistah Blistah, paradise was a place called La-La Land, a swath of earth in a secluded corner of Coral Bay. Once hidden by trees, the land was now raw and exposed, like acreage stripped clean for a shopping mall developer. After Irmaria, Sistah Blistah's house—a shackteau called Ooh-la-la—was underwater.

Sistah Blistah's son knew the caretaker of a villa up in exclusive Peter Bay. The connection meant that's where Sistah Blistah rode out the hurricanes and, for 10 months, where she'd been living, "riding out" the aftermath while she rebuilt Ooh-la-la.

"Peter Bay? Wow. Sweet!" I had said when I heard she landed in a castle with a killer view. She had her own room—called it the Princess Tower—and full run of the gourmet kitchen.

"How is it up there?" I asked.

She gave me a look. "Not how I could live."

She used to clean Peter Bay houses. Now being up there full-time? Seeing the other side? Surreal. It seemed nobody *lived* up there! Even the foliage was imported. And the kitchen! The kitchen was about the size of her entire house, and it was in fine condition—she knew because she'd been cooking for the construction crews—but they were doing a total renovation.

She was telling me this as we walked around her property. In contrast to the manicured landscaping of Peter Bay, Sistah Blistah's land was wild. Carnival beads hung from bougainvillea branches. Sistah Blistah checked the water level in her cistern and a family of frogs jumped out.

Nearly a year after the hurricanes, she was finally getting a new house, but it was not quite habitable. She's lucky she wasn't in her own house when Irma hit. During the height of the storm, even that stone mansion where she sheltered was shaking. She thought they were going down the mountain in that fortress. The pressure was so intense. And when they came out? You couldn't believe it. You just could not believe what you were looking at. Everything was gone.

"I've never really talked about it," she said. "Just ... Gone."

Sistah Blistah was paranoid that I'd write something negative, disparage the villa owner who had been so generous. She was over-the-moon grateful. But she wanted to go home.

I had assumed—wrongly—that my old neighbor would relish living in luxury for a while. For her, Coral Bay proper was paradise, though there are plenty who would disagree. When I lived at the Cliffhanger, we had a word to describe certain house-guests: over-expectant. As in, you don't want your visitors to be over-expectant, so you try to paint an accurate picture ahead of time. It is 85 degrees and sunny. And we do not have air conditioning. We do have bugs. Big ones, the size of small rodents, and some of them fly. Yes, we live in paradise, but not necessarily the one you see in glossy brochures about Paradise. The resorts are on the other side of the island. Along with the maid service, the pool, and the cocktail servers who swing by your hammock with piña coladas. The cost of living is exorbitant. That means we can't take off work every day of your vacation. Oh, and we don't shower all that much. That's not a problem, is it?

When my mother came to visit (in the rainy season. I honestly did not know. It seemed better than hurricane season?) I did my best to prepare her, but there was no denying it: She got one of the hottest, rainiest, buggiest weeks of the year. She got eaten alive. Some paradise. One of my coworkers told her gin was a great mosquito repellent. Just apply it directly to your skin. Mom thought drinking it worked better. Just add tonic and lime. Mom was a good sport.

"Is your mom having a good time?" asked everyone I knew,

everywhere I went, because everyone knew within 24 hours that she was on island.

I didn't think so. But more germane to the discussion is that I wanted her to be head over heels for my St. John. Anything less would not suffice. Turned out I was the over-expectant one.

There are no words to express my joy in seeing you thrive in your new digs, my mother wrote when she got home. *Paradise is wherever you are and when you are sharing your zest for life with those around you.*

Paradise, it would seem, should be a place where you feel safe and loved. With as few worries as possible. A sunny day under a palm tree on a pristine beach? That's a no-brainer. But I've been to a nirvana in the North where a brother gives his sister a place to stay rent-free, an uncle loans his niece his car, and a mother makes sure her grown-up daughter has cash for groceries. When I left St. John, Philadelphia was a metropolitan oasis where friends buy you dinner, remind you it's OK to let your family take care of you once in a while, then push you out the door, beseeching you to go do whatever it is you're still trying to do.

Paradise might be having two places to come home to: One that grounds you, nurtures you, gives you roots. One that buoys you, challenges you, goads you into not being a candy ass.

Coral Bay embraced me, then sent me off on a great adventure. Living there changed the course of my life. No wonder it keeps calling me back.

Most of what I found in Coral Bay—friendship, perspective, a larger sense of self—I carry with me. Maybe it is, now, part of my DNA. Coral Bay certainly taught me that storytelling is part of my DNA. But St. John, the place, is a touchstone. Like a favorite passage from a treasured book, it's a comfort to have it within reach, to remember how and why it inspired. To be able to go back again and again to see it, touch it, get the meaning just right.

In Sistah Blistah's case, one man's trash was another woman's treasure. Her new shack-teau would be outfitted with thousands of dollars' worth of high-end stainless appliances discarded from the Peter Bay villa's kitchen remodel. She scrolled through photos on her phone to show me. Her construction pictures were mixed in with hurricane aftermath and the occasional nature shot. The photos went something like this: Debris. Wrecks. Trash. *Frog!* Destruction. Devastation. More Destruction. *Flower!* Through the cracks we see the light.

It was a blistering July day, but it was comfortable inside her work-in-progress home. Sistah Blistah told the builders she didn't need fans. There was always a breeze in her corner of paradise. As we sat in the cool dark, the sun outside illuminated a patch of garden—hot pink bougainvillea, bright young greenery, radiant blue sky. Framed by the door-less doorway, it was a miniature portrait, a harbinger of *Better Days Ahead.* I took a snapshot, and this one turned out.

18

THE ELIXIR

It was stormy the day I flew down for the visit that would mark the one-year anniversary of Irma. As the plane approached the Virgin Islands, there was no Caribbean blue beckoning. From my window seat I saw smoky-gray sky dissolving into the horizon, blurring into the navy of the sea, which darkened as I looked lower, deeper, until, straight down, everything came into focus and I could see whitecaps, the detail on the turbulent sea in fine relief, even through three panes of hazy acrylic. Later, in one more attempt to describe the hues, I'll ditch my thesaurus and Google "colors," getting help from Benjamin Moore (*Gentleman's Gray, Stunning*), Ralph Lauren (*Club Navy, Washed Denim*), and Sherwin Williams (*Naval, In the Navy, Blackened Blue*), but when we landed, the flight attendant went with a simple "crummy."

Aren't you worried about hurricanes? people asked before this latest trip down.

It was, of course, possible there would be another hurricane while I was there. If so, I would hunker down with Cruz Bay Julia at Coqui Cove, the house that survived Irma. For the time being, it was just rain and gloom. When my ferry docked in St. John, there were no hurricane watches, no tropical storm warnings, just a flood advisory. I'd be fine if I got to Fort Julia before the roads got too bad.

Crummy was right. Nearly four inches of rain fell that first night, something we learned the next morning during the ham radio check-in, a new part of Julia's routine. For two solid days it was tempestuous, miserable, and then the sun came out. Julia and I went to the beach at Jumbie where the water, 85 degrees, was teeming with fish—violet and gold fairy basslets, and jillions of glittery little silversides, more than either of us had ever seen before. We snorkeled through vast schools of them, just sitting there, so plentiful even the giant tarpon, their predators—looking like sharks, the way they cruised leisurely around—couldn't chase them off. The big fish must have had their fill. We were swimming in an aquarium and when we emerged, pelicans soared overhead against a sky so blue it mocked any suggestion that everything wasn't back to being perfect in paradise.

ON THE EVE of the anniversary, I drove out to the Annaberg sugar mill and three great egrets took flight in front of my Jeep, their pure white feathers a surreal beauty against the starkness of barren mangroves. A symbol of the mixed message that was this island one year after Irma tore her apart.

Two days earlier, at the eight-vehicle Coral Bay Labor Day "parade," the biggest cheers had gone to the BBC truck. A year after the hurricanes, the imported linemen were still fixing power lines, still the heroes of Coral Bay. Spectators took pictures of a Carnival princess, about eight years old, resplendent beneath her lace umbrella and tall-as-her-head tiara. The backdrop for this otherwise adorable Instagram moment was the faded sea-foam green and coral pastels of what used to be Island Blues—where I interviewed Santa—and was now a heap of splintered wood, overgrown with weeds, untouched since the hurricanes hit, the whole mess looking like it just happened. Through a missing door you could see the only thing left inside—a toilet, lid up. The remaining walls were defaced with graffiti: *Fuck you, pay me,* someone scrawled. *You little spies.* The princess, posing atop an electric-blue dune buggy, smiled, oblivious to the profanity behind her, the vandal's warning to *Trust no one.*

Every day things were better and every day there was so much more to do. There was prudent, sustainable rebuilding, and there were hundreds of homes without roofs. For some people life was getting back to normal, if a little rough around the edges. For others, life was still very hard, the repercussions manifold. The island and its people were both remarkably resilient and breathtakingly fragile.

One year after Irma, the main clinic was still shut down. A banner over the sign for the Myra Keating Smith Community Health Center read *CLOSED FOR RENOVATIONS. We're working hard to serve you better!* as if the de facto hospital was just in need of a paint job.

One year after Irma, there were no shelters. Zero. Should another storm warning be issued, the *St. John Tradewinds* reported, Virgin Islands government officials were advising St. John residents to go to shelters on St. Thomas, a boat ride away, never mind that on many days there was only one barge running between the two islands.

One year after Irma, the ritzy Caneel Bay resort looked much as it did the day the hurricane hit—rotting wood and shards of glass and crap just sitting, right where Irma left it. Ditto for the Cinnamon Bay campground. Mr. Otis, who I had played darts with, had been caretaking at Cinnamon and wasn't even allowed on the neglected property to retrieve his possessions out of a locker. Not even his work boots. The whole situation vexed him. There was so much he could do to help clean up the mess. Instead, nobody was doing anything. Both Caneel and Cinnamon were privately run, on National Park land leased in apparently complicated deals, those deals being the prevailing explanation, or excuse, for the sorry state of both properties. Both sat, desolate, as disputes about insurance and leases and who should be responsible dragged on. Wasn't it desecration to leave park property in this condition? *SHAME* someone etched into a piece of wood propped up at the entrance to Cinnamon Bay. Sacrilege.

One year after Irma, tourism officials pronounced the island ready for business—and in many ways it was. Not just ready, but necessary, given that tourist dollars were the island's lifeblood. Much had changed for the better and progress would continue in the years to come. But a lot of what had changed could only be measured by what you didn't see. What was no longer there. There was an acute absence of things. Palm trees. The particular curve of a favorite beach. People. Familiar faces had simply disappeared. New faces filled the void. Green grew over the remains.

ON SEPTEMBER 6, 2018, someone with one of those quote-of-the-day calendars posted a photo on Facebook of that day's quote: *Take Life By Storm.* You can't make this stuff up.

I met up with Badlands Frances at Aqua Bistro for the "Irma Day" pig roast. It was a fundraiser for two favorite charities: St. John Rescue, the first responders; and Island Health and Wellness Center, which provided affordable medical care. Most of the people donating were hurricane victims, people who could benefit from their own GoFundMe campaigns (or a "Go-Me!" fund, as one local kept calling it). I saw Birdie, a guy who lost everything—his house, his boat, even his anonymity when his girlfriend, desperate for news of survivors post-storm, posted his real name online—open his wallet and put cash in the jar.

From where we were sitting, I could see *Silver Cloud* floating in the harbor and, swaying off her stern, the American flag. So many Coral Bay survivors had mentioned that flag. Immediately after Irma, as they emerged from wherever they had sheltered and tried to make sense of the transmuted world they stepped into, people looked out to the water and found a shred of comfort in that one familiar sight. Captain Elliot had raised the flag as soon as he was able to get on board his damaged and dismasted ship. The harbor needed some color, he thought. And some hope.

After lunch we hopped into Frances's tricked-out Jeep, Big Blue. The car was her pride and joy, burnished to a sheen, lug nuts meticulously painted with blue nail polish. She handed me three small bottles—*Sturdy Sapphire* by Sally Hansen, *Why Not* by Sinful Colors, and L.A. Colors's *Aqua Crystals*.

"Wrong shades," she said.

I guess she figured I'd be able to use them in my other life. I thanked her and tossed the nail polish in my bag. Something to add to my paint chips and thesaurus.

We drove the two minutes over to the Dinghy Dock, where there was a subdued gathering of weary sailors. What will happen if another storm does hit? seemed to be the main topic of conversation and a foreboding subtext to everything else.

I don't have to worry about trees blowing down and falling on my house, said Lord Thatcher, because I don't have any trees.

We don't have to worry about the boats, said Captain Elliot, gesturing toward the harbor, because there aren't any.

Elliot was preoccupied with his smartphone. There was something out there. It wasn't Florence (named September 1) or Gordon (already up by the Keys). It was behind those. Didn't even have a name yet, wasn't technically a storm, but it was out there, coming off the coast of Africa, first a yellow X on the National Hurricane Center map, then an orange X, now a red one, each color change indicating its chances of becoming something bigger just got a little better.

September is the worst. There's always "something out there" in the height of hurricane season. Marilyn, Hugo, Irma, Maria—they all hit in September. The latest "something" was forecast to turn north before hitting the Caribbean, but you never know.

"Where are your X's now?" someone asked Elliot.

In the silence that followed, I asked about the second boater who died. One year after Irma, there still had not been anything written about him. Maybe I could do that.

Ardis, someone said. His name was Ardis. He was tall. Barrel-chested. He used to sing at open mic night. He died trying to outrun Maria. Reticent talkers started throwing out bits of information, enough that I wanted to jot down a few notes. *Don't quote me on that* was as common a refrain as ever—even when people had so much to say—so I made a big show of taking out my notebook, a warning that I was writing stuff down. Ardis built his boat. A trimaran, someone said. The boat was called the *Carolinian,* or *Carolina.* Talk to Ray who took over Crabby's, they were friends.

Frances and I headed over to the potluck at Pickles where I saw lots of old-timers, including the Save Coral Bay activists leading the fight against a major construction project proposed for the harbor. Someone wanted to build a megayacht marina on the Island Blues property, the profane backdrop for the parade princess. One year after Irma that site wasn't just an eyesore but a blight on the psyche of a community trying to move on. Did no one with a claim to this valuable waterfront land feel an obligation to clean it up? Meanwhile, the permit process inched forward. The island was being threatened by twin evils: climate change and commercialism. Development may yet prove more destructive than any hurricane. An architect issued a warning about greed: "If we let the bulldozers take over, there's no future."

At the end of the day, I met up with Julia. In a year's worth of visits, she hadn't once sat to let me formally interview her, and she won't this time, either. Instead, she took me up a grassy hill to a sugar mill ruin on private property—a place I'd never seen before—to watch the sunset. The expansive view of sea and surrounding islands was enhanced by the newness of the angle. I sauntered around taking photos, and I caught Julia framed in a doorway of the crumbling mill, a silhouette. She struck a goddess pose and the rays of light streaming through the opening gave my tireless friend a halo.

ONE YEAR AFTER IRMA, the traumas of that day were, for many, still unspeakable, even the source of existential crisis. There were people I did not see out at any of the events marking the milestone anniversary who, later that night, and in the days after, surfaced on social media, sending ripples of agony, and gratitude, across the ether.

Lori wrote:

> One year ago I sat in a closet and prayed to live. I hope to
> live my life in a way that justifies being saved.

Erin posted before-and-after photos of her house and yard, framed by cartoon tropical flowers and a *Fuck You Irma* caption:

> I can't even list the hundreds of people who have helped
> me along the way. I'm so incredibly grateful.

And from Pat, from Shipwreck:

> We have physically and mentally moved to south Florida ...
> That photo makes me very homesick but we have decided
> to put our house on the market and make the best of it here
> ... Thanks for thinking of me on this very sad week.

IT TOOK another full day for the island to recover from what felt like a collective psychological hangover, but by the weekend it was time, again, to look forward. On Saturday I was supposed to get together with Ivy League Abby. Our plans were loose. She wanted to get her dinghy in the water. Was that OK? Sure. I'd help! I just needed to stop by Erin's first. Great, Abby said. How is Erin? Invite Erin. I stopped by Erin's house but she wasn't there, I just missed her. She didn't answer her phone or my texts. I called Abby back to tell her, but now I couldn't reach her either. I made a pass around Coral Bay—Skinny's, Connections, the Love City Mini Mart, Oasis, Aqua Bistro—but no sign of Erin or Abby or anyone else I knew. I was sitting in my broiling Jeep, frustrated, when I realized I was parked in front of Crabby's and someone was inside. I introduced myself to Ray, the new owner, and asked about Ardis.

He was a philosopher, Ray told me. He had met Ardis Perrins about 10 years earlier, in a bay in St. Thomas where Ardis's boat got stuck in the shallows after a storm. Ray dropped his extra anchor in deep water, took the bitter end of the anchor line over to the beleaguered captain, and told him if he was ever in Coral Bay, he could give it back. A couple of months later, Ardis did just that and, in the process, fell in love with Coral Bay. He also loved dancing and reading, and he remembered everything. You could have a conversation with him about any subject. Ardis was from Lithuania and had come over on a ship with his mother and father as a child. He was a gifted mechanic and a woodworker. He was married for a short time, somewhere near San Francisco. He had no family when he died. But no man is an island, and Ardis had Coral Bay.

Ardis survived Hurricane Irma by sailing south, past St. Croix. People told him he was crazy, but it turned out to be a good plan, one that kept him safe and his boat intact, allowing him to come home a few days later and help his St. John neighbors who weren't so lucky. When Maria threatened, he thought he'd try a similar strategy and sail away, out of the storm's path, but something went wrong. He never came back.

Ray wanted to go out looking for his friend, but his own boat was too badly damaged. He reported him missing to the Coast Guard. About a month later, Ardis's boat was found upside down near the Dominican Republic. His body was never recovered. Lost at sea. He would have wanted it that way.

A TEXT POPPED up from Erin. She's sorry she missed me! But she's getting out on the water! Something about Bob De BOP and Ivy League Abby. I couldn't find Ivy League Abby or Erin, but it was OK because Erin had found Ivy League Abby. This was extra good news because Erin could actually do the stuff on Abby's boat that I had volunteered to help out with.

Somehow we all met up and drove out to Johnson Bay where the dinghy was beached. I was trying to decide whether to leave my phone and wallet in the car and asked if the vessel was seaworthy, which Erin and Abby both found hilarious, but admitted was a valid question. We waded through tangles of sargassum that thickened the water and flipped over a pitiful, soggy rubber raft. It had broken boards for seats and looked dreadfully underinflated, but Ivy League Abby threw in snorkel gear, a cooler of beer, and a pair of oars. Ivy League Abby's a badass—a submarine captain who has also circumnavigated the Earth in a sailboat—but don't even bother trying to get her to talk about any of it. She pushed off and all three of us hopped in.

I settled my wet ass and grabbed an oar. Ivy League Abby picked up the other one. I'm sure my rowing was subpar, but I wanted to do my part. Do you know where we're going? Ivy League Abby asked, a polite way, I suspected, of hinting that I was rowing in the wrong direction. I didn't. Moreover, I was skeptical of getting anywhere in that saggy vessel, but in Coral Bay, it helps to be game for anything.

Abby gestured up ahead. Turns out *Bop She Bop* was not the pathetic dinghy we were in danger of capsizing, it was the sleek little powerboat we were rowing out to. We climbed aboard and one, two, three, lickety-split, Captain Badass had the engine in the water, the Bimini up, and we were off to Hurricane Hole, skating across water so flat it looked like a sheet of glass.

When we got to the most ideal of multiple ideal spots, Abby cut the engine. We drifted up to a mooring and tied up. It was a seamless, almost silent, operation, executed perfectly (by the other two). We took a moment to consider the amount of yelling that might have accompanied this maneuver had some other (male) captains we know been at the helm, and then Erin jumped overboard. With that splash, a year's worth of sorrow—for one evanescent breath—dissipated. The Elixir. She emerged from the water all smiles, a vision of joy, however brief.

Hurricane Hole hadn't looked this pristine since Irma. The Navy had only just finished, maybe the week before, towing away the wrecked boats that had sat in heaps for some 50 weeks. We snorkeled into the mangroves and saw little fish and corals, a baby barracuda. There were some colorful sponges that no one recognized. Odd, tiny signs of new life, but new life nonetheless. We glided wordlessly under the water. I watched my friends—survivors—swim through transparent sea and wondered if they felt as light as I did.

Back on board, we motored slowly around the coves, enjoying the serenity, and the companionship. When it started to get dark, we headed in and continued on shore our small celebration of not just a little normalcy, but what turned out to be a rather spectacular afternoon. That's the thing about Coral Bay. One minute you're driving in circles in the blazing heat, looking for people you can't find, missed connections all over the place. Next thing you know, you're out on the water with two of your favorite people, banking a strong contender for the top-10-days-of-your-life list.

SKINNY'S WAS OFFICIALLY CLOSED for the height of hurricane season, but James, the cook, was opening on Sundays for football. The smell of burgers wafted through the stagnant air. Chickens clucked and scattered as I walked in, following the scent, and I've time-traveled. I knew everybody there.

Erin was at the grill. Anna Banana was tending bar. James was supervising from a table where he was engrossed in a game of dominoes with Big Steve and Kathy, my old Cliffhanger neighbor. James was wearing his do-rag. I was wearing my do-rag. Did we still look like twins?

"We look like husband and wife," he said.

I had been trying all year to talk to James. I knew how crucial he had been to Skinny's rebuild, but anytime I asked about his home, how he was doing, I'd get the same answer—*I'm busy. 24-7!*—and no more. He still wasn't answering questions, but did I want to be on his team?

Belle came in, complaining about the heat. It was hot as fuck under Skinny's new roof, she grumbled.

It had been a similar hot, calm, clear September day when I first went sailing on *O'dege*. Back then it was all so new and curious and wonderful. Practicing for the Virgins' Cup and learning about Fighting Lady Yellow and sail trim and boundaries. Getting to know the woman who lived on this small boat and didn't seem to need much else. Who had no closet for clothes but enough dresses to share; no shelves for books yet seemed to have read everything.

In the end, Belle cried. She cried in June, nine months after the hurricanes, when she was getting her first break off island. She was alone in the St. Thomas airport when the tears came.

"I don't know what to do. I really don't," she said, when we finally talked about it.

Belle had heard second-hand about *O'dege*'s fate. "Well, she's floating," someone told her after Irma, which was more than the bearer of the news could say for his own boat. She had cut the rigging free and tried to work up the grit to do more, but no. It was demoralizing. Every time she started cleaning, *O'dege* took on more water and her captain lost a little more heart. Belle had felt indestructible in that boat, may even be indestructible, but her boat was not. One year after Irma, *O'dege* was still stranded in the harbor, mastless and disgusting down below, full of brackish water. Hull scratched to shit. Fighting Lady Yellow paint faded and peeling. Sinking would have been better. This limbo, this in-between shit, was the worst, worse than sinking.

Belle calculated the thousands of dollars she'd put into *O'dege*. Asinine, on the one hand, considering what she cost to buy. On the other hand, when you spread it out over 15 years, it wasn't that bad. Cheaper than rent and sailing her had been her favorite thing to do. She had done it again—sunk more money into her, more sweat, more time—right before hurricane season. A new mast. New rigging. Only to have Irma take it all away.

It was all salvageable. She could have *O'dege* back in racing form in a month. Spend a shit ton of money. Work her ass off, sunup to sundown. But wasn't that asinine too? You went into the boatyard November or December and by the time you came back you only had five fucking months until it was hurricane season again and what if it happened again?

Maybe if she had a partner. Did I want to rescue *O'dege*? She always thought I would be a great next owner. She would help with the work, she'd even help with the money, she just needed somebody else to be responsible. To make the emotional investment. "Think about *O'dege*," was the last thing Belle said when we said goodbye.

Late in the day I was eating a blue cheese burger, medium rare, sitting next to Badlands Frances at the bar. Erin and Anna were on the other side—right where I met them. What were we talking about? I can't recollect, but it felt like the old days, like nothing at all had happened, not two hurricanes, not even the past 14 years.

It was dark when I left. Driving out of Coral Bay, I encountered a gang of feral donkeys, hee-hawing up the hill. Two of them were fighting in the middle of the road, so I stopped. From where I waited, I could just make out the road to Harry and Kelly's, where their Labor of Love sat waiting for a buyer. Off to the right, high up in the cliffs, Arlene was tucked into her sanctuary, for six more weeks anyway, safe in a place where no jumbies could torment her.

When the beasts calmed down, I passed the herd, slowly, and continued up Centerline. At the Smoothie Stand I turned right and headed down the dark incline of North Shore, where my headlights caught crabs scuttling out of the way. At the bottom of the hill, near Maho, there was a stag, frozen in the light, antlers branching skyward like the trees there used to do. I inched past him, parked, and walked out to the deserted beach.

There was one lone boat on the water, its bright light impairing my vision, but then whoever was on board turned the light out and with that switch revealed a panoply of constellations, like an illuminated scrim. The Big Dipper was tilted low, scooping seawater out of Maho Bay. It was silent except for murmuring surf, kissing the shore. I stood there, barely breathing. There was no denying the energy in this still-sacred place.

Continuing home to Fort Julia in the moonless stillness, I passed Peter Bay, where Sistah Blistah was imprisoned in her palace, and wondered if she was out counting stars, too, or merely counting the days until she could return home to La-La Land and her little piece of paradise.

MONDAY WAS A CRAM-IT-ALL-IN-LIKE-A-TOURIST DAY. Every time it's the same. I get Last Day Syndrome. I'm wistful. I need to do everything, see everyone, take pictures of it all. I was up before dawn. I wanted to watch the sun come up over Coral Bay.

Among the photos I took at sunrise, there's one that shows all of Coral Bay from the overlook on Centerline, where I first laid eyes on the place. In the image I can see the boats in the harbor, and Hurricane Hole, and the mountains of the BVIs beyond. Skinny Legs and the Dinghy Dock. The road that goes from the Triangle to the Cliffhanger, past where Shipwreck stood and out to Salt Pond. Almost everyone I know on island lives—or lived—in this picture. For a small sliver of time, nearly everything of any significance in my life happened within the perimeter of this frame. It might never be the same. But on that magnificent morning, from a distance, it was starting to look familiar.

Next I was on to Trunk, where the pelicans dove for breakfast and the gulls' staccato laugh punctuated the sound of the waves. I was the only one there. In the early morning solitude, it was not the overrun tourist favorite, it was simply this: an inarguably stunning beach. I was close to God right there. After a swim, I stopped at another overlook to look back down one more time and take more pictures. With a year's worth of new growth and the brilliant sky—100-mile visibility, someone said—my photo of Trunk Bay looked just like all the postcards.

Later, people will look at that photo and want to know: Is the water really that blue?

And I will answer, unequivocally: It is.

At least for now.

There would be eight more named storms that season. Hurricane Helene veered north without getting near the Caribbean. Hurricane Isaac lost steam near the Dominican Republic. Tropical storms Joyce and Kirk posed no threat to St. John. Hurricane Leslie formed in the North Atlantic and, as weather forecasters described it, wandered around like a zombie for weeks before hitting Portugal, Spain, and France. Hurricane Michael formed well west of the Virgins, then slammed into the Florida Panhandle as a Cat 4, one of the most intense storms ever to make landfall in the contiguous U.S., causing destruction and death all the way up to Virginia. Tropical Storm Nadine fizzled out. Oscar became a hurricane on October 28, but far out in the Atlantic, away from land. In all, there were 15 named storms, eight of which were hurricanes—above that year's NOAA predictions and, like 2017, above the average. None of the 2018 storms did serious harm in the Virgin Islands, but no one could have predicted that. You never know what's going to be The One.

Patty, Rafael, Sara, and Tony never materialized, but there would be more storms the next year. And the year after that. Already named.

Andrea, Barry, Chantal ...

Arthur, Bertha, Cristobal ...

Ana, Bill, Claudette ...

There won't be another Irma or Maria, but only because the names are retired.

In 2019 Hurricane Dorian, a Category 5 storm, will devastate the Bahamas and surpass Irma as the most powerful Atlantic hurricane ever recorded.

In 2020 there will be a record-breaking 30 named storms.

In 2021 the United Nations World Meteorological Organization, because of that new record, will stop using the Greek alphabet for late-season storms and instead add an entire second list of names.

In 2022 Hurricane Ian will slam into Florida with 150-mph sustained winds, the deadliest storm to hit the state in nearly a century.

Paradise in its truest form may be a state of mind to which you can always go back; but paradise, the place, is under siege.

MEAN JEAN and I spent our last afternoon together with a swim at Maho.

The ocean was opalescent, its surface a prism, shooting light in all directions. Sun sparkled on top of that crystal clear water like a billion flawless diamonds.

I dove under.

Hitting the water, I felt what I always feel: A letting go. A sense of flying and freedom and being fully alive. The exhilarating act of living.

I can't swear that there were pelicans an arm's distance away when I surfaced, but that's how I remember it. That's how I always remember it.

I licked my lips to taste the salt and, adjusting my mask and snorkel, looked out toward shore. If I squinted, letting in just a glint of sunlight, I could see the shadows of phantom palms reaching across the fotty-two shades of blue.

When the bugs started biting we packed up and Mean Jean drove back to Skinny's where my Jeep was parked. A few donkeys moseyed around. There might have been music playing in the distance. Maybe Bob Marley, "One Love."

We didn't want to say goodbye. I'd be leaving island soon and didn't know when I'd see her next, so we sat in the car and talked. The sun was going down. We could have been watching the sunset from one of St. John's many fabulous locations, any of a dozen overlooks within a few minutes' drive, but we sat in Skinny's parking lot, next to a dirty, white Suzuki Sidekick missing its rear axle, among other vital parts, and supported by concrete blocks. *Positive is How I Live* proclaimed the bumper sticker on the back. Directly in front of us was a battered boat, hard aground, but the flamboyant tree in front of Connections was in full bloom, electric red against a fiery, flamingo-pink sky.

ACKNOWLEDGMENTS

First and foremost, I want to thank my mom, Marge Smith, who has been my #1 fan longer than anybody and didn't even blink when I told her, at age 39.5, that I was quitting my very good job and moving to an island without one. I'm especially grateful for the Christmas conversation she had with her mother, Margaret Gradel Crowe, my beloved grandmom, that gave me the push and support I needed to finish this as an independent publisher. Providence really does move in mysterious ways.

The pinnacle of my journalism career was working with the insanely brilliant Bill Knoedelseder in Philadelphia in the '90s. He made a surprise return 20 years later, first telling me it was my calling to return to St. John after hurricanes Irma and Maria to get the story and then following through in spectacular fashion by agreeing to be my editor again. He took multiple drafts and made them a book. If these acknowledgments lack poetry, it's only because he didn't edit them.

St. John filmmaker William Stelzer not only designed the beautiful cover but also was the first person to hand me money ($40 cash, when I arrived home after sailing across the Atlantic) as advance payment for two copies of the book he thought I should write. Bryan McKinney shared his harrowing Hurricane Irma story and hilarious Coral Bay observations in addition to the artistic talents that produced a map so perfectly fanciful, it belongs in a book called *Not On Any Map*. Dear friend, captain, and artist Billie Denise Wright treated me to countless glorious sails, then let me have the pick of her paintings for the cover art.

I'm most grateful to Melanie Burney and Kevin Ferris at the *Philadelphia Inquirer* for publishing the essay that led to the completion of this book. Huge thanks to Darrin Britting for his unparalleled eagle eye in copy editing. All mistakes are mine and due to compulsive tinkering. Thank you to all my early readers for their input, insights, and friendship, especially Kim Glovas, Fernando Mendez, and Terry and Maryjane Ruggles. Judith Kelman, being a writing mentor in Visible Ink is an honor and a privilege. Jennifer Lewis-Hall, I definitely want you on my trip.

So many people on St. John shared their hurricane experiences —some in formal interviews, some indirectly. I'm beholden to all of them. I'm honored that they trusted me with their stories and hope that I've done them justice. They are all survivors.

Moe Chabuz, Doug Sica, and Pat and Dennis Rizzo gave waitressing jobs to a woman with no waitressing experience, making it possible for me to live in Coral Bay, and then an endless list of people made it a home including a boatload of badass women and a treasured group of old—and young—salts. I'll refrain from listing them all here since many are already in the pages of this book and some wish to remain anonymous. Also, I still, honestly, do not know everybody's last name. St. John Sun Times editors Tom Paine, Shirley Reid, and Eloise Anderson all believed I had something to say. Special shout out to Chris Bast who so fervently insisted that I belonged at Yaddo and, when I didn't get accepted, one-upped them and gave me his beautiful villa as a writing retreat.

Erin Pryor Durrell—*Bosom buddy! Terrific and sexy!*—is a friend to the end. Sara O'Neill and Martha Hollander bailed me out on a momentous sail to the women's regatta in St. Martin. My snorkeling buddy Mean Jean Vance is the reason I have a writing business, and the mermaid-angel Celia Kalousek keeps it (and me) on track. Jenn Robinson continues to share tears, tales, and precious office space at Connections. Kim McCoy taught me how far I could go with a lucky $5 in my pocket. Jim Donovan, the finest sailor I know, helped me set my course.

During my time traveling, and afterward, inspiring words from Connie Abrams, Howard Altman, Mark Angeles, Katherine Blodgett, Theresa Conroy, Melissa Coopersmith, Robin Culverwell, Wendy Daughenbaugh, Katie Friesen, Ron Goldwyn, Naomi Grabel, Judith Kurnick, John Kwasek, Jay Lloyd, Will Lloyd, Reenie Lynch, Richard Maloney, Jennifer Urbano, Toni Yates, and Tracy Galligher Young sailed in out of the blue at crucial moments. Mark Abel encouraged my journey but met me at the airport when I needed to come home. My brother, George Smith, gave me a place to live and my uncle, Fr. George Crowe, let me drive the Popemobile. Thank you to everyone who urged me to just keep going and/or otherwise "fuck the job." If you're one of them and I forgot to acknowledge you, please call me up and yell at me. I am still underemployed and always have time to talk.

I wouldn't be breathing if it weren't for the OG girl gangs from PW (carpe diem Cynthia Friedman, Cindy Firing, and Lisa Firing Lenze—my original partners in creative crime) and NYU (Trish Baillargeon, Amy Brennan, and Cinder Miller—yes, I'm the slowest, but I do eventually cross the finish line). In Philly I laughed all through chemo thanks to Dr. Lisa Grunebaum, Lilly Schwartz, and the inimitable Ellen Hutton, who was first to give me permission to use her real name and I thanked her by cutting most of her pages. (Sorry!) I hope one day all my nieces—Kayleigh, Abby, Evie, Louise, and Caroline—will read this and, no matter what their adventures, know to surround themselves with strong women who love them, champion them, and remind them constantly how fabulous they are.

Finally, from the bottom of my heart, thank you to my husband, Steve Holt, who reads every word I write with thoughtfulness, perspective, and wisdom. He's had to listen to me talk about this book since the day we met but gave me my happy ending anyway.

ABOUT THE AUTHOR

Margie Smith Holt is an Emmy-winning journalist. Her work has appeared on television and radio, in print, and online. This is her first book. Visit margiesmithholt.com for more.